AFRICAN APPRENTICESHIP

Works of Dame Margery Perham, D.C.M.G., C.B.E.,
D.Litt., F.B.A.

THE PROTECTORATES OF SOUTH AFRICA
(with Lionel Curtis)

NATIVE ADMINISTRATION IN NIGERIA

TEN AFRICANS
(editor)

AFRICAN DISCOVERY

AFRICANS AND BRITISH RULE
(with J. Simmons)

RACE AND POLITICS IN KENYA
(with Elspeth Huxley)

AFRICAN OUTLINE

THE GOVERNMENT OF ETHIOPIA
(first published in 1948)
new edition in 1968

LUGARD: THE YEARS OF ADVENTURE 1859–1898

LUGARD: THE YEARS OF AUTHORITY 1898–1945

THE DIARIES OF LORD LUGARD
(editor, with Mary Bull)

THE COLONIAL RECKONING
(Reith Lectures)

THE COLONIAL SEQUENCE 1967

THE COLONIAL SEQUENCE 1970

Margery Perham in 1929

AFRICAN APPRENTICESHIP

An Autobiographical Journey
in Southern Africa 1929

Margery Perham

FABER AND FABER
3 Queen Square
London

First published in 1974
by Faber and Faber Limited
3 Queen Square London WCI
Printed in Great Britain by
Latimer Trend & Company Ltd Plymouth

ISBN 0 571 10535 1

Contents

Illustrations

Nos. 3, 5, 8 and 13 from photographs by the author. Photographs 1, 8, 9 by Satour.

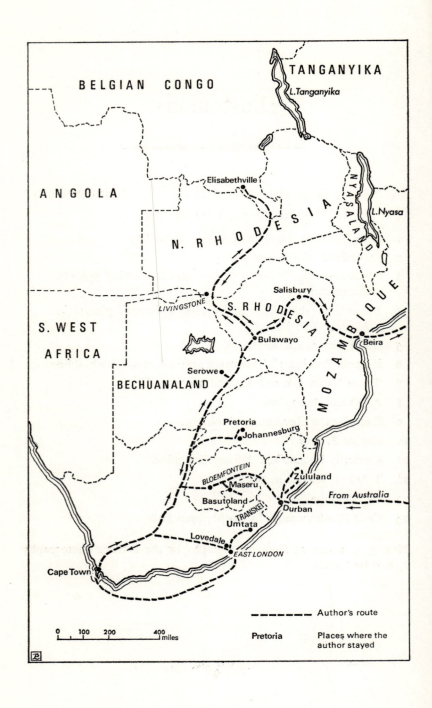

BELGIAN CONGO

TANGANYIKA

L.Tanganyika

ANGOLA

Elisabethville

N. RHODESIA

NYASALAND

L.Nyasa

S. WEST

AFRICA

LIVINGSTONE

S. RHODESIA

Salisbury

Bulawayo

Beira

MOZAMBIQUE

BECHUANALAND

Serowe

Pretoria

Johannesburg

BLOEMFONTEIN

Maseru

Basutoland

Zululand

From Australia

TRANSKEI

Umtata

Durban

Lovedale

EAST LONDON

Cape Town

– – – – – – Author's route

Pretoria   Places where the
author stayed

0   100   200   400 miles

Foreword

This book contains the diary I wrote when I travelled round the world in 1929–30. The journey was made possible by the grant of a Rhodes Trust Travelling Fellowship. These awards were made to Oxford dons to enable them to spend a year away from the University seeing the world. There were no precise instructions as to the use to be made of the opportunity. Whether or not because the experiment was regarded as being unfruitful it was discontinued after a few years.

The award came to me as a great surprise. I still do not know what led the Trust to give me, a young and obscure female don, this exciting opportunity. It may have been due to my having given lectures on such subjects as British policy towards native races and also upon the working of the Mandates system which I had studied in Geneva. The two Rhodes Trustees whom I met gave vague replies when I asked for instructions. One said I could broaden my mind; another that I could go wherever I liked in pursuit of 'colour problems'. I think it was the Secretary of the Trust, Philip Kerr, later Lord Lothian, who said I would be 'an ambassador for Oxford'.

One reason for the grant may have been that, shortly after my first appointment to Sheffield University and a breakdown in health, I spent a year in British Somaliland. This experience, hardly a rest-cure, aroused in me a strong interest in the problems of colonial government. At that period there was no widely accepted routine for young academics to develop a chosen subject with a view to a university appointment or to promotion by way of a D.Phil. degree. As I did not know how else to express what was to me an enthralling experience, being my first contact with Africa and 'native administration', I wrote a novel.[1] More than forty years later, in March 1970, I gave a talk about my experiences in Somaliland in a B.B.C. Radio 4 series called 'The Time of my Life'. My present publishers suggested that it would

[1] *Major Dane's Garden*, published by Hutchinson in 1924 and republished by R. Collings in 1970.

be appropriate for this account of my first contact with Africa and its administrative problems to be included in this volume.

I started my travels in the midsummer of 1929. I was by no means an experienced traveller or what is called 'a woman of the world'. Nor was world travel so well organized then as it is today. My commitment was vague and I had no instructions. I started with the United States where I learned what I could of negro questions and collected some information about the American Indians whose history had long interested me. I then sailed from San Francisco to Hawaii. Hearing there was some kind of trouble among the natives (a word not then regarded as being loaded with any sense of inferiority) in both the American-ruled Samoan Islands and those under New Zealand's United Nations' Mandate, I visited both these beautiful and deeply interesting dependencies. I wrote articles about them which were the first of my writings to appear in *The Times*.[1] In the North Island of New Zealand I followed up the Samoan trouble and saw what I could of the Maoris. I then went across Australia where there was little opportunity to learn much about the neglected aborigines. And so on across the Pacific to South Africa.

During all these travels I made such notes as I could and collected documents for further study. I also wrote a diary letter which I sent home to be typed and distributed to four or five close friends and members of my family. It is this diary, covering my travels in southern Africa, which is contained in this book. During a journey which needed all my time and strength the diary letter was written whenever I could snatch the time, often in trains or late at night. I had no idea of writing it for publication. As my more serious investigations—and travelling at speed even these could not be very serious—went into my notebooks, the diary contained the more general impressions and personal experiences which might interest my friends, but often ran on to deal with politics and public figures. When the question arose of publishing this diary I thought it better not to load it with explanatory notes but to let the story, with its possible exaggerations or occasional gaps and inaccuracies, remain as it was written.

It may be useful to remind readers of the general situation in South Africa at the time of my visit. This, with extensions into Basutoland, Bechuanaland, the two Rhodesias and the Southern Congo, covered a period from October 1929 to March 1930.

After the languors, the transitory friendships and the deck games

---

[1] 'White Rule in Samoa', *The Times*, 10 and 11 April 1930.

of a long ocean voyage I had to brace myself to confront the situation I was to encounter in southern Africa. The Boer War had ended twenty-seven years before, followed by the amazing success of the two Boer generals, Botha and Smuts, in bringing their people into effective co-operation with the victors. Then had come the movement towards unification. The Governor-General, Lord Milner, had collected a group of able young men, mostly from Oxford, generally known as his Kindergarten, to help him in the task of repairing the war-shattered conditions and preparing the ground for unity. Philip Kerr had been one of these young men and I hoped that his name would commend me. I was a little less happy about carrying the label of Cecil Rhodes but could quote to myself the Latin tag, *pecunia non olet*.

The South Africa I was to encounter had passed out of the political euphoria within which the Union had generated. Botha had died in 1919, leaving Smuts to carry alone the great work of reconciliation. For this task in spite—perhaps because—of his becoming a world statesman, and incidentally directing the conquest of German East Africa, he was less successful than Botha in keeping the allegiance of his own people. In 1923 he failed to win the incorporation of the Southern Rhodesians into the Union. He had to face also the rising assertion of the white miners on the Rand. In 1923 his party, allied with the Unionists, representing the British element, was defeated by a coalition of Afrikaner nationalists and the new white Labour Party. The hard shape of the new South Africa was taking form thrusting aside the liberal and reconciling elements out of which the Union had been born. When I reached South Africa Smuts was abroad, exercising there his wider influence and, incidentally, lecturing in Oxford about the future of white civilization in eastern Africa in terms with which I strongly disagreed. In South Africa the more liberal English-speaking element, especially in the Cape, was increasingly perturbed about the native policy of the Hertzog government and especially the threat to the limited native franchise in the Cape. Added to this was the demand for the incorporation into the Union of the three native protectorates directly ruled by Britain—Basutoland, Bechuanaland and Swaziland. It was thus a complex and ominous South Africa upon which I disembarked in October 1929.

Prologue

Talk given on B.B.C. Radio 4 on January 11th 1972 in the series 'The Time of my Life'.

'The time of my life.' Yes—but what sort of time? The time when I did my best work—or what I *thought* was the best? Or the time that was most decisive in my career? Or the time I enjoyed most? Fortunately I have no difficulty in choosing the time which meets numbers two and three of these criteria. The time of my life which was at once the most enjoyable and the most decisive for my future was the year 1922 which I spent in the then British Somaliland. I can make this clear only by trying to give some picture of what I was before and after this experience.

I am told that very early in my childhood I used to answer the usual grown-ups' question of what I meant to be when I grew up with the answer—'a big-game hunter in Africa'. This, of course, was the result of my favourite reading. About Kipling's *Mowgli* and *Lives of the Hunted*—admittedly neither in Africa and both of which should have turned me against hunting. But *Jock of the Bushveld* and Rider Haggard's romances—these gave me the Africa about which I dreamed. But what hope could there be for a child, a female child at that, and at the turn of the century, of getting to Africa, least of all of becoming a hunter?

I had better begin by explaining what sort of child I was and in what setting I grew up. My father was the youngest son of a large family farming in the south-west. No land was left for the last two boys so one went as a missionary to Malaya, became Archdeacon of Singapore and translated the prayer-book into Dyak, while my father went into business in the north and we lived quite prosperously in Harrogate. I was one of seven children: three boys, one girl, two more boys and then me. I need mention only two names, my sister, Ethel, and my youngest brother, Edgar. (My father had a passion for our Anglo-Saxon origins.) My mother came of a family of French

15

extraction, and her mother, Mrs. J. H. Needell, wrote novels, mostly long three-volume ones. These were said to have been a great success in the seventies and eighties and to have won the approval of Gladstone. One can't help feeling glad that he got that much light relief.

Looking back it seems to me that we had a more exciting and self-contained life than many children today. We owed little in early days to our schools. We had a nursery and nurses and as we grew older, led a busy and tumultuous life of our own. The big boys took us on immense walks over the Yorkshire moors, twenty miles was regarded as a norm. The nursery was always full of firearms and sometimes we went out to what was then a wild crag and fought campaigns among the rocks and trees with blank cartridges. I can't think how we all survived. My eldest brother—in a row over his teasing my cat—did once shoot me deliberately with an airgun but the bullet hit the calf of my leg without doing much damage.

My father was a keen churchman, an adherent of the Oxford movement. He sent most of us to Christian boarding-schools and wanted us to have the university education he had missed. In early days I saw little of my sister as she was eight years older and away doing well at school and, later, university. My great friend was my youngest brother, Edgar, three years older than myself. His enthusiasms were for music and classical studies. Though he communicated neither of these to me, I think he was the main educational influence in my life. We were inseparable except for the cruel divorce of our boarding schools from which we wrote long diary letters to each other, sometimes in verse. We composed operas—I provided the words and he the music. We invented a world of our own, with its own maps, and built up its history in conversations on our long walks. And we joined together in every imaginable sport, birds' nesting, butterflying, fishing, swimming, golf, cricket at the nets, tennis. But my African dreams were my own secret—even from him.

My education was at first rather chaotic. My mother often went abroad in the winter. She did not like leaving me alone with a nurse and so sent me to boarding-school and then brought me back home on her return. So I had four or five changes before I finally went to St. Anne's, Abbots Bromley. Here, Miss Rice, the headmistress, a stately, splendidly aristocratic, devout and authoritarian woman, took firm hold of my hitherto meandering education. I had no academic ambitions. But she lured me to stay on to be head of my house and to fill the time by working for an Oxford scholarship—interesting work, she said, and no need to take it even if I won it. In those days scholarships meant something, especially to girls. When I won it she persuaded me again to stay on to be head of the school and to take Responsions, the then entrance exam to Oxford. It was a hard year as I had to swot up Latin and Greek from zero. I must confess that even to the end I hated school. It was not the fault of the school. It separated me from the holidays, from freedom and my brother. I used to cross off the days, often even the half-days.

Well, Miss Rice got me to Oxford—just as World War I broke out. My brother injured himself diving on our last summer holiday. So, before being able to join the army, he had his last year at Oxford taking Greats while I had my first year taking history. Then he joined up and was killed at Delville Wood.

Naturally I wanted to do some war-work. I did what bits and pieces I could while at college and as my time ended I managed to get out with the army lecturing on Salisbury Plain and in northern France. This last assignment was pretty hair-raising as I had no uniform: there was no one with much responsibility for me and I was far more unsophisticated than girls of my age today. The question for me, with the war coming to an end, was 'what next?' I definitely did *not* want to teach—I wanted something more active and adventurous. But some of the men who had taught me at Oxford persuaded me that it was my duty to fill a war-vacancy at a university ready for the flood of men which demobilization would release.

So, unwillingly, I went to Sheffield. If I am certain about the best time of my life this was just as certainly the worst. I was alone in a strange grimy city. I was not welcomed at the University. I was the first woman appointed to the academic staff. One of my first experiences was to be led out of the large warm Senior Common Room by its president, an old professor, and shown into a very small, barely furnished room next door which never had a fire. 'This', he said, 'is to be the Ladies' Common Room.' Add to that I had my first and, I am sure, very reformative, experience of poverty. My half-time salary —can you believe it?—was £100 a year. My now ageing parents did not approve of what I was doing and were planning to retire to the Channel Islands. And I was determined to be independent. So I took cheap rooms on the edge of the city. Every evening I went out to them on a clanging tram, walked half a mile and sat down to the piece of steak and a pudding both of which I had cut up into four portions to last for four days. My one recreation was to walk out on to the rather grim moorland and sit down amongst the wiry inhospitable heather which was grimed with soot, and contemplate, physically and mentally, the dark bare horizon.

But as the war came to an end demobilization released a flood of men to invade the University. Many were married with young children. Their government grant depended upon their passing their exams—but some were war-weary, some were below standard. Lodgings were sometimes uncomfortable—babies could keep them awake at night. They were desperate to pass their intermediate exam and so keep their grants and so I rashly offered to give the individual tuition which was not provided by the University. I should have foreseen the result. I was crushed by overwork and this on top, I suppose, of my personal troubles and isolation, led to a breakdown and stern doctor's orders for a year's complete rest. But what to do with it? The answer—go to Africa and fulfil my childhood's dream!

How could this be possible? Providence intervened through my sister. But how she was able to get me not only to Africa, but to what was then, perhaps, the most exciting part of the continent I could have chosen, demands quite a bit of explanation.

My sister, as I said, was—is, for we live together now—eight years older than myself. After university she was drawn by missionary ambitions to work abroad and in 1910 she took ship for East Africa. But alas! for the plans of mice and women. On the ship she got engaged and was married in Mombasa Cathedral not long after her arrival. It was through her husband, Major Henry Rayne, D.S.O., M.C., that I was now able not only to go to Africa but to go to one of the wildest, most romantic places—according to my idea—in the whole continent. And also to learn through him a great deal about a still earlier and even more romantically adventurous Africa.

I must therefore put him in the picture. Henry Rayne—he died some years ago—had run away from his New Zealand home as a boy and lied about his age in order to get into the New Zealand Mounted Infantry (I hope I have the name right). After a full and exciting Boer War he found his way up north to the then newly annexed East African Protectorate. Here he played his full part in the rough-and-tumble of opening up that beautiful, controversial acquisition. It happened that perhaps the most famous of all elephant-hunters was at work in the wild, almost virgin region—virgin as regards rape by Europeans—where the Belgian, Sudanese, Ugandan and Kenyan frontiers met (met at least on the map). Bell was a Scot of Lord Dewar's family. He was known as Karamoja Bell from his main shooting ground: he was the greatest exponent in action and on paper of the brain-shot and he wrote a book, *Wanderings of an Elephant Hunter*.

At that time, round about 1908, the Belgians were incensed at British criticism of King Leopold's dealing with the Congo—the controversy over Belgian Atrocities and Red Rubber. (I remember my young brother and I being mobbed on the sands near Ostend when we were heard speaking English.) The Belgians naturally made the most of a lawless Britisher poaching in their virgin annexation and making a fortune out of their ivory. Rayne volunteered for the long and dangerous job of tracking down the intruder, arresting him and bringing him to Nairobi. This he did. But on the way back he and his prisoner became firm friends and Bell tried to persuade him to join his next expedition. It appears that when, later, Rayne made his first visit to England, he called at the Colonial Office about his pay, considered himself insulted by the official concerned, hit him (one version is that he knocked him down) and rushed outside to telephone Bell in Scotland 'I'm your man!'

You might object at this point that I am supposed to be telling my own story, not my sister's or my brother-in-law's. But I must tell you a little more of them in order to show how I did at last achieve 'the time of my life'. For Rayne and Bell, after glutting themselves with ivory in the same wild region of Bell's former wanderings, decided to become the first settlers on the Juba river, the then boundary between the Italian and British territories in wild, hardly tamed Somali country. It was on the return journey from their visit to London to sell their first cotton that Rayne met my sister. Immediately after their marriage in Mombasa Cathedral he took her up to this wild country to live in bush full of lions beside a river full of crocodiles, to experience a Somali rising in which their nearest British official was murdered, and to have her first baby.

I must refer to a little story about this baby. I was at my boarding-school, enormously excited, as you may imagine, by my sister so dramatically forestalling me on the road to adventure. She wrote me long letters about her experiences and her husband sent me a bracelet made from the hairs of an elephant which he had shot, clasped with gold and inscribed with my name. Needless to say I had regaled the girls in my house with these adventures. So when, one day, about five months after her marriage, my sister wrote 'When I come home you will be an aunt', I put down the letter and joyfully announced 'My sister has had a baby.' There was a rather hushed reaction from school-fellows who were a little more sophisticated than myself.

Marriage did not divert my brother-in-law from his adventurous career. He returned to the army in World War I and in the inter-war years mcomanded a joint expedition from the Sudan, Uganda and Kenya to clear raiders from Abyssinia—as Ethiopia was then called—out of the wild dry hinterland round Lake Rudolf. He wrote a book about it called *The Ivory Raiders*. And it is worth recording that in face of red-tape objections that Somalis were too excitable to make good soldiers, he trained a Somali Company *and* held them steady in a square attacked all day long by a greatly superior and well-armed force of raiders from Abyssinia.

His next employment was in the expedition of 1919–20 which at last destroyed the power of the so-called Mad Mullah who had dominated Somaliland for twenty years and, after a series of campaigns, had forced the British to retire to the coast. So 1920 saw him posted as District Commissioner of the newly regained frontier district of Hargeisa. My sister was to join him. Here, at last, was my chance! My mother tried taking me to rest in a luxurious hotel in the Lake District. No good! I almost hated the hills and waters as much as I hated the hotel. To me Somaliland was the obvious, the only, the predestined place. It was not so obvious to medical opinion that immediate post Mad Mullah Somaliland was ideal for rest and recuperation. But I had to win and in 1921—I forget the exact date—at twenty-four (and, as I see now, a very young and uninitiated twenty-four), my sister and I left Tilbury in a P. & O. liner.

We disembarked at Aden and my first experience of tropical heat was to have it thrown back at me like a blow from this place of solid rock. We stayed at a dingy hotel in the middle of the town—hellishly hot. I looked out from a rickety balcony on to the crowds seething below—Yemenis and Arabs of many other kinds, Somalis, Jews, Indians—also of many kinds—and Negroes—all dark, brown to black, alien, unknown, unknowable. Next day we were to cross the Gulf of Aden to Berbera to live almost alone and far inland among a population of dark people. I had an overwhelming spasm of recoil, of something more than physical fear. I referred to this in one of my Reith Lectures—a revulsion against the thought that I—how can I express it?—I, so white, so vulnerable, so sensitive, so complex, was about to commit myself to that black continent across the water; one, almost alone, among tens of thousands of strange, dark, fierce, uncomprehending people, and live away on that far frontier, utterly cut off from my own race. It was more like a nightmare than a natural revulsion. I suppose it was racial fear. It passed and I have never felt it again, not on the Somali frontier or later in any situation of danger or isolation in any part of Africa. Even, when alone in remote almost unadministered pagan areas in northern Nigeria, or at night alone in the African slums of Durban.

We boarded the dingy little Indian-owned cattle boat which fed foodless Aden from Somali flocks and herds. It was now on its empty run. We disembarked at Berbera, the headquarters of the Protectorate—a few white bungalows in some irrigated greenery with the native town a discreet distance up-shore. A shock awaited us. The Mad Mullah had been defeated but some of the tribes into which the Somalis were divided—there was no unity—were giving trouble. And this was down in the south along the Abyssinian frontier—my brother-in-law's district. He was in danger—I forget now whether the trouble this time was an attempt to register the too-numerous firearms, or the first taxation in this newly occupied district. Whatever it was, the Governor told us no women were to go there and we had better turn round and go home. Here was a stunning disappointment! We pleaded for a little delay. And got it. So we kicked our heels in the pitiless heat of Berbera, riding on the shore or sailing the shark-infested sea or dining in or out with the handful of officials.

At last the situation cleared—Major Rayne came up to Berbera and persuaded the Governor to let us go back. After all it was upon my brother-in-law's judgement that our safety depended. I have already mentioned his faith in Somalis as soldiers. He knew them well and had then just written a book about them and the recent final expedition in which he had taken part. It made no difference to his affection for them that Somalis had more than once tried to murder him and in one attempt killed his colleague beside him. So, backing his D.C.'s judgement, the Governor let us go. First across the burning coastal plain, then 5,000 feet up the terrifying masses of rock which led to the plateau—past Sheikh, the Governor's little hot-season retreat. On again through a sandy waste, dotted with thorn trees, rocks, ant-hills and spiky aloes. We met Somalis, very few, travelling with the mats and poles of their huts strapped on their camels. Sometimes through dim aisles of the thorn trees there would be a scurry of buck or an ugly wart-hog trundling off. And always birds, doves of many kinds and sizes. Now, for me in England, the voice of doves always recalls Africa—a harsh setting for such a gentle sound. There were other birds—why are they so numerous in semi-desert lands?—storks, vultures, hoopoes, hornbills, carrion crows and the glorious jays with feathers of a dozen iridescent blues.

At last, after threading a route of nearly two hundred miles and seeing buildings only at Sheikh, we reached Hargeisa. It is still a magic word to me. Yet there wasn't much to see—sand, thorn-trees, aloes, a few stony hills, a *tug* or dry water-course. On the other side of this *tug* from our bungalow the Camel Corps were living in tents, two Somali companies and half-a-dozen British officers.

You might well ask how such a place could give me 'the time of my life'. Yet it did. Whatever my later travels in more beautiful and dramatic parts of the continent, this was my *first* Africa. The people— few enough of them—were at once fierce and beautiful. I think the people of Africa's north-east are, by our own standards, the most beautiful in the world—slim, upright, with dry polished skins, dark hawkish eyes, fine-cut features and proud carriage. They are hard people in a hard land. I used to watch them in my brother-in-law's court litigating tenaciously for compensation after inter-tribal fights— 100 camels for a man, 50 for a woman. But they could be loyal to Europeans they respected. Even gentle. We made friends with the Somali leader who had backed the British against the Mullah, Haji Musa Farah. He once expounded to me the habits of the weaver birds who were making their nests in a tree over his tent. He treated his ponies like children. We bought a lovely grey from him, which we called Griselda, marvellous on trek and over the jumps and a real member of the family.

Why was I so gloriously happy in Hargeisa? There was little enough to do. We had to stay indoors during the heat of the day. But there were books to read, letters to write, and a menagerie to play with, young buck, cheetahs, two young lions and an irreconcilable little leopard. There were tennis, riding and steeple-chasing. There were the Camel Corps officers across the river-bed to be dined with in their mess tent. Or they would come across to drinks or dinner with us. There were buck and guinea-fowl to shoot for the pot. No rule against shooting sitting birds! I once shot seven with one shot—they were all bunched together and rather young. I felt like Herod. Above all there were the nights. I slept in the open on the roof. We had a breed of very large hyenas there and at night they came snooping round. They could bite off half the face of a sleeping man. Their extraordinary howl punctuated my dreams. And if the moon was up I could see them slinking around the bungalow like grey ghosts.

The rains broke late that year. I saw the misery this meant for man and beast in this desiccated land—and the satisfaction to the vultures! Then the first huge drops fell. The shrivelled land drank them in and gave out a strange, acrid, never-to-be-forgotten smell. The first soupy water came fingering down the dry river-bed followed by a torrent full of branches and dead creatures. One night the river rose high enough to cut us off from the Camel Corps and dinner. I had to mount a camel and tuck my long dress—of course we dressed for dinner!—round my waist.

Among many memories of Hargeisa three events stand out. One was the day we found a document stuck on a tree near our house. It was a call to the Somali soldiers in the Camel Corps to cut all white throats and go with their weapons across the border into Abyssinian Somaliland and join those fighting for the deposed Muslim emperor, Lij Yasu, against the Christian contender, Haile Selassie. Obviously our throats were *not* cut: the Somali soldiers remained loyal. Lij Yasu's star sank while that of Haile Selassie rose to shine for nearly half a century and is still shining.

It may have been in some relation to this threat that the military authorities decided to add an Indian Company to the two Somali ones, and this led to my second thrill—the right word I think. The newly arrived Indians needed training in Somali bush warfare. It happened that just before we arrived, many of the Mullah's soldiers had been captured and it was difficult to know what to do with them. So some of them were drafted into the Camel Corps. They were now told to take off their uniforms, put on their dervish clothes and play-act the part of the enemy. The officer in charge of them was rather a special friend of mine and he said I could go with them. I am sure he must have got into trouble afterwards. But could anything have been more gloriously exciting than galloping around with this wild-looking troop, ambushing the enemy in a narrow rocky defile and later dashing madly around them like Red Indians as they formed up, and almost breaking a British square?

The third thrill was the best. Major Rayne had to beat the bounds of his newly reconquered district up to the Abyssinian frontier. I was allowed to go with him. This meant setting off into the blue with a string of camels, ponies and mules, a handful of Somali police looking splendid in their uniforms, and a few cooks and orderlies. We could keep up the pace by shifting from one kind of mount to another—camel, lofty and romantic but liable to let you get swept off by a branch of a tree if you got sleepy and you had a long way to fall—mule, tireless but rather dull—pony, handsome and sensitive. I remember caressing my pony's neck—crisp, chestnut hairs, burnished in the sunlight—in gratitude for his gallant responsiveness in spite of the blazing heat. It was generally a matter of going single file, weaving our way through the universal thorn trees.

The sun decided our routine. The cook and orderlies got up in the dark and set off with the baggage camels. We rose just as there was the first low hint of light through the trees and jogged along generally in that strange silence which the mystery of an African dawn seems to impose. We would catch up the advance guard for our breakfast. We would rest in the midday heat. Perhaps we shot something for the pot—a buck for the men, birds for ourselves. But we also had a little flock of sheep with us, the hardy Somali fat-tailed sheep. I thought this was rather horrible. They well knew the dangers of the bush and panted along after the baggage train in order to keep up with us and preserve their lives—only, one by one, to lose them to the knife as they reached camp.

We carried wonderful tents. They had been made for King Edward VII's great Indian Durbar and later distributed to appropriate colonies. They were large, with a decorated blue lining, two rooms in each, blue druggets on the floor and a lavatory bathroom leading out. Only there was no water! We could be sure only of what little we carried for drinking. I remember stopping at a so-called well in a dry river-bed—just a very deep hole with a man at the bottom scraping up what looked like cocoa—yet I drank it.

Night was the zenith of adventure. I slept on a camp-bed in the open with large fires on each side of me to scare potential carnivores—lions, hyenas or leopards. The police built a high *zareba* of thorn branches round our camp. They would sing themselves gutterally to sleep. Then that miracle of the tropical night of stars! If the moon was up the sand turned the colour of milk. These nights utterly fulfilled the heart's desire of my childhood for adventure in Africa.

The adventure *could* have ended there. One night some trekking Somalis asked if they could build their *zareba* alongside ours for extra protection. They did. But just before dawn lions came and chose to jump *their* defences rather than ours and seize a man. The racket that broke out caused them to drop him but he was dead. My brother-in-law said we must go after them. So in the first light we started out on our ponies to follow the tracks. We followed them nearly all day. Late in the afternoon the lions must have got tired of being hunted and began to slow up. We dismounted. My brother-in-law became separated from me by a bit of thick bush. One of the lions stepped out of this. I reached to my bearer for my gun but he had silently stolen away. It was just as well, for if I *had* fired I should probably have done no more than wound the lion and this might have ended in serious trouble for me or someone else. Fortunately the lion made a noise—neither a roar, a growl, or a grunt, but something between all three. Major Rayne was, of course, a very experienced hunter and knew the meaning of this particular utterance of the lion. He therefore fired in the air and the lion, not relishing enemies behind and in front, sheered off into the bush. Not much of an incident to any experienced hunters but, for me, the climax of adventure.

But the whole trek was to me, in the full sense of the word, thrilling. What especially appealed to me was that on our very blank map the word 'Unexplored' was printed right across the area we were traversing. At some points there was no way of knowing for certain whether we were in British Somaliland or Abyssinia. As it was all just Somaliland and unadministered on the Abyssinian side it was only by geodetic survey that we knew where we were. As far as I knew no Europeans had ever followed our route, yet when, from time to time, we met a few Somali nomads filing through the bush with their camels they hardly turned their eyes to look at us—strangely snubbing encounters!

My Somali trip came to an end. I had to leave Hargeisa, pass again through that grim thorny wilderness, and across the oven-hot plain to reach Berbera. I had still one more very minor adventure. The little Indian cattle-ship was loaded with animals for the return journey and I had to walk among and on top of its living cargoes destined to nourish foodless Aden, in order to reach my cabin. Worse than that, the Scottish captain—his post was hardly an élitist one—was reeling drunk. I was the only passenger and he followed me around with a glass of whisky in one hand and a photograph in the other with the ceaseless refrain—'Have a drink! Look at my wife!' He was clearly quite unable to take the right line out of the harbour.

Fortunately I had done a lot of sailing around Berbera and I knew the line the Arab dhows followed out of and beyond the harbour. But the night, thick with animal stink, was hardly restful. And in the morning I got up early to find that the skipper had achieved the impossible—he had failed to find Aden—a pretty obvious landmark. Between us we located it in the end, arriving very late; I had to witness the unpleasant scene—doubly unpleasant in the racial atmosphere of those days—of the Indian owner coming aboard to curse the erring captain and sack him on the spot.

But that was the last adventure—at least in this particular 'time of my life'.

It will be obvious to anyone that the reason why this harsh corner of Africa was Heaven to me was that it provided the perfect stage in which to play the romantic role of which I had dreamed as a child. I delighted even in the costume needed then for the part I was playing—the high leather boots, the breeches—the short circular khaki skirt, the becoming double terai hat—long since discarded as an unnecessary protection; above all the rifle over the shoulder and the pistol under the pillow.

But now I was back in—of all places—Sheffield, and the lecture room, the winter slush and the clanging trams. True, things improved a little. I took a house in which my sister could spend her leave. I played games. I dabbled in repertory, wrote a play about Anglo-Saxon England, produced it at the University and shamelessly commandeered the best part for myself. I experimented with a motor-bike until it crashed, and then with a horse—which didn't. I began to make friends, especially amongst the medical fraternity. But this was not enough. I wanted to *do* something about Africa—about the problems of what is now called colonialism which were thrashing about aimlessly in my mind. Today, of course, I should have been encouraged to do a D.Phil. on Somali administration. But I had hardly ever heard of that magic abbreviation by virtue of which a graduate now becomes a lecturer, or a lecturer a reader. So I wrote a novel and poured into it the problems of Somaliland as well as the adventure and the harsh beloved setting. It was the story of the rivalry between the medalhunting colonel of the Camel Corps and the good District Commissioner devoted to his people and full of plans for irrigation—that is why I called it *Major Dane's Garden*—and how he dealt with a native rising and how the colonel's young wife transferred her affections to the D.C. The story has been forgotten for about half a century but, astonishingly, it has been resurrected as the first of a new series of colonial novels.

Prologue

Was 'the time of my life' in Somaliland to be nothing but a wonderful episode looked back to with bitter nostalgia? The rosy hues of
personal adventure and self-romantization started to fade and I began
to discern some of the realities which lay underneath them—the rights
and needs of our African subjects—Britain's capacity to meet them—
the quality of our colonial service—the ultimate goal of our imperial
rule, if indeed we were aware of ultimates. What could I do about
Africa in Sheffield except read and meditate about such problems.
Suddenly there occurred an internal convulsion in my college at
Oxford, St. Hugh's, one which shook the whole University. But that is
another story of which much has been said and written. There was a
large re-arrangement of staff and I found myself back again there as
Fellow and Tutor in Modern History. This was my chance! There
was now time to do more than dream about Africa—I could study it.
You can—or you could then—lecture upon almost anything irres-
pective of attracting any audience. So I indulged myself with such
subjects as 'British Policy towards Native Races', or the 'Mandates
System'. After a year or two of this there came another utterly un-
expected intervention of fate—a letter from Philip Kerr offering me
a Rhodes Trust Travelling Fellowship for a year's travel round the
world looking at—I forget the definition—native or colour questions,
then an almost unknown subject of academic study.

So I set off round the world *en route* for Africa by way of America—
Red Indians and Negroes—Hawaii, Fiji, Samoa, New Zealand, Australia and then at last Africa. And just as I reached East Africa I
found a cable from The Rhodes Trust offering me a year's extension of
my travelling Fellowship.

Since then I have been travelling in Africa, trying to see it at all
levels from the lowest bush-station to Government House and the
Colonial Office. The University invented posts for me and then
Nuffield College gave me a Fellowship which allowed me to combine
travel with lecturing and writing at Oxford. I went through all the
colonialist's attitudes—the belief that we had almost unlimited time
in which to develop our administrative methods—the growing realization of the need to prepare our wards—not *too* urgently—for *eventual*
self-government—then helter-skelter rush over the edge and into
independence when our African friends and pupils became ministers,
top secretaries and even Heads of State overnight. But this abrupt
conclusion has not changed my unfashionable view that, by any
balanced historical judgement of the history of imperialism and the

character of the Africa we annexed, our colonial rule was, on balance, an immense and essential service to Africa. I shall not forget the privilege I had at Oxford of teaching the colonial administrators back from the field for a year's so-called second course. Teaching?— of course they were teaching me, and not only about Africa and their work but about the spirit of devotion most of them brought to it. I learned about something else in Africa—the selfless work of the Christian missionaries and came to believe that the faith they gave to those peoples able to receive it may prove the most precious service of all.

And what about my beloved Somaliland? Alas! I never got back to study it in my new role of student. South, West and East Africa, and an interesting extension into the West Indies, were too demanding. But I thought much about it and did what one writer could to project the case for the unity of all Somalis at the end of World War II. You can imagine my pleasure when I was invited to attend as the guest of the new government the independence celebrations of the united British and Italian Somalilands in the summer of 1960. So I could see again that harsh land and those handsome, high-spirited people rejoicing in their freedom and unity. The unity was almost unbelievable to anyone who had known them in the days of frequent inter-tribal fighting over the scarce water and grazing. Such conflict had been a theme of my novel. It is sad indeed to see the weakening of our ties with Somalia, and their substitution by Communist influences. But nothing can change my purely personal and perhaps rather egotistical attitude to Somaliland as the place where I fulfilled so ecstatically my childhood's dream and also found a guiding purpose for my life and work—truly that year was 'the time of my life'.

Arrival in South Africa

October 1929

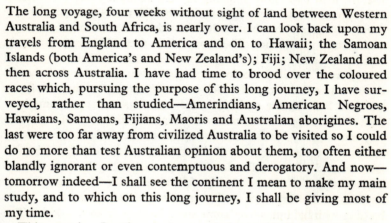

The long voyage, four weeks without sight of land between Western Australia and South Africa, is nearly over. I can look back upon my travels from England to America and on to Hawaii; the Samoan Islands (both America's and New Zealand's); Fiji; New Zealand and then across Australia. I have had time to brood over the coloured races which, pursuing the purpose of this long journey, I have surveyed, rather than studied—Amerindians, American Negroes, Hawaians, Samoans, Fijians, Maoris and Australian aborigines. The last were too far away from civilized Australia to be visited so I could do no more than test Australian opinion about them, too often either blandly ignorant or even contemptuous and derogatory. And now—tomorrow indeed—I shall see the continent I mean to make my main study, and to which on this long journey, I shall be giving most of my time.

This morning I woke up at 5 a.m. being suddenly aware that the ship was slowing down. I knew that this would be an important day for me. I had seen no land since we left Western Australia two weeks ago and after the long emptiness of the sea it was with a sense of shock that, looking out of my porthole, I saw great blocks of concrete sliding past almost perilously close to us. Then, squatting on the concrete, I saw black men with fishing-rods—the first Negroes I had seen since I left America. Behind them was a low green hill. And what a new value the green of earth offers after weeks at sea! The hill was capped by a lighthouse and in front of this the disreputable-looking flotilla and implements of what I later learned was a whaling station.

I dressed hurriedly and went on deck. The ship was making her way across a great dull enclosed sheet of water, with docks and a town smudging the coast at one point—Durban! So this was Africa! Except for those black fishermen there was nothing so far to suggest it. Dull

29

skies, dull colours, dull town, not a scrap of foliage or an architectural feature to distinguish it from a port in America, England or Europe. I thought of the only other part of Africa upon which I had landed, the almost empty white-hot desert coast of Somaliland with its few thousand slender, handsome, fierce Hamitic nomads.

When we had breakfasted I went up on deck. I found we were now berthed and that the wharf was alive with black men, Zulus, I assumed. How like, and yet unlike, the Negroes of America! Two or three centuries of life in that country have set a stamp upon the faces of Africans. Gone is the unrestrained expressiveness and merriment. Not that the men I was now watching showed no dignity but it was something brought with them from their tribal life and—so I speculated— deeply threatened by their inclusion within a world they cannot yet understand or influence. These men were dressed almost entirely in black coal sacks, which hung, toga-like, from their shoulders, and every sort of battered, borrowed headgear was stuck on their heads, down to an officer's cap of which not much more than the wire frame was left. Beneath the coal-blackened jute, legs and arms sometimes flashed with copper wire; ears were weighed with lumps of wood and tin; some woolly heads were shaved in strange designs. Even to my ignorant eye the men were of different tribes, mostly Zulu, but—I later learned—Basuto, Pondo, Fingo as well. They looked up at us impudently, their faces nearly fell apart with their continuous laughter and every now and then they hurled themselves into a battling whirl of limbs over some small largesse from the decks. The people on the boat laughed and commented:

'Look at the niggers!' 'Aren't they priceless?' 'Throw them a penny and see them fight for it.'

I went below after a bit and sat in my cabin. I felt faint but the cause was mental rather than physical. Whether my mind had become softened with three weeks' isolation from the puzzling world, I don't know. But the sight of the Kaffirs on the docks was like a stunning blow. I seemed to feel the immensity of the problem they represented and the absurdity of my attempting to understand it. How could any humane relationship be established between the people on the wharf and ourselves, the people on the decks? And this was only a sample, only the first corner of the continent which I could visualize spreading west and north, the whole terrifying map, with its enormous distances, its oppressions and cruelties, its voiceless, primitive people, its senseless political divisions. I wanted to lock myself in my cabin, hide

under the blankets. Understand this ? Study it ? Report on it ? I felt
I dared not face this ridiculous enterprise, could hardly dare to step
off the ship on to the docks, in order to begin it.

But Africa now came right on to the ship. The black faces, bleared
with coal dust, unfamiliar, grinning, were passing, peering into my
window, and the shouting, singing, groaning, whining, and thumping
of coaling was in full swing. So I went out to keep my appointment
with the two or three passengers I knew best, English, German and
American. I was foolish enough to marvel that none of them shared
my feelings—not that I asked them!—that people stepped so cheerfully for the first time on to the black continent, as if Durban were
just like any other port, and the dockers around us like any other
dockers.

Certainly the natives showed no such sense of gloom. It would be
hard to imagine men who looked on better terms with their world as
they seethed on the coal barges, laughing and singing, lay smiling
on the wharf, or ran and jumped at dangerous speed with their porters' trolleys.

Two or three of us, including Underberg, a German friend I had
made, hired a car and went a long drive for three hours. I thought the
town of Durban quite uninteresting: the suburbs had the usual
pleasant roads, the houses perhaps a little bigger than in Australia and
New Zealand, and made more distinctive by the Dutch influence, for
the curving gables and pillared *stoep* are easy to mould in concrete. To
anyone fresh from Australia the most striking feature was that all this
European life was built on a black foundation. Black errand boys,
street sweepers, nurse girls, maids in doorways, gardeners in gardens.
Yet this black labour is, I soon learned, rigidly controlled: no native
may enter or leave the town without a pass: if he has to stay for his
work it must either be on European premises or in the native compound. Entering this he is dipped and his clothes fumigated; the same
on leaving.

We stopped by the beach—it was Sunday—and had a good opportunity to study the physique of the bathing and sun-bathing crowds.
To me it seemed poor. I saw scores of rather weedy men, pale, with
weak blue eyes and dark hair; it almost seemed as though a type had
been evolved, at least in the city. They looked very different from the
big, beefy, Australians I had lately been visiting.

I dined in town and at night walked along the 'front' which a Black-
pool expert, imported for the purpose, had bedizened with coloured

lights and littered with band-stands and shelters, all the tawdry bric-à-brac which in Britain so often, and so lamentably, borders the majesty of the sea and amongst which the Zulu rickshaw boys looked very strange objects.

I made contact with one or two of the white 'gaugers' in charge of the dock labour and through them I went to see the manager of one of the biggest of the firms which recruits labour from the reserves and contracts for the work on the docks. He was a hard, stringy Scot, with gimlet eyes and a mouth like a rat-trap, working in an office full of Indian clerks and Zulu foremen. Queues of natives, looking bewildered as cattle in a pen, waited their approach to the big counter behind which he sat. He could speak to them, such words as were needed, in any Bantu language and did so with a voice like a machine gun. It was impossible to tell from his tone whether he were cursing, dismissing or accepting them and equally difficult to interpret their manner as they wavered up to the counter. Some were clearly straight from the bush, others had been there before. He distinguished them, Pondos, Basutos and Zulus, down from their kraals for six or nine months, forty-five shillings a month and their keep in the compound. He explained to me:

'I have been at this for forty years and I can tell you I know my job. My firm can get all the labour it wants because we have a good reputation. They know where they are with us. We are firm but just; we give a boy his rights, no more and no less. I accept only the raw bush native. No mission boy is allowed inside this place, no so-called educated boy. Any suggestion that a boy has had the faintest connection with the I.C.U. [the native Industrial and Commercial Union which, I have since learned, is just struggling into existence] and out he goes! But the I.C.U. has been pretty well dealt with in Durban, I'm glad to say. To his shame, a white man has been mixed up with it.'

'No,' in answer to questions, 'there is no government inspection of our compounds, nor do the government lay down any conditions. Our natives are perfectly happy so long as they don't get interfered with. Yes, breaking of contract is a criminal offence and I always see to it that they get jailed for it or, better, fined, then they have to stay longer to work off the fine.'

Rather unwillingly he agreed to let me look at the compounds. But at this moment a policeman came in. He reported the death of a man who had just been killed. A rope had broken and a basket of coal had fallen on him and he had died almost at once. The policeman described the condition in which he found the body and handed over the man's belt, wallet, etc., all dripping with blood. The manager took them, excused himself from coming with me and shook hands. I withdrew mine to find it stained with the blood of No. 1102. There was nowhere to wash it off so I had to go as I was, carrying the mark. I went with one of the Zulus. We threaded our way through some dirty back-quarters until we found the compounds. My companion, questioned about the I.C.U., seemed afraid to speak, except to disavow all connection with it.

The compound, though gloomy and prison-like, was not too bad. My entry caused a good deal of excitement among the men who had just come off night-shift and were lounging about in a state of undress. I looked into everything—the kitchens where huge vats of white 'mealie-meal' were cooking or cooling: the shower-baths through which they must pass on their way in from the docks: the dormitories where two rows of wooden shelves have been polished to ebony by sweat and coal dust and where groups of men were squatting, gambling, or cooking their own food in native cooking-pots. Then I went to the sick-wards, where 'flu, fever, and bronchitis had turned black men grey, and where they lay on rather dirty grids under tattered blankets. The native pharmacist, however, looked clean and efficient and was very proud of his cupboard of medicines and his long experience. I asked him if he were going to be a doctor. He looked at me in surprise and said: 'How can a native be a doctor?'

Then aboard again *en route* for Capetown. We had had three days with flat, sandy coasts slipping past to the north. On the fourth, in the morning, I stood on deck looking at some very interesting shaped rocks sticking up out of the mist and sea, apparently quite close to the boat. I could hardly believe this was Table Mountain hanging over Capetown and still some thirty miles or more away. We had to run very close before the magnitude of the rocks was indicated by the town at their base coming into view. When I did see the whole thing I was simply amazed. Nothing had prepared me for the grandeur and strangeness of the site. It was, I think, the first time on my journey that the real thing was so far beyond my most brilliant expectations. The mountain looked unreal, like an impressive piece of painted scenery. For me it was the gateway to a continent. I knew that north and north-east of it there stretched a thousand miles of racial problems deeper and more complex than any I had yet surveyed.

Capetown

October 1929

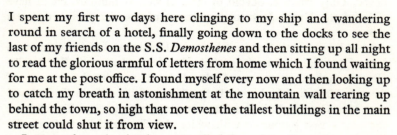

I spent my first two days here clinging to my ship and wandering round in search of a hotel, finally going down to the docks to see the last of my friends on the S.S. *Demosthenes* and then sitting up all night to read the glorious armful of letters from home which I found waiting for me at the post office. I found myself every now and then looking up to catch my breath in astonishment at the mountain wall rearing up behind the town, so high that not even the tallest buildings in the main street could shut it from view.

I engaged a room in the part called Seapoint where the open sea breaks on the rocks and rows of hotels and pleasant villas cluster along this favourable site like shellfish. The Lion Mountain, as rounded as Table Mountain is square, lies behind, and its couchant, rocky lines against the brilliant South African sky save this suburb from looking commonplace. Also, the architecture is good; simple houses are washed in pale grey or lemon: they have gardens and pergolas brimming over with blossoms, wide pillared verandahs, and often a red-flagged terrace garden climbing up the hill. Household standards can be high for cheap coloured labour makes possible what is denied to the Australasian colonist.

The crowd is motley in Capetown streets. I saw the English in all degrees of acclimatization; brawny, tanned harsh-faced Dutchmen in big hats; Jews of all kinds, white and prosperous-looking Jews or lean, dark Jews from eastern Europe: well-dressed Malays in black or red tar-booshes; Indians; 'Cape coloured' people, only a degree less respectable-looking, and very various in type and tint; and, of course, every kind of African drawn from all parts of the Union and beyond, including bare-legged women balancing pots and bundles on their heads.

One of the first things that strikes the newcomer is the thoroughness with which the new bilingual rule is carried out. Every single public notice of every kind, however long or large, has to be duplicated, and what this means in a big town, in the post office, the railway station, and even in the museum, can be imagined. All blue-books are printed double at huge cost. Even on the Official maps they Dutchify English names—East London becomes Oos London, though why does Johannesburg not become Johnstown? The size needed for the stamps defeated the Afrikaners until they thought of having alternate stamps in Afrikaans and English, getting the balance in their favour by abolishing the king's head. As for the flag, it has to be seen to be believed. Only fanatics, devoid of taste as well as humour, could have reduced the Union Jack to its present minute size within the new stripes.

I had hardly settled into my Seapoint Hotel than I was rung up by a Mrs. Cartwright, sister-in-law of Monsieur Marzorati, the Anglo-German-Italian governor of the Belgian mandated territory of Ruanda-Urundi. I had looked after him and his wife in Oxford and now Mrs. Cartwright insisted upon my staying with her. To fetch me she sent a vast limousine with white chauffeur and he took me the sixteen miles out of Capetown to Fernwood in Claremont. Here I relaxed into hospitality so luxurious that, in this country, and with my commitment, I felt almost guilty in enjoying it. The house stands in a beautiful garden with a bathing pool. There is plenty of social life and a car at my disposal.

One of my first engagements was a visit to the beautiful racecourse, Kenilworth, for *the* race of the year, the Metropolitan. Here I saw the extraordinary mixture that makes up Capetown society in the enclosure. Incidentally it was my first race meeting ever. There was one horse that to me was quite obviously *not* a racehorse, an enormous, thick-set, grey, which looked almost absurd in the string of twenty slender, silk-skinned aristocrats. So I tried to be very clever and staked on the slenderest and satinest. The grey simply romped home. I saw my first big crowd of natives there, hundreds and hundreds, thronging their own special part. Horseracing seems a taste easily acquired.

The Rhodes Memorial was up the hill behind the house. The area of the Rhodes estate is kept free from all buildings except public ones. This means that the whole steep slope up to the towers of mountain rock is an unbroken forest of pines, mostly the beautiful chalice-shaped stone pine or the lofty *pinus insignis*. This is the outcome, of course, of wise plantation long ago. The result is rich in colour. The sky here is famed for its almost constant and radiant blue which is given its full depth by the dry air while it has not the white glare of the tropics. From its earthy bases the towering crest of rock springs straight up in walls and towers: it loses all grimness from the variety of its colours. Then comes the sheath of pinewoods reaching further up the slopes, green as only southern pines are green. The earth, when it shows itself bare, is almost flaming with colour; where men are levelling a site for the new hospital you can see it, changing in fifty yards from bright sienna to crimson and from crimson to orange and salmon-pink. At rare intervals, in a high creek on the mountain, the dark moss of the pines is streaked with the palest silver-green, the colour of the last, lingering indigenous trees, crowded out as the Bushmen and Hottentots have been crowded out, by alien growths. It is worth a climb to see them. Each soft green leaf is bound in a close silver net which can be rubbed away from it and when the evening sun catches the upheld branches the whole tree does, in truth, turn silver.

I was not quite isolated from history in my luxurious setting. My hosts' place was close to the beautiful old Dutch house Groote Schuur. (The Afrikaners' domestic architecture was one of the few good things they brought to the sub-continent.) This house was restored and modernized by the young architect, Herbert Baker, whom Rhodes selected to work with him, and who later designed impressive public buildings elsewhere in South and East Africa and, in Oxford, Rhodes House, my own place of work. Close by Groote Schuur is the house of Rudd, the man Rhodes sent up to Lobengula's kraal to obtain the concession which led to the foundation of Rhodesia and so to the destruction of this African chief and the loss of his tribe's lands to white settlers.

I think I must just remind you of the general situation in South Africa as I arrive here in its political capital. (Pretoria is, of course, the administrative capital, Bloemfontein the judicial. South Africa is too nationalist in its provinces to agree, like Australia, upon a single capital.) The two unifying Boer generals are now out of action, Botha by death and Smuts by electoral defeat in 1924. General Hertzog, with the help of the Labour Party, is in power and is determined to swing policy in a pro-Boer and anti-African direction. Above all he plans legislation to destroy the remaining limited voting rights of Africans in Cape Province, the last stronghold of those Cape liberals who, during the making of a united South Africa out of the four provinces (Transvaal, Orange Free State, Natal and the Cape) have struggled to save this last relic of racial equality. My object in the Cape is to make contact with the British leaders, both those who worked to achieve the Union which is now taking on such an unfavourable shape for them with their religion of the British Empire, but especially with the Cape liberals who are trying to defend the native franchise. I don't yet know whether I shall be able to meet the Afrikaner leaders.

It was easy enough to meet what I must call the British element. Among them is Sir Drummond Chaplin, once Administrator of Rhodesia, friend and associate of Rhodes, an M.P. and now director of the Rhodesian railways. He asked me to dinner at the palace he has built twenty miles from Capetown, with a mountain behind and the ocean in front, and gardens, terraces, and loggias round a house of which one might dream but never hope to see. There, Lady Chaplin sleeps in a luxurious bedroom crowded with parrots and love-birds and pekinese, the room stinking like a fowl-house with stale feathers and wet bird-sand. I called *en route* at the house of the Archbishop of Capetown to pick up two bishops. One of these was Bishop Paget, whom I knew. When Dean Church left his books to my college, St. Hugh's, I had been deputed to select what we wanted for the library and Bishop Paget had followed me anxiously round the bookshelves to glean my leavings.

From the Church to the Law in the person of Sir James Rose-Innes who asked me to lunch. He is a great champion of the Cape franchise and represents the Cape-British tradition in native affairs. I did not realize that he was the Chief Justice and lightly engaged him in debate on the subject of the whereabouts of sovereignty in a mandated territory. I rather fancy myself on this issue and brashly tried to make him see sense. I was told only afterwards that he had given judgement in the famous international case about the status of South West Africa. He could hardly reverse it at my suggestion! His daughter, Countess Molkte, was there, wife of *the* Molkte's son (or grandson, I suppose ?). Her son has been chosen, very fittingly, as the first German Rhodes Scholar to go to Oxford since the war. She is very thrilled about this. I promised to look him up. But I imagine he will be a bit of a lion.

I was entertained also by Mr. B. K. Long, editor of the leading South African newspaper, the *Cape Times*. He is very much in the limelight at the moment because, backed by his intelligent wife, he has published very strong comments upon the character of a lately deceased millionaire, Mr. J. B. Robinson, with regard to the terms of his will. The scandal has, I think reached the British Press. This multi-millionaire, his fortune having been made in South Africa, is accused of having left nothing to any South African cause. He is reported to have left £1,000 to one daughter on condition that she did not receive money from any other source. His other daughter, Countess Labbia, married to an Italian, is said to have got £3,000,000. Mr. Long said what he thought of this in his paper. And all Capetown is buzzing with it. B. K. Long printed all Countess Labbia's furious letters to his paper and added this note to her final one: 'In view of the writer being a lady, I have erased the more abusive expressions.'[1]

Next came Professor Eric Walker, author of the best history of South Africa, an extremely handsome giant of some six foot three. He took me over the splendid new buildings of Capetown University. If Berkeley, California, is supposed to be the finest (modern) university building in the world, taken in relation to its site, then it will have to be demoted to second place. Right in the centre of that mountain-slope which I have described, the pine trees have been cut away and three terraces excavated. Along these run low, simple Italianate buildings with soft red-tiled roofs. This, again, is the work of Rhodes' friend, Baker. Inside I found good taste and simplicity. I went to the girls' wing, talked to some of them in their studies, drew them on native questions and found them quite liberal.

Then there was Professor Barnard (the pupil of Professor Radcliffe-Brown, the Sydney professor of anthropology). To him I had been specially recommended. He is a blue-eyed, fair-haired, poetic-looking person. He asked me to lunch to meet the Director of Education in the Cape Province, the last of three generations of pro-native Britishers, who has done an immense amount for native education. It is very hard for all these men to have to work now under a Dutch Nationalist government, especially when they can still remember the happy days of working under an autonomous Cape government, free to follow their own traditions and in close contact with Britain. Doubts about the future hang like a cloud over the Cape British and, I expect, over all liberal-minded British in South Africa.

I could well understand their feelings when at last I made contact with the Boer Government. This was not easy. Twice I had appointments with the Prime Minister, Hertzog, and twice these were cancelled at the last moment. Finally I did have an interview with his

---

[1] The later story is that the Countess gave £3,000,000 to Mussolini who made her husband a count.

Minister for Native Affairs. His hard face and hard voice were intimidating. As I could get no response about the current and repressive
native policy I urged him to look ahead, twenty-five, fifty years, with
the natives growing in numbers and resentment. This angered him.
He said, 'Don't worry your pretty little head about such things', in a
voice which made 'pretty' an insult rather than a compliment.

On my last day Mrs. Cartwright took me the seventy-mile drive
round the Cape Peninsula. I shall not forget that drive. I have now
been driven on this tour round San Francisco, Auckland, Wellington,
Sydney, Melbourne, Adelaide and Perth, but none of them, nor all
their individual beauties put together, can come near this. Nearly the
whole of the coast is a natural rock-garden, its steep, tumbling masses
of red and brown rock netted with flowers and spicy shrubs. The sands
are, in real truth, almost as white as snow, and the sea is all the colours
the sea can be when it is sparkling with sunlight, with cloud-shadows
above and a changing floor of weed, rock and sand below. You double
and circle round the rocky heights of the peninsula: away inland are
the smoky-blue, comb-shaped crests of the Hottentots' Holland
Mountains and between them and the peninsula the flats, where,
clearly, once the seas met to make the Cape an island. Coming back to
Capetown you pass the Naval Station at Simonstown, where two little
sloops seemed to make up the South African navy; then the famous
surfing beach of Muizenburg and the cottage where Rhodes died, so
prematurely, before the Boer War was ended. It is a gay place now,
generally called Jewsenburg, because on the sands, in the season, the
Jewish girls are said to be walked up and down and round and round,
to be judged and selected by the Jewish men. At least, so goes the
story; but prejudice may have told it, for national prejudices of all
kinds are strong here.

One thing I have noticed about the South African light. The beauty
of the air in Australia, and especially in New Zealand, comes from its
being so liquid-clear that every colour gets its utmost value as it never
does in England. But in South Africa the light is different: clear and
dry, it seems to have a quality of its own with which it dowers the
country. It is a golden light and has the power to gild, but at the first
touch of evening it is infused with red and this, so it seems, long before
the sinking sun has any red to offer. Distances in New Zealand were
surprising to my English eyes by the depth of their blue, a green-blue:
the red-gold of South African light makes a violet-blue and at sunset
there seem no limits to the extravagance of the colours it can create.

I have not forgotten how in Somaliland the mountains turned opal and amethyst but here no jewel would make a simile. It is colour from the paint box, as crude and clear as colour can be. I have seen a big turret of rock catching the last shaft of the sun over the curve of the earth and its face was orange and crimson and the shadows purple. Superlatives become stale, I can only say that I stood like an idiot, struck motionless, my brain refusing to credit my eyes.

I snatched odd hours to work at the parliamentary library where I was given a special permit to read and the staff were very good to me and smothered me with 'native' literature, all very depressing. In the intervals I rode a lovely ex-racehorse called Fuschia, belonging to my hosts, winding through paths in the pine woods. I bathed in my hosts' swimming pool and played some tennis. There were two beautiful creatures in the house to play with: the daughter, Yolande, and the son, d'Arcy who was having a term off from Oxford. I made contact with the Governor-General, the Earl of Athlone and his attractive wife, Princess Alice. I rode for hours with the highly intelligent Imperial Secretary, Captain Birch-Reynardson, my chief informant on South African affairs, at least as seen from the top.

All this, packed within a fortnight, has been marvellous experience but very exhausting so, not surprisingly, one of my visits has been to the doctor. The unseen Afrikaners, now the real rulers of the country; the vast dark background of the Africans—these are the forces to be understood and I do not see how it is to be done. But tomorrow I leave this lovely curtain-raiser of Capetown. I have chosen to go to the famous missionary school for Africans, Lovedale, founded in 1841, and the new University College of Fort Hare which has lately been founded alongside the school. Here at least I shall meet Africans of a kind, I hope, with whom I can talk freely.

It may be a long time before I can get off my next diary letter.

Lovedale and Fort Hare

November 1929

I left Capetown at four o'clock on 12 November, seen off by my hostess, she, splendid in a red picture-hat trailing red and white chiffon. To my joy, Professor Barnard, the young and brilliant anthropologist, was on my train.

But the train! Travelling luxury has been in a descending scale since I left America. The gauge here is, I gather, only three feet odd and the equipment is most primitive. There is no gauze to keep out the grime: the berths are hard; lavatories and wash-basins all crude and rather dirty; no hot water; no emergency chain and no locks. All that can be said in defence is that travelling here is fairly cheap. I feel a bit gloomy as I shall have to spend so much time on trains. And this was a main line train to Johannesburg and most of my travels will be on branch lines.

Professor Barnard travelled with me for a day and a half in the same train as far as the junction at De Aar. Then I turned back south-east towards the coast and he went on north-east to Johannesburg. We met for all meals and morning tea so I got the chance of picking the brains of the man who, Professor Radcliffe-Brown said to me in Sydney, was the only other real anthropologist in the world—and his pupil! No, I think he included Malinowski among the select.

Barnard was much harder to draw than Radcliffe-Brown. He wanted to draw *me* on Samoa and the Maoris so I had hard work to keep him to it. Like his master, he has been unable to establish a regular course in anthropology at the University and can only get it in as a subject among others for B.A. with an advanced course afterwards. But he has succeeded in establishing a summer school to which administrators are sent from Basutoland, the Rhodesias, South-West Africa and the Transkei. Missionaries also attend. In his opinion such a course is more necessary than even the appointment of government anthropologists. He would like to get men from Tanganyika and we agreed that it was strange that Sir Donald Cameron, with his liberal views, has not, it seems, even one government anthropologist on his staff. We grieved that Oxford should be so woefully backward in anthropology and decided that the best scheme was that Oxford should be the world's centre for the subject, radiating field workers, and soaking the central imperial administration in the right scientific spirit. At present, by his account, anyone in England who wants to study anthropology must go either to London, where he will get something from Malinowski, to Sydney or to Capetown.

I arrived at Alice the third day in the train. I was met at the station by the Principals of both Lovedale and Fort Hare. They had decided that I should start with the potential university, Fort Hare.

Heavens, what a day! I was up soon after seven, and we had breakfast at seven forty-five. I then went over to prayers with the Principal and sat with one of the staff. The hundred or so students filed in, including the first eight women students. I looked along the lines. The faces were of all types, a few undoubtedly, from their appearance, would support the controversial and superficial view that the African black man had smaller brain capacity than the white. But how far do such appearances count? All the students were dressed in conventional European clothes but nearly all of the suits, though neat, were, upon closer inspection, shiny and even threadbare.

The Bible lesson was very appropriate—how does it go?—'Do good to them that hurt you—pray for them that despitefully use you and persecute you'. I wondered whether Christianity could and would enable these people to exercise the almost unimaginable restraint that will increasingly be demanded of them. One item in this morning's paper contains news of a raid with machine-guns and tear-gas upon natives in Durban—I must try to get there. Another, a new stringent bill against native agitation. A third item reports a strike, quite an orderly one, in which the strikers were surrounded by two or three hundred police and given five minutes in which to decide whether to go to jail or continue work.

The Principal offered an extempore prayer in which he thanked God for the day in which they lived; for the League of Nations and the new hopes of peace and co-operation, above all for the great opportunity that had come to them at Fort Hare. The students filed out to their lectures and I went with the Principal to his study. Here

I sat down opposite his desk with pencil and paper and interviewed him.

The Principal, of course, is a Scot, a fairly young, fit, vigorous man, liberal-minded, cultured, Scottishly rugged. He seems sensible and able. I asked him first how the Union Government, so opposed to native education, could have made such an exception to its own policy as to establish anything so dangerous as a native university college. He explained that there had been plans and propaganda by friends of the natives for years before 1916 and that the surrender made by the Government, that is by Botha, was partly political. In the War, the fear of native trouble was intensified, and the establishment of the College was a sop, an amicable gesture. Also, because otherwise they would get higher education in the United States and were, indeed, already beginning to go there. Botha showed great courage by coming down to open Fort Hare himself. Since then it had been supported partly by a grant from the Union Government, partly by endowments from Carnegie, Rockefeller and the Rhodes Trust—the latter for £2,000 only. The students pay £30 a year and more than half of them are on bursaries raised by the natives of the Transkei, Basutoland, and one or two other sources. One is sent every year by a Negro 'Sorority' in the United States. £30 is not much as an all-inclusive fee and the students live a very simple life, their food consisting largely of native 'mealie-pap' and a loaf of bread a day. They live in hostels that have been built by the missionary societies; there is a Presbyterian, a Wesleyan, and an Anglican hostel and one which is central and undenominational.

It must not be imagined that the hundred students are all doing degree work as external students of the University of South Africa. About 75 per cent are working for two years at matriculation; others at an agricultural course; others for a special College Diploma in Arts, a kind of adapted matric course. Others are doing a theological course at their denominational hostels and only join in occasional work at the college. Finally, a very small minority are doing the three years of the South African University B.A., a mixed pass degree, with exams at the end of each year. So far about eight men and one woman have taken the degree, the latter being the first of all South African women—of all African women?—to become a graduate. Them en were mostly medical and went on to get the degree at Edinburgh where they are all said to be doing good work. The policy of the College is of course to increase gradually the proportion of degree students. But they are very much at the beginning of things. Only some 20 per cent of African children go even to the elementary schools and as, until lately, there has been practically no provision for secondary education, higher education was almost an impossibility. At present the majority of students come to Fort Hare from the old-established mission schools of Lovedale and Healdtown.

The students are of all tribes, mostly Fingoes and Xosas, some Zulus, Basutos and Tembus, a few coloured, and one or two Indians. Discipline presents no difficulties; they do not fight and they work only too hard.

The Principal took me round the College. In a corner in the library we found a graduate, now doing an advanced course in English literature. A very dark, shy man from Basutoland, it was a little difficult to get him talking. But he told me that he had not found Anglo-Saxon very difficult—he had already passed in it—that his favourite period was the eighteenth century and that in that period his favourite poets were Pope and Addison. I thought this very surprising, as if a starving beggar had expressed a preference for truffles and caviare over bread and beef-steak. But he stuck to his point; the vitality and humanity of the Elizabethans seemed to leave him cold, as did the romanticism and sentimentality of the nineteenth century. I wanted to go on talking to him but the Principal dragged me away to a lecture-room where a huge Irishman was giving senior matric mathematics. The Bantu excel in maths and yet hate them. They have to give great time and effort to the subject but they get excellent results. I went down among them and asked an Indian boy what he was doing. He explained, and there were shouts of laughter when it became clear that, being no mathematician, I could not understand his explanation. All the time I was struck with the cheerful atmosphere the African seems to bring with him. These people are not cowed; they *seem* free and lusty.

All the same I found occasion to criticize the Principal, to fear that he was not all pure metal unalloyed. In one class he showed off a little, teased the men for my supposed benefit. He made them stand up in tribes and was very jocular with the Zulus because they were so proud of their fighting record and strength and yet this lot happened to be smaller than the other students. It was all in fun and the men laughed and yet I imagined they were laughing to please us and not themselves. He picked out one small man, put his hand on his woolly hair, twisted his head about and said, 'Look at this representative of the great Zulu nation!' If ever a black man can blush, this man did.

On to the labs, where five men and one girl were cutting up snails and making diagrams. Then to the business and commercial class. Here I was introduced to a huge Nyasaland native, a government clerk in Rhodesia, spending the whole of his holidays at Fort Hare to improve himself. He is the uncle of Clements Kadalie, the notorious 'agitator', who has been head of the I.C.U. and is said to have pocketed some of the funds. This great giant, so black that one realized how little black most of these southern Bantu are, rose from beside the tiny white woman who was teaching him, gazed at us with hostility, whether learned in Nyasaland or from his nephew, I do not know. Questioned by the Principal he told us, unsmiling, that he had lately been to see the sea for the first time.

'And did you like it ?'

'Yes, but I do not like the taste of it.'

'But you surely did not drink it ?'

'Yes, I did. My nephew Kadalie told me to go and drink the sea because the sea was medicine.'

We found another man in the library, a thin, alert creature, with gentle brown eyes. He was from Johannesburg.

'How are things there now ? Are they better in the last few years ?'

'Oh yes. Europeans sometimes come into our compounds and locations, a thing which never happened before.'

'Have you any water or light ?'

'They have put on a little water but we have no light. We use candles.'

'Do they still push you off the pavement into the gutter ?'

'That is becoming difficult. They have brought so many of us into the town that there is no room in the gutter.'

We left the building again, passing the Principal's office, where his secretary, who was an African, was handling all the work and plant of the big office with what seemed to be quiet efficiency. He brought a sheaf of beautifully typed letters for the Principal's signature.

We then went out to run up to a native village to see a bush-school. Five or six miles over appalling tracks in a sturdy Buick brought us to a big village on a hillside. The one square house among the round ones was the school. Here were rows of woolly heads and beady eyes, all a slightly different heights, ranged in forms, Sub A; Sub B; Standards I, II, and III. We told the teacher to carry on. She was a young, loud-voiced, stout African girl. At the top of her voice, in slow, laboured words, she bellowed, with suitable gestures:

'Dees — ees — ma — HAD.'

They screamed the repetition:

'Dees — ees — ma — NAWSE.'

I cathechized Standard III. Quite a decent map hung on the wall and they picked out the main towns of South Africa, darting like lizards to the spots. The reading-book alas! was an English one, wholly unadapted to their use, and dealing mainly with objects and events that would always be foreign to them. It is strange that though we have been in South Africa for a hundred and thirty years we have not been able to produce adequate text-books for the native children, while the Americans have a whole elaborate series for the Philippines— which we borrow for Fiji! In Samoa they have done better than this.

Mr. Ker asked one of the children to read. He read well. Then Mr. Ker held the book upside down, the boy seemed to think something was wrong but, at a second order, continued with the story.

Then we went into a native hut close by. Two women, clean and dressed in flowing garments to the feet, ushered us in. The hut was beautifully clean and neat both inside and out, and the mud walls decorated with a spotted pattern of lime and polished. On the walls hung faded photographs of the family and a picture of Lord Haig. There was an iron bed and mattress, a chair, and a kettle. On the floor was a child of three, covered with flies, its bronze having turned to sickly green. It was gasping out its life in little coughs.

In the afternoon from two to four I worked at the literature of the place, reports, syllabus, etc. At four I went out to review the 'Wayfarers', the Guides. All the women students studying for the degree— and there are only eight—are Guides. But they are not allowed to wear the same uniform as the whites. They wear rather ugly brown cotton faced with orange, with big straw hats. A nice half-Dutch, half-English woman presented them, Miss Maritz. I was told that she had had a great struggle with herself and her friends before she came but that she had been 'converted' and it was clear that she was devoted to her students. I was told that she had had a sick girl to sleep in her own room with her. She is leaving now to take up a lectureship in science at Wellington College in order to keep up her standards but she told me that she hoped to come back again to Fort Hare. She was rather apprehensive about my request to be left alone with her girls for fear we should not hit it off and certainly they were shy with the two of us. At last I got her to go. I put them in a circle round me on chairs.

We talked for an hour. It was astonishing how quickly as I talked to them the impression of their ugliness faded and the intelligence and beauty of some of the faces appeared. They were soon most animated and though at first they would answer me in whispers, all at once, so that I could distinguish nothing, they soon improved, and one after another began to speak out and stand out as individuals.

Only one was a 'coloured' girl, and she was different from the rest. The strain of white blood was enough to make her look very different and enough, too, to make her slicker, and more self-conscious. The knowledge of that almost unrecognizable kinship with myself was enough to introduce a slight confusion into our relationship. I felt it, and I am sure she felt it too. With the native girls it was different. They were almost too good to be true, responsive, quick to pick up points, intelligent, courteous, attractive.

I asked them first about their work. They sketched in a hard day with little room for recreation. Were they never tired or bored? No, they liked it all so much. Their favourite subjects? Not history! 'Not as *we* learn it—we are not interested in the war of the Spanish succession. Perhaps, if we did it in more detail.' No, science was the favourite and perhaps it is well that it should be so as it is probably the best corrective to the non-reason that has dominated many concepts of the tribal past. English, too, they like: especially Dickens, Jane Austen and Charlotte Brontë. Two of them smiled at each other in joint appreciation as they said, 'Oh, yes, we *love* Jane Austen.' Miss Austen —and Zululand![1]

They questioned me eagerly about Oxford and listened with gleaming eyes to what I said of the life and the students. It was clear that dimly, far away, English student life was their ideal. It is upon *that* we shall founder with all our theories of differentiation, of adaptation to native society, etc., upon their passionate determination to accept nothing but that which will give them not only the right but the power to gain equality.

Presently, rather tentatively, I probed more deeply. Did they not find the life here strange? How and why had they come? What would they hope to do? 'There is nothing we should be allowed to do

---

[1] Many years later, when visiting the University of Puerto Rico, I had the same enthusiastic response about Jane Austen from the students of this island, descendants of slaves with some Spanish blood and influence.

in South Africa, Miss, except teach.' And when they went home to their tribes did they not feel strange—different—from their own people? No, they said, they loved to go back. And what about the customs and ideas they found there? Here at last I got an answer that went to the essential point. One girl, whose keen, clear eyes denied the impression given—to us—by her thick purple mouth, said:

'Yes, we *do* find it difficult. Do you know, Miss, that smelling out witches has not died out at all. Even round here, within five—one—mile, it is going on. They do not often kill the witch now but they lie in wait and beat him or her, burn the house and drive them out. It is when something happens that cannot be explained.'

'But *you* have studied science. *You* know the reasons for what happens.'

'Yes, Miss, but when things happen that we do *not* know the reason for—'

'But you know that there *is* a reason and that you could find it out if you had the knowledge.'

There was a pause.

'Yes, but, Miss, there *are* things that happen that cannot be explained. I am afraid—I know that if I went back and lived among my own people I should believe these things again. I know I should. I feel it.'

'Do you know', said another girl, thrusting her dark face forward in the ring, 'that among my people were two, a man and a woman, married, who had both been educated. They were both teachers. And someone died suddenly and they smelled out the woman as a witch. And in the night the husband cut off her legs, and put knives into her body, and then cut off her head.'

The first girl, who was very wise, said:

'Miss, if the Europeans would only be more sympathetic and *explain* things. When I was at school (a mission school, of course), one of the girls suddenly found some funny little marks on her arms and leg. She thought she was bewitched and she went in great terror to the white head-mistress. But the mistress was annoyed and said, "Don't be silly. That's nothing at all." So the girl went on believing she was bewitched and she died. The Europeans don't seem to understand.'

I wanted so much to go on talking to the girls. They, too, wanted me to stay. But five o'clock struck, and I had to go and talk to seven selected degree course men on the verandah of the Principal's house.

D   49

I found the men waiting, two Basuto, two Zulu, two Xosa and a Fingo. It was really not so different from talking to a group of students at home. It was impossible to remember that most of them were fresh from the mud-hut in the bush and that the brother of one had just been killed in a tribal affray. And that another, when he got back, would have to struggle to turn out a chief who had dispossessed him.

First, they asked me all about Oxford, a rain of eager, detailed questions, the answers received with reverence. (Oh, the responsibilities of Oxford!) India we discussed, and then Somaliland and the League of Nations. Then they began to ask me for detailed information about the exact constitutional relations between South Africa and England. It was pathetic to see in what a hopeless direction their minds were working. Soon they came into the open. They asked me terrible questions.

'What does England think of the situation out here?'

I explained that we were quite detached, that we were more liberal than South Africans but that it was easy for us to be so as our interests were not involved.

'Can England do *nothing*, then?'

I explained how, even with the recent South African–German trade treaty which so closely affected us, we had not so much as protested.

'But South Africa is a possession of England.'

I tried hard to explain.

'But the *King*! He is King of South Africa. What does he think? Will *he* do nothing?'

More constitutional history. Then:

'But, Miss, what do you yourself think of the way we are treated?'

Now for it! I had already asked the Principal if he objected to my talking politics in the College, and he made the very proper reply, '*Magna est veritas et praevalet*'.

I said I thought the policy was wrong: that every consideration, religious, social, economic, directed us to put all our energies into raising the black people; that so long as the reward of effort was a share in the best we had to offer, so long would they be attached to our civilization, would feel a stake in it. But then, it was easy for me, coming in from outside, to be impartial. Could they not make the effort, great though it was, to understand what the whites felt about it. Did they not realize, now they were educated, how great was still the gulf between their people and ours; and how the whites, one to four, feared to be swamped by a race so different from their own.

'Are they *afraid* of us?' It seemed a new idea. They were spell-bound. I began to get a cold feeling. I had before me the first of Africa's university men, all about to take their degrees and go out, marked men and leaders of these masses, the still backward masses. I felt I had got into a position into which I must go further because I could not retreat.

'You are going out into the world highly educated, feeling and thinking almost as we do and yet you will be treated—well, you know far better than I how that will be. You will have every temptation to become embittered, to become agitators and to take short cuts. Your lives cannot be altogether happy; you have had this great privilege of education and it is going to cut you off and mark you out among your own people and among the whites. But if you do try to take short cuts the results could be disastrous. If you do all you can to make relations worse instead of better, do you know what will happen? Supposing it leads to outbreaks of violence, do you imagine for a moment you can succeed? I want you to look up and answer me. Even if there were a temporary success? England would have to back law and order in South Africa—as the whites see it. It is *your* people who would suffer, not the whites. They would crush you easily, in spite of numbers. You know that?' They all said 'Yes'. 'A very heavy responsibility rests upon you. All your effort should go back into your people to raise them. They are not ready yet to claim and make effective use of political power. What your race is capable of will be judged largely by what you, the first few highly educated members of it, do with your leadership. Where you have now a dozen you will need hundreds, then thousands, educated and united, to win and use your rights. And remember, too, that all the white people who are working for you will be defeated unless you work with them. If you make mistakes they may become helpless.'

That is the gist of what I felt driven to say and from that we went on and spoke with the greatest frankness of the whole situation. I do not know if they felt the same sense of solemnity that I did because the subject was so heavy with dread. I felt it was almost unfair of me to talk or to let them talk of it. It was like talking of the hills and sea to a man chained hand and foot in a dungeon. I think I shall have hard work to keep my emotions in order while in this country. What I had felt for American Negroes, Samoans, Maoris, was nothing to what must be felt for these people, especially for these few to whom we have given this terrible gift of intellectual training. Was it fair to talk to them like this, in full social and intellectual equality, when outside of the charmed circle of Fort Hare, they may not sit in the same railway carriage, or eat at the same table, but must live under a different law, in a semi-servile state? Hertzog and even Smuts refer to the blacks as barbarians.

They seemed to me intelligent, patient, earnest people; perhaps patience and a sense of humour may save them from the envenomed hostility shown by some Indian leaders towards whites which would have made such a conversation as this impossible. (I have often tried it in Geneva and elsewhere.) Yet one trembles to think how little the Indian has to accuse us with, in comparison with these people.

I was already late for an appointment at the Presbyterian Hostel, Iona, where the Warden had asked me to dinner to meet the students. They were all working in the common room. I peeped over one tufted head. *Undirectional Reflexes. The Thorndike Theory.* Over another, a larger tome, Lowel's *Primitive Society.* Some had sat their exams that day in social anthropology. They produced the papers, with questions ticked, explained what they had done, and complained about the unfairness of the paper. At the Warden's request I made an appeal to them to rest before exams and not to work late. Evidently human nature, however different racially, makes the same reactions to examinations. I saw their shower-baths and went up to their dormitories. Some have rooms for three. There were books on or by every bed.

The hostel is a pleasant new building. Two sides of a quadrangle, with Moorish arches, have been built. The rest is to come. Through the arches was seen the open country under the clear night sky, ridge upon ridge of dusty blue veld. It will be a great pity when they build up that quadrangle. Why should people live in a box on the veld?

I now had to motor over three-quarters of a mile away to Lovedale, the most famous of all South African missionary institutions, a Presbyterian foundation begun in 1840. Here I again met Dr. Henderson, who took me up to the big hall, which can seat about 800 of the 1,000 pupils of all ages who fill Lovedale.

I found myself, all unprepared, addressing the Lovedale Literary Society. It seemed to consist of several hundred boys and girls from about fifteen to twenty-four years of age. I had forgotten that I had been asked that morning if I would speak. I said I would tell them about Samoa if I could have a chance to think for ten minutes what I would say. I never had that chance, so I decided to talk about Somaliland. However, Dr. Henderson made a very formal introductory speech about my lecture on Samoa, so I found myself forced into the position of giving a lecture upon Samoa without one moment to consider what to say. Had these rows of black heads, with flashing white of eyes and teeth, been my only audience I should not have minded. But in front, sitting rather stiffly, was a row of the Scottish Presbyterian Church, the staff, full of missionary lore and, perhaps, inclined to disapprove of my appreciation of the languorous delights of Samoa. However, I could only plunge and hope to come out the other end. So I rambled on and drew for the Africans, the slave-race of the world, a picture of a people who need not work and, for the most part, will not work, but prefer to dance and sleep. And for a people who dare hardly think of the injustices of their lot how could they credit the story of the Samoans' light-hearted rebellion and the indulgence of the New Zealand Government. I felt it was all rather like a fairy tale. I was very conscious of the gravity of the faces in the front row, of the lines cut into the fine head of my chairman, the headmaster, by the sorrows of Africa. At the end he rose, spoke briefly, and then made them all stand and pray for me. He prayed that I might use my great opportunity wisely; that God would be in my heart and mind and that He would guard my health when I went up into the dangers of Central Africa. The Africans are demonstrative; I could not help but see that all the rows of them with closed eyes, bent heads and puckered brows, were wrestling in prayer for me.

Back again to Fort Hare to another talk with the Principal in his study, and then to my room, not to bed, but to read literature about the place and make notes before all the day's material slipped out of a mind too sleepy to hold it.

The next morning I was up early in order that I might call upon two native members of the staff before I transferred myself completely to Lovedale. First we went to see Professor Jabavu, perhaps the most famous living South African native. His father was famous, too, for the production of a South African newspaper, and both were educated at Lovedale. Jabavu is very black and rather squat-faced. I have found both here and in America that the highly intelligent and refined-looking African is not necessarily the one we should pick out for intelligence when we judge their faces by our standards.

The interview was marred for me by Mr. Ker staying with us the whole time. I could not lead Jabavu on to the fundamental subjects I wanted, nor, had I attempted it, could he have answered. I complimented him upon his books. I had recently read his collected political articles and found them very clear and vigorous, humorous too, full of those pricks at the bubble of our complacency which the underdog can so well inflict. He spoke with glowing admiration of Professor Radcliffe-Brown and, by implication, I thought, in depreciation of Barnard. But that, perhaps, was not surprising, since his pupils had just taken an examination paper set by Barnard which Jabavu considered most unfair. I got the impression of a highly educated man, clear-headed, and lively, with an important part to play as an intellectual pioneer of the Bantu but not, perhaps, a man of great wisdom or force. If I go to the advanced vacation course on anthropology at Capetown University I shall meet him again, and may revise my hasty judgement. But Ker confirmed it, saying that the father was the bigger man. I looked with interest at Jabavu's house, European in style and furnishing, in what we should call a very suburban style and not very well ordered. But then the standards of taste round him are not very high. Also his wife was away. She is the leader of a social movement among the women around here.

We hurried on to call upon Max Jurgeon, an American negro who has recently come to Fort Hare, paid for by the International Y.M.C.A. He is a man with a very wide reputation and has played a great part in the Students Christian Movement. He has been sent all over the world, to East Africa during the War, to Egypt, India and South Africa. Enough, it might, and probably has been, said, 'to give a nigger a swollen head'. But it is impossible to shake hands with Jurgeon and exchange a few words without liking him. He is lighter skinned than his country cousins here, with a very smooth skin, a broad, open face, Caucasian lips and nose, and very fine eyes, dark, full of spiritual intelligence and very thoughtful. No cocksureness here and no self-assertion. Yet he looks young, not much more than thirty. We had a most interesting talk, and yet, strangely enough, I cannot remember what it was all about. I can only remember the tone of the conversation which was very serious. We must, of course, have been surveying the racial question, the causes for anxiety and those for hope. I gathered that Jurgeon had come to Africa to throw himself into the task of heading off the vanguard of the educated Bantu from materialism and political agitation. Yet he was suspect by the Union Government, has been carefully watched and kept on the end of a short string as far as leave to stay in the country is concerned. His house was in perfect order, his children self-confident and charming.

The joke is that with American money a new house is being built for him near the College, and his American standards demand two bathrooms. The old-time authorities cannot help but smile that the first man in the valley to obtain this luxury should be a Negro.

From him we went to call on the Anglican Hostel. Compared with the Scottish Presbyterians the Anglicans have been backward as far as advanced education is concerned: their hostel is very small and overcrowded, an ordinary bungalow with bits built on haphazard and with students' sleeping quarters all over the house and garden. The chapel is a large Kaffir hut, round and thatched, in which the furnishings of an Anglo-Catholic altar glow richly. The bishop, Smyth, was away, but I was shown his cell-like study and his iron bedstead, one of a long row in a verandah dormitory. His sister and some other female relation, tall, faded, well-bred women, brought into this valley, otherwise Scottish and Bantu, the atmosphere of a West Country rectory. I imagine they may feel a little alien to the rather dour, democratic, pedagogic, Presbyterian spirit of the mission. Yet it is an excellent idea in this infant Bantu university to allow any denomination to build its own hostel and so get the rich variety of the different missions in the hostel life with the unity and broadness of the University encircling them.

It was now time to leave Fort Hare and transfer myself entirely to Lovedale. Mr. Ker took me. From the gate we went up a long avenue of trees into the untidy litter of buildings, built at many times and in many styles between 1840 and 1925, that make up Lovedale—solid stone with clock tower, modern technical block, cracked mud and tin dormitories like shabby stables and a warren of workshops. In this new country, the whole place positively smelt of tradition and was most attractive after the rather glaring newness of Fort Hare.

The Principal came out to meet us and took us in to morning tea. (Is it the Scots who have carried morning tea all over the world?) Dr. Henderson is a man of about fifty. He is reputed to be the wisest authority on the native question in Africa. He has worked also in Nyasaland and East Africa, and has been connected with Lovedale for about thirty years. He shows you first the Scots layer, undemonstrative, silent, almost repressive. It is with surprise that you learn that he is highly strung, almost nervous. A deeply religious man, big of heart and brain, but physically not very strong. (The train, as I write, is bumping badly. It is unfortunate that most of this diary-letter has to be written in trains or late at night.) The African problem has scored deep lines on his face, increasing the natural ruggedness and giving a sad expression. For he has not merely looked out upon affairs from Lovedale; he has gone out and joined in the wide struggle, writing, speaking, attending government committees, knocking on departmental doors, urged by moral indignation into activities that must be repugnant to him. What such men as he—there are not many —suffer in and for Africa! Busy, harassed, unwell, he now put himself entirely at my service for the week-end, answering my ceaseless and leading questions very slowly and thoughtfully; sometimes refusing to answer, pleading bias or inadequate knowledge. An adoring wife, anxious for his health, but with deep respect for the mysterious activities that dominate his life, watched from a distance, mostly in silence, her occasional interpositions in the interests of his food or rest waved away, not harshly, but with a gesture and look that seemed to be habitual. I thought him a great man, a great Scot, product of forces peculiar to his country and creed. Are they now ceasing to operate? Will the new exports be so good? Export we must, from England or from Scotland for the future of Africa lies partly in our schools and universities. As he said, when moved (and he was often moved because, rather remorselessly, I kept him to the fundamentals of the situation):

'Can *you* do nothing in England so that your people shall not be corrupted on the boat coming out, before they even set foot in the country?'

We went round the workshops. Lovedale operates on a very large scale, accepting contracts for big buildings and carrying through the whole work, making all the doors and window-frames in their own shops. They built part of Fort Hare and have now a contract for a big government agricultural school. All this work, of course, is work only for African purposes. What they perform is a proof of the capacity of the native to do the skilled work. All the work I saw, carpentry, metal work, waggon-making, counts as skilled in this country and where the colour-bar works, which is almost everywhere, the native is automatically shut out from it.

Most striking is the printing shop where I saw an African in sole charge of a type-making machine just bought from America and costing nearly £2,000. In a huge shop natives were printing and binding books in seven languages with illustrations and music, with only two white men to supervise. They are all apprentices. I asked Dr. Henderson what became of them afterwards. He said they could try to get jobs in the Cape wherever the colour-bar still does not yet operate or work independently among their own people. But this is not always easy because of their own communal attitude to their service—as with Maoris. Or else they could go north to Nyasaland or the Congo where the colour-bar does not operate. I read a very interesting letter from a Lovedale old boy who had gone up into the Congo and was astonished to find natives allowed to do any work they were capable of doing, there being little or no white artisan class to be preserved from competition. He tells how in the Congo 'the engine and locomotive drivers and guards are all natives, but, in the case of the mail trains they generally add one or two European guards so as to avoid trouble in examining the tickets of Europeans. The Lovedale students could see that the government of the Belgian Congo had made a splendid system for letting the natives to improve in every work in the country. I want the students to think about their brothers here who manage to do all all sorts of work in every department with such little education they have. The question of the unskilled and skilled labour is not in the least recognized by the government here. . . . The students should know this. A King was born a ruler, but the President was never born a ruler, yet he became ruler through working hard and cleverness'.

In the afternoon, as I had asked Dr. Henderson to interpret the country to me, he decided to take me up the hill from which a wide view of the district can be seen. First we passed through the Lovedale farm in the bottom of the valley, irrigated from the stream which is called, by courtesy, a river. Here we saw wheat and lucerne and the dairy herd of magnificent Shorthorns kept in condition by feeding on lucerne and on concentrates and by very careful breeding. The land looked fairly green but then they had had the best spring rains for very many years. A whole field given up to the cultivation of hideous spineless cactus, as a last resort by which to keep animals alive in case of drought, brought home the realities of farming here.

This country, the Ciskei, is the area where Bantu and European first met in serious contact, and where, after a long series of wars, they were settled down side by side in uneasy neighbourhood. Land that was barely adequate for the Africans in 1875 is ludicrously inadequate for more than double the population in 1929. A people used to extensive farming, to shifting their ground in order to rest the poor land (a sanitary precaution also) are now left congested and impoverished. They are ignorant of intensive farming, even if intensive farming on such poor land could support their numbers.

The view from a spur of our hill, as interpreted by Dr. Henderson, was a most striking chart of the situation in South Africa. I do not pretend that it is typical of all South Africa; there are parts, three-quarters of the whole, where the natives, in overall numbers of four to one, hold no land; there are some reserved areas where few if any Europeans hold land, though many of these are poor and congested. But here, in the Ciskei, is a meeting place of the two races.

You must imagine one of those enormous views, clear almost to the horizon, which seem peculiar to South Africa, the country lying like a map on three sides of us, low hills hummocking round the wriggling line made by the muddy little Tynnice river. The greater part of the valley alongside the river, and the best part, was cut into European farms, with their tree-girt homesteads, squares of verdant lucerne and yellow corn. The grazing land behind, fenced into squares to allow rotation of pasture, was spotted with mimosa scrub in just the right proportion to grip the slopes and give food in the drought. Higher up the slopes, or in other depressions away from the river, was the patchwork of native cultivation, above which were the villages, the round mud huts with conical thatched roofs and the square cattle kraals made of grey-green cactus or prickly pear. Even to a novice the distribution of land was preposterous. But some of the effects were also visible. The native pasture land was denuded of scrub, the grass eaten down to the roots and this had been followed by erosion which had left great wounds in the sides of the hills. Overstocking, exhaustion, denudation, erosion—this had been the sequence, and now a yellow weed, beautiful, harmful and apparently invincible, was creeping from the pasture on to the arable and gleaming like an evil halo upon the native lands. Nature had sketched out as vivid a chart of the unjust racial situation as if a man with bold strokes of coloured crayons had tried to illustrate it.

When the sun slipped down a little the picture became even more vivid, for the outcrop of little huts, whose soft grey thatching made them almost invisible from above, were now picked out in double fashion, for the light caught one half of their circle and made it shine and threw a dark shadow behind the other. All over the hills and slopes they began to appear, like an eruption of pustules breaking out, emphasizing the enormous size of the native population the land was bearing. I should not say 'bearing': it cannot do that. More than 60 per cent of the able-bodied men are always away in the mines and even so the people of the district are in a state of semi-starvation, strangled with debt and crowding the Lovedale hospital with ever-growing cases of malnutrition, scurvy and tuberculosis. In the local Commissioner's office, into which I went, there are figures which show that in 1875, with half the population, and without money earned from the mines, the people were producing and spending more, very much more, than now, if the difference in the value of money is allowed for. Yet I read this same day General Smuts's plea for more white settlement as a panacea for all ills.

I have given you the long-distance view from the hill. A closer view showed us large numbers of goats and donkeys, abhorrent to Dr. Henderson as signs of bad farming. The cattle, beloved of the Bantu, woven into his history, measure of his status and the price of his wives, were enjoying the best moment of their hazardous year. They looked rather fine and glossy to my uninitiated eyes but I was told that they were quite useless except for the plough. The cows, depreciated stock, improperly fed and used, produce hardly any milk; the oxen are never eaten except when they die (which, in a series of recent droughts, is generally of starvation). I gather that the Bantu attitude to cattle, plus the congestion, has filled all native areas with almost valueless beasts. A return could only be got from them if their numbers were cut down to a third or a quarter.

There was another way in which this countryside offers a chart easy to read. The heathen women conveniently and artistically are dressed in flaming umber; the Christians in anything but that, and generally in white or blue print. So startling is the umber that, from above, from up to almost a mile away, you can detect whether a village has been converted or not. Some villages seem to be mixed; so, apparently, are some women, for I saw one who must have found herself in difficult situations for she was heathen below the waist and Christian upwards.

When the car could go no further I went up the hill alone, and having had no exercise for days, I ran as hard as I could up the rugged track. Round a corner of rocks I ran into some native women balancing big logs of wood upon pads on their heads. So great was their astonishment to see a white woman up in this place and running that they all but dropped their logs. They broke into ejaculatory talk and, seemingly, tried to warn me against going any further. When, going down, they saw the car, they went in a state of great excitement to Mr. Henderson to tell them where the runaway had gone.

We got back just in time for me to change, have some supper and motor back again to Fort Hare, where I had that morning rashly promised to give a lecture. The students were to choose the subject. They chose 'Oxford'. As soon as I heard this I was paralysed with horror, realizing that I knew hardly a single, lecturable fact about my university. However, on condition that I had half an hour with the *Encyclopaedia Britannica* beforehand, I agreed. But I never had the half-hour, not half a minute, and so, two nights running, I had to speak without time to think what I was going to say.

In the hall there were about a hundred and twenty students, and most of the staff. I did all I could to make them realize the age of Oxford. This was difficult for tribesmen, without much accurate history, but by looking ahead to Fort Hare in the twenty-seventh century I got across some dim idea. I told them all I knew of Oxford's history and of its present rather complex working and quite brought down the house with a picture of the tutorial with teachers and students chatting in armchairs once a week. I referred to our highly optional lectures and to the luxurious conditions in some of the colleges. To students whose first lecture is at 7 a.m., and whose diet is mainly mealie-pap and dry bread, this contrast must be rather startling. Games, higher education for women—how they consumed it all, gazing up at me as if I were talking of heaven. At the end, having asked permission of my chairman (the Principal) to turn a lecture into a sermon, I could not resist suggesting to them the greatness of their own opportunities, and the responsibilities which rested on them, in view of the possibilities, almost beyond imagination, of education in Africa. (But alas! how far away!) Then we motored up on to a plateau to see the veld and the mountain ranges in the moonlight, an exercise which gave me a chance to cool off.

I had some fear of a Lovedale Presbyterian Sunday. However it was all very pleasant. We had service, some 1,200 of us, in the open-air church, its aisles made of oak trees. The service was all in the native language, Xosa, except the sermon. I never saw a congregation listen to a sermon more attentively than those children. There were some very little girls in front of me who never took their eyes from the preacher, never fidgeted, although of course it was all in a foreign language, understood with difficulty. Moreover it was one of a series on the commandments and this being the eighth, the preacher was upholding the sacred rights of property, warning them against Communism. It is almost pathetic how the missionaries as pastors struggle to repress discontent with one hand while, as teachers, they give the African the fuel for this fire.

At the service in the front row of close-cropped woolly heads, white tunics, navy skirts, bare brown legs and feet, was one child who stood out as different; she was a little paler, her hair was long and silky, and she had a beautiful, earnest face. I found out afterwards that she was the result of an unusual scandal in Kenya—white mother, native father, and had been taken over completely by Lovedale.

An afternoon's work; a long talk with the Principal; then to dinner with a member of the staff, old in missionary work, and extraordinarily well-informed from long reading of missionary literature. (Incidentally I remember reading their daughter's, Monica Hunter's, entrance papers, passed on from Somerville, and we accepted her, but she got an exhibition at Girton, and became one of South Africa's leading anthropologists.)

Then we all went to the big hall where the Principal had got the old 1912 film, *From Manger to Cross*, to show the students. (He was much criticized for showing *any* film on a Sunday evening!) The hall was simply packed, and slowly the smell of the African began to issue, accumulate and at last fill the hall. I do not find it nauseating as some white people seem to do. It is a little like coconut oil, slightly singed, but with something elese, sweet, heavy, and indefinable. A native to whom this was mentioned replied that, as far as he could understand, our smell was to them even more repellent. Asked to define it he said that they all agreed that we smelt like dead bodies. I think we lose on the comparison.

The film was less interesting than its reception. I remembered, in a far-away period, seeing the film in the Kursaal at Harrogate. I remembered the effeminate Christ, closely based on the traditional pictures, chosen for looks rather than ability and expressing divinity by behaving like an automaton. I remembered Judas, the heavy film villain. The big audience was very rapt and still; many of them were seeing a cinema film for the first time. I confirmed a discovery that in moments of excitement the Bantu laughs, not meaning to express amusement; at the expulsion of the money-changers, performed with sudden and quite violent energy by the automaton, there was an outburst of laughter. But with the sufferings of Christ, with the scourging, the audience, now thoroughly roused, broke out into groans of indignant sympathy and muttered protests. At one point, on the road to Calvary, the feeling was so strong that I thought the pictured crowd of mocking Jews would find a real crowd of Africans precipitated upon them.

Next morning I was up soon after six o'clock and went down to the steps and balcony in front of the main building, to see the whole lot of the students assemble. They marched up in detachments from their dormitories, according to their place in the school—high school—standards VII and VIII—First and Second Year matric—teachers training —industrial apprentices—girls and boys separate. They were all dressed in European clothes, all decent, but many of them worn and darned. They marched up in perfect order, prefects walking beside to give the commands. When they were all ranged up the Principal prayed for God's help in the day's work, a very earnest, simple, extempore prayer. Then he said a few words and in the same order, and the same silence, they marched off to work in the various buildings.

Dr. Henderson and I changed into riding clothes and went off at full speed on his horses so that he could continue his exposition on agriculture, by taking me round the farm, a very important item of education—for those who would have any land.

After breakfast I went off to see all I could before I had to catch my train at 11.45 a.m. First we inspected the elementary school, hundreds of children from all the surrounding districts. The lesson at the moment consisted of bread and milk, to enable the little things to face up to the morning's work, some being in a very dubious state of health and many having walked six miles with six to go back. In charge of them was a native woman of much charm and dignity. She gave an impression of reserves of power. She had spent two years in America studying social and welfare work. She told me that she thought education at Lovedale was better than in America, it was much sounder, with less advertisement. She said that she was a great joke among the American Negroes, being one of the first real African women they had seen. Also, they were amused by her accent, English or rather Scots, for in Lovedale all the children talk with a Scots accent.

From the little ones I went to a matric class on the Xosa language, a young graduate from Fort Hare teaching a big class the niceties of their own language. It is, by all accounts, rich and beautiful. I heard it maintained that the Old Testament is a finer rendering of the Hebrew than the English, their life as semi-nomadic cattle-owners being so much nearer that of the Israelites than that of Tudor England.

I slipped out soon, and wandered into the grounds. In the shade of a tree, on a seat, three Indian boys were sitting, their heads bowed over books. I sat beside them. They were reading detective books. It was a free period. They were all from Durban or nearby. They responded very politely. I marked their slender, delicate figures contrasting with those of the African. They were all sons or grandsons of Indian emigrants. They had no intention of going back to India; they recognized that in spite of the colour-bar they were much better off economically than in India. They were bright, and keen on politics. We discussed the recent Durban police raids and they expressed themselves strongly on the side of the native. I asked them about their relations with the natives here, among whom the Indians are hardly fifty per thousand. Two said they felt very lonely and out of it. Yet they would not say they did not like the Africans: they said they felt different, and though they got on well enough, could not make friends. The third boy said he was not lonely; that the natives were very good to them; they never quarrelled. They described the same relations in Natal, detached but not unfriendly. They said that the Natal Indians had now collected money to build a school of their own in Durban, but even so they would rather come to Lovedale. And what was their religion? They were Hindu. And was their Hinduism untouched by all the Christian preaching and services they had attended? Yes, entirely. The bell rang and with polite apologies they went in to work.

The next encounter was even more interesting. It was a class in teacher-training for girls. It was in the open air under some trees. Fortunately the teacher was late and I had the chance of talking for ten minutes to the group of fifteen girls of between sixteen and twenty, who crowded eagerly round me.

I asked them many questions, especially about their homes. They told me that they never grew their hair, they kept it short all their lives, only wrapped up their heads when they married. They loved their short skirts but when they married they would have to wear long skirts to the ground. (Is this a relic of Victorian influence?) Also they would have to go barefooted, and they hated that, as most of them had tried shoes and liked them.

'And when you go home, do you go back to carry heavy loads and work in the fields?'

'Yes.'

'And do you not mind that?'

'No. Our parents have to work so hard and give up so much to send us here that we like to do all the work we can when we get home. Sometimes our parents say that now we have been to school we ought not to do so much work, but we don't think that.'

Then the little ones arrived to be practised upon and were seated on little benches round a squat table. One student gave the lesson, the others stood in a circle. It was an English lesson and the girl told these mites the story of the fox and the crane. It was really rather painful to see the teacher and the children straining after the meaning and the accent. And the white teacher reinforced the impression. She said that far too much time had to be given to English. That it would be better if it were taught as a foreign language. As it was, nearly all their lessons were in English and they were bound to talk it all the week except Sundays. It was as though the lessons in an English school were in French. The loss in education was great, the strain and the time spent enormous. In her opinion all the white teachers ought to learn Xosa. It was all the sadder, she said, as the children were so *teachable*, so eager, and docile; they could accept all that we would give.

It is a difficult problem. The pure educationalist would say, and say indignantly, that education should be adapted to their needs, that language is custom, tradition, history, expression, most of all to a primitive people whose way of life is so different from ours that their thoughts are distorted in translation. Nor is it only that they teach them so much English and teach them all their subjects in English. They are also teaching them on a syllabus set for English children. If in their reader they learnt about things familiar and interesting, or at least related to their own lives, the strain would be less, but the subjects are as remote as Mars and the moon to the kraal child. I have seen them at it. I saw Standard V struggling with *Oliver Twist*. They were at the most-quoted incident. Progress was impossible. The passage should be recalled in order to appreciate what Dickens' style means to the native child—a porringer—thin gruel—this festive composition—an almshouse. I asked one girl what an almshouse was. She stood up, with the usual respect, and in her deep voice coughed out awkwardly 'A workhouse, Miss.'

'And what is a workhouse?'

'An almshouse, Miss.'

In another class, a higher one, they had written up on the board all the expressions that were incomprehensible. They covered two sides of the board, culled out of one lesson. This was a teachers' class. I remember only the two top ones—'a sop to Cerberus' and 'showinp the white feather'. And yet these children—the lazy Africans—jump the centuries and by dogged labour, some of them pass exams on the same syllabus as the whites—the various standards, the Junior and Higher Teacher's Certificate, the matric and now, for the few, the B.A.

It seems from all this that differentiation, a special syllabus, separate exams, if exams there must be, are urgently demanded, if we are to stop what is almost a cruelty. But there is another set of considerations. The English language is the gateway to a new culture; they have, of course, no written literature of their own, next to no history, as we define it. And the exams are the gateway to all the professions, and even to many more lowly jobs. You cannot be a carpenter without some knowledge of maths. You cannot run any shop or small business without some knowledge of book-keeping. The South African native is in a peculiar position: he must adapt himself to white civilization and to do that he must show that he can face the same tests, hold the same ground. Not only 'progress', but mere self-defence seems to demand this.

If any leaders are to hold their own with us then there must be men who have trodden the whole intellectual round and reached the goal; have taken the very best we have to offer. In higher education there can be no differentiation, no adaptation, or very little. And to build up even to a small pinnacle, at this stage of the Bantu, means a very big base for the pyramid. It seems to mean that the greater part of the syllabus for native education must be dominated by the matric and the B.A. We have the same problem in less extreme form in England and have we yet found the answer?

There is another consideration that I should have put in and which I may have mentioned before for I saw it in Samoa. At the very moment when we are developing theories about differentiation, taught by the anthropologists, the natives have found their voices and clamour for identity. 'We want to be like you.' The teachers tell us they are almost fanatical about it. They refuse any soft options; are most suspicious if a teacher omits or adapts at her own discretion. 'Why did you leave that out? We want to go back and do it.' They absolutely rejected the idea of a special matriculation adopted to their needs.

It was time to go. We motored down to the station, and I took my leave of the two Principals, deeply impressed by their work and their spirit and by all I had seen of Scotland's gift to Africa.

Transskei[1]

November 1929

<hr>

To reach this, to me, all-important territory, I have had to go right down to the sea-coast and change trains at East London. Here I picked up with a businessman living there. He motored me all over the dapper little port, with its clean front, cheerful hotels, model schools, etc. But I wanted to see the native location, so I interrupted his many speeches: 'This is our new technical school . . . it cost £x,ooo . . .' etc. His citizen's pride was annoyed. He had grown up with East London and loved it because he had helped to make it. What did I want with the native locations—dirty, stinking places? However I got my way in the end. One of the blocks of native quarters was fairly decent, rows and rows of Kaffir huts. But the other and bigger one was awful. It was very old and made of the refuse of European houses—odd bits of wood and iron and biscuit tins, all jumbled anyhow, and simply crammed with humanity. The stench was awful. I got out of the car and walked among the houses, looking in. There were pathetic attempts at decency, newspaper cut in patterns on the shelves, cheap and hideous pictures on the walls. But most huts were bare or full of ugly litter. Yet African girls living in this warren cross the river to the smart, shining town and tend white

<hr>

[1] I must add a note here as in my diary-letter I was obliged to leave too much to be taken for granted. The Transkei was—and is—much the largest and most important native area in South Africa. In 1929 it was still very much a legacy of the British Cape tradition. It is the result, after much preliminary conflict, of various experiments in administration. These had led by degrees to a unique, though still very limited, degree of self-government in the councils of each tribal area. In 1895 representatives from these districts were brought together in a General Council in which white officials and native representatives sat together. Powers, both local and central, were very limited. But the Transkei was the creation of the relatively liberal Cape tradition. By the time I visited the region the officials in charge, still mainly British, were beginning to feel the influence of the Hertzog Government, with its repressive attitude in native affairs.

children or work in the houses. The contrast is really horrible. Yet my host made it clear that no one was interested, no one cared.

I went back with him to his pleasant house. We had supper there and at 10 p.m. he drove me back to the train, which would take all night and all next day to get into Umtata in the heart of the Transkeian native territory. From East London I carried in my mind an unhappy picture.

I had a beast of a night in the train; I was icy cold and bitten to death by mosquitoes. But the next day was most interesting. I woke to find a noisy train. Several coaches, loaded with Africans from the mines, had been added and these men were hanging out of the windows, yelling and singing at the top of their voices, and shouting and waving to every native they passed on the line. At the first stop I walked up to have a look at them. The carriages were crowded beyond anything I have seen, even the London Tube at the end of the War about six o'clock. They were so choked with black men that heads and half of their bodies were shoved out of the windows. The variety of garments out of which their black brawniness was bursting defies listing: there was every kind of dress from shabby but conventional European, through gaudy blankets, women's discarded jumpers, knitted helmets, cerise and peacock, down to ragged vests, copper wire and beads. Some had wooden boxes, about the size of a school tuck-box, but painted in gaudy colours reminiscent of gypsy art in England. All day long from sunrise to sunset, as the train would painfully round the curves of the hills, this excited company filled the air with song and shout and made the little naked shepherds on the veld run beside the train until they tripped over a hole or fell in exhaustion. Every now and then some men would get off at a halt, wave good-bye to the train and start loping away over the downs to their villages, each carrying his box. Or perhaps his women would meet him and carry his belongings. He is a great man who returns from the mines with £6 or £10 in his pocket and full of tales of Johannesburg or Kimberley. He can now buy a wife, or a second one if he is already blessed, or he can invest it in the Kaffir bank—cattle.

The country we went through all day was that into which the advancing Bantu, pushed on by the Zulus from the east, were penned in by Boer and Briton from the west. It was here Sir Harry Smith fought and marched; this was the land he and Sir Benjamin d'Urban annexed and which, in 1835, Lord Glenelg, one of a unique group of humanitarians, gave back on the grounds that we were the aggressors and the natives more sinned against than sinning. Later in life Sir Harry had to conquer it again and Sir George Grey to devise a system of government for it. And by degrees, with much trouble and many risings, it was annexed piecemeal until, in 1895, Rhodes took over the last bit, Pondoland. Meanwhile, the comparatively liberal Cape Government, imbued with British traditions, and in close touch with the mother-country, treated the land as native reserve, and built up in it, year by year, at the hands of some very good and true administrators, a system of government, which was adapted in some measure to the needs of the tribes. And now that there is the Union and, more to the point, motor traffic, men down from the Transvaal and Orange Free State are discovering the Transkei, and saying, 'Good Heavens!' (or whatever the Afrikaans equivalent is), 'Why, this is a magnificent stretch of country, about the best in the Union. And it all belongs to natives! It's monstrous.' (I did not invent this. I heard it more than once.)

It certainly is good *looking* country. In parts it is rather like the Berkshire Downs, only grander, with here and there a spine of rock sticking out as it never does in our chalk downs. In this wonderful air you can see some forty miles of these rolling grassy slopes, dotted with cattle and kraals, so that the phrase 'the cattle upon a thousand hills' comes to one's mind. As the huts are mere dun-coloured mounds, not much bigger than the cattle, they do nothing to break the sense of space. And over all these huge stretches there is not a fence, nothing but the square kraals made of cactus in which the cattle are herded at night. The fences are the little herd-boys, dressed in a leather thong and a bead, who dash across country to intercept the train and run and scream and dance and sometimes roll on the ground with glee and excitement.

Yet further knowledge takes much of the pleasure out of the picture. The cattle, which to the ignorant eye look quite fine and glossy, are 'scrub' cattle, almost useless for milking purposes, good only for 'compound' meat for the mines, or (a more recent outlet) as a low-grade tinned export to Italy. The country, though not so ruinously overstocked as the Ciskei, is overburdened, with the consequent results of erosion and the growth of the yellow pest resembling ragwort. There is now hardly grass long enough to thatch the mud huts. Much of the beautiful-seeming grass is *sawerveld*. The flocks of goats, whose funny square shapes go bobbing away from the train, are of little use except for ritual feasts. For this purpose, it is said, their advantage, in contrast to the sheep and the cow, which die silently, is that they scream when being killed. Yet, with more intensive farming, the country could bear many more than its present number of inhabitants, which is about a million in 16,000 square miles. But to introduce more intensive farming is easier said than done. But I expect I shall have to return to farming.

There was no fence beside the railway and every now and then the slow, noisily puffing engine, on rounding one of the frequent curves, would find cattle or sheep all over the line. The brakes would be put on, the engine would burst into frenzied hoots and every passenger would stick his head out of the window to watch the fun. The natives in the front vans could see best and treated the whole thing as a treat arranged for their benefit. Could the cattle get across in time? The herd, of course, must follow the leader. And there were limits to what the engine driver could or would do by way of braking, especially running downhill. The horses were always safe; the goats hopped out, well able to save their glossy skins; the sheep generally escaped with a last, desperate leap, even at the cost of allowing their flock to be cut in two. But the cattle were lethargic and stupid. I do not know how many we ran down. I did not much enjoy watching at the last critical moment. But I saw one herd overtaken and the dying and wounded scattered over the veldt. Not that it mattered. The native—I hope?— got compensation, and the village a feast.

I did not have much luck on this train. I picked up only a telephone supervisor, Hartz, a mixture of Welsh, German and Dutch, whose only items of interest were the cruelty shown to the native in Portuguese territory and the indignation of the Germans in East Africa that we should fight with black troops against them.

Arrival at Umtata was rather grim. No one met me and I had counted on some kind of reception, being recommended to the authorities by Dr. J. H. Oldham and the Colonial Office. So I asked for the hotel and drove there. I found the Chief Magistrate, Mr. Welsh, had booked a room there for me. He had also sent his secretary to the station. But the young man had accosted an elderly woman, saying, 'Are you Miss Perm?' To which she sensibly replied 'I am, and this is my husband', and so drove off in the Chief Magistrate's car to the hotel. The secretary—looking rather foolish—told me to be ready at nine in the morning, as the Chief Magistrate would call and take me to Buntingville. He then disappeared without telling me where and what was this unattractively named place. It sounded more

like the Middle West than South Africa. But as I had been poisoned at
the place where the train stopped for us to eat, I tottered to bed without more speculation.

(Perhaps I should explain that the train having stopped at a small
European settlement, I got out, when I was instantly accosted by a
gross-looking white with a coloured servant who insisted that I should
come and have lunch at his place. The guard, clearly an accomplice,
said it was a good idea and cheerfully promised to keep the train waiting until I returned. I was put in a ramshackle car and run half a mile
out to the 'Hotel'. Here I sat down alone at a table set for thirty, while
mine host stood over me, drinking and a native servant brought me
disgusting food, which, under the eye of the hotelier, I had at least
to nibble. Meanwhile he blasted the niggers, which did not improve
my appetite. I was then run back, and the waiting train went on.)

I am not sure what poison I had imbibed, strychnine I should think,
from the convulsive nature of the pangs. The next morning saw me in
no state to meet the Chief Magistrate, still less did I read any attraction into the unromantic place-name, Buntingville. But time was short,
and I dared not rebuff the first courtesy of the administration, so I
dressed and stood on the cold, wind-swept porch to await the car.

The Chief Magistrate, Mr. Welsh, was small, unexpansive, but
natural and sensible, a grey-haired, sallow, dark-eyed man; at first
sight not impressive, yet somehow adequate. There were other officials
with us in the car and their relations with him (to judge by my
experience in Somaliland) were freer than those in a British colony
with the governor, a status to which the Chief Magistrate's position
approximates.

Buntingville, eighteen miles away, turned out to be the headquarters of the Wesleyan Mission in Pondoland, the last tribal area
to be associated to the Transkei. The mission was celebrating the
arrival of the first missionary a hundred years ago. In the solid, old-
fashioned stone house we were greeted by men and women preserved
from another generation by their isolation in Africa. Furniture,
clothes, even the food, spoke of a bygone age. We went to the church,
stuffed to suffocation with the devout Christians of the Pondo tribe,
and were wedged close to the platform. Then began the speeches, the
pitiless speeches of nonconformist ministers, followed by the remorseless eloquence of native orators. Yet, perhaps, if I had not felt so ill,
I might have appreciated all this eloquence for it recalled the turbu-
lent and bloody past of this disputed region: of Zulus massacring

Pondos; of English punishing Xosas; and of later days when, as a child, Mr. Welsh himself was cut off in a beleaguered mission station. I must say, however, that the ministers who spoke did not make the best of their missionary history. Lists of achievements, mostly in figures of souls and money, were read off to mark growth and there was overmuch complacency and repetition. The most interesting thing was the translation: the native preachers who interpreted put a passion and, it seemed, a beauty into the colourless English statements that made me think of French translations of English speeches at Geneva.

Two speeches were interesting. The Chief Magistrate spoke quietly and sensibly and was frankly political. He warned the people against agitation, against imagining that they could yet stand by themselves; reiterated that the only way of salvation lay in co-operation between white and black. He repeated the old simile of the black and white notes of a piano.

Then the paramount chief of the Pondos, Victor Poto, rose; a youngish and educated man, with an earnest, rather shy manner. It was clear in a minute that he did not belong to the older generation of his people to whom oratory was meat and drink: with the education of the European, the self-consciousness of the European had come. He spoke English and if the eyes were shut, the diffident, quiet voice, groping for the right word, might have been that of an Englishman. Yet his meaning was not diffident. He, like the Chief Magistrate, went straight to the point, without compliments.

'My people', he said, 'are grateful to you white men for coming to help us. We needed your help and we know you made great sacrifices to come and live among heathen and savage people like ourselves. But we were not altogether benighted heathens. We were told all our customs were bad, that they must all be swept away. But now we know that among the bad there were good customs and we are very sad that we let them go. We want to hold on to whatever is left. Moreover, we think that the time is coming when no longer should everything be done for us. We want to do things for ourselves. We want to feel our self-respect again. The Chief Magistrate spoke of co-operation but that surely means a sharing of responsibility.'[1]

The audience gave subdued applause to this but the rows of sparkling African eyes showed pride in their chief and pleasure at what he

---

[1] Chief Victor Poto had, and still has, a courageous and distinguished career as a critic of Government policy.

said. Even the oratorical black parsons on the platform (and how black they look in their conventional clerical clothes!) applauded with smiles.

Whether I am becoming over-subtle I know not, but it seemed to me that there was being exhibited in that crowded church, on this occasion of compliments and prayers, the opposition, one that can hardly be kept for long within such moderate bounds, between the paternalism of the white, both in religion and politics, and the new self-assertion of the Bantu.

But we had now been crouched breathlessly upon narrow benches from 11 a.m. until after 2 p.m. Mrs. Welsh, the Chief Magistrate's wife, amiable mother of four daughters, saw that I was near collapse and with much fighting we got out, and I cut the centenary feast and went back to Umtata in someone's car to fall into bed. The hotel was horrible: the bed was a board with a deep hole in the middle; the servants were speechless black women who ran like hares from my desperate gesticulations. Clearly no one of importance or affluence can ever visit this centre of the most important of the native territories.

When, after a day and night of misery, I had to get up, I was handed over, body and soul, to one Mr. Barrett, the second man in the administration. He was not at first very encouraging. He was a quiet, lean, rather awkward individual, with a drawn, leathery face, and eyes too shy to meet one's own for more than a moment. He never seemed to have tried smiling: he thought for a minute before speaking, and then spoke with great deliberation in a husky, rather high-pitched voice, keeping his hands and body quite motionless.

He took me into his office, sat me before his spacious desk and said he was entirely at my service. It is, however, difficult, at least for me, to command, at a moment's notice, services offered so joylessly. The Transkei officials, I thought, are, of course, wholly independent of the Colonial Office (which had commended me to them) and may have some feelings of professional jealousy. Perhaps they think it damned cheek to foist a young unknown English woman on them. So I let him down gently with what has now become my usual demand for a place in the office where I can spend two or three days studying all the documents they think fit to put before me. The response was immediate: all this was now done. I was given a large room of my own; a huge desk was piled with records and blue-books and a clerk was told off to fetch and carry. Moreover, I was put in telephonic communication with Mr. Barrett, the chief officer, in case any questions arose.

Under these ideal conditions I sat down to read up the minutes of the rather unique Council—the Bunga—in which native chiefs and representatives sit with government officials, and which has now been working in the Transkei for about twenty-five years. Here comes a problem. I do not know how far I should plunge into my subject proper in this circular letter. I think on the whole I had better keep out of it as it is bound to be rather heavy stuff and difficult to abbreviate. And whenever I get the chance, perhaps at Pretoria, I want to sit down for a week and write articles on the Transkei as well as upon Samoa and also Basutoland—if I ever get there. But I must say here how fascinating I have found this kind of work wherever I have been. Never since I was in the examination schools at Oxford has the big hand of the clock jumped so rapidly from point to point as it has in these hours, whether in the Governor's office at Pango, in Apia, Wellington and other places. Barrie says that when you find the work that is not work to you, but sheer pleasure, then you have found your vocation. But I am afraid that even the Rhodes Trust will not pay for me to revolve indefinitely round the world studying blue-books in their places of origin. It is, of course, the ideal way to study such a subject. You have at hand all the officials to answer questions, to expound policy, and to give you, unconsciously as well as consciously, the spirit and traditions of the administration. Then, all round you is the country, spread like a map, with experts to interpret the pattern and the colour and missionaries to give you, from their own distinct angle, their stored knowledge of the dark inhabitants.

If only at interviews I could always take notes, as I sometimes do! That would save me from straining my memory and from sitting up all hours to write down what I have heard during the day. But I find that many men, perhaps most, shy at a notebook. One has to learn to guess their reaction by instinct for to ask and be refused almost wholly negates the value of an interview for some men. Others are too halting to speak well to the top of your head: you have to face them, and give them whatever prompting you can with the expression of your face. I must say that on the whole I have been very fortunate and have met with singularly little prejudice on account of my sex and a great deal of sensible courtesy and helpfulness. Fortunately for me, most people like to talk about their job, and very often men have said, when I thanked them, 'But it is so wonderful to meet anyone who takes an

73

interest in these things.' The excellent American writer, Raymond Buell,[1] whose recent footsteps I discern from time to time, has not muddied the path. But I do not think he did very much talking, or rather listening, to officials. He seems to have tackled No. 1 only, and neglected the rest. Perhaps he had no time. (I shall see the result in due course.) At any rate he made a mistake. The old-established district officer—by whatever title he is called—often knows the detailed working of the administration better than the top man, even though he cannot write reports and weave policies so well. And it is vital always to get into touch with agriculture, the basis of all native life and, if possible, with police and education as well. It is all of breathless interest and I cannot count how often I give thanks to those to whom thanks are due—first to Cecil Rhodes and Barbara Gwyer[2]—secondly to my sponsors, H. A. L. Fisher and Philip Kerr.

All this explaining arose, I believe, from the taciturnity of Mr. Barrett. Well, Mr. Barrett behaved with more than correct courtesy. He called for me at the hotel in his car and always returned me thither. He called at my office in the Secretariat at intervals to put himself at my service. And this was all the more remarkable because the first day, when he had taken me in to introduce me to the Treasurer, the latter had pointed out a paragraph in the daily newspaper entitled 'Promotion of Popular Transkei Official'. Then, with much eulogy, followed the news of the promotion of Mr. Barrett to the central Native Affairs Department of the Union Government. He read it through, apparently unmoved, and it was only later that I learned that it was the first he had heard of it. 'I think it is better in these cases', he remarked to me later in his dry voice, 'to inform the official concerned first.'

I do not know whether, at the start, I quite misjudged Mr. Barrett, or whether he changed, but at a certain stage it dawned upon me that this man, always the busiest man in any administration, and now immensely occupied by rounding off all his jobs before being transferred, was sacrificing himself to an extraordinary degree on my behalf. Presently he transferred me from my first office into his own, which led out of the Chief's, and there, for two days, in all the intervals between calls from next door and urgent interviews, he patiently expounded the administration, looked up documents and answered

[1] Raymond L. Buell, author of *The Native Problem in Africa*, 2 vols., New York, 1928. A very able and thorough investigation.
[2] Miss Barbara Gwyer, Principal of my college, St. Hugh's.

my many questions. When I asked for an educated native, he produced one: when I demanded an old trader of long experience, he
dug one out in half an hour. Meanwhile work was piling up on his
desk to be dealt with, heaven knows when! And because it rained on
Friday, he gave up his Saturday to take me out to see the Cowley
Fathers' Mission and the Agricultural School.

Here I am tonight, very much in the wilds, after a long and tiring
day. I got up in good time this morning. I had been up writing late at
night; the conversation I had had with the man from Leeds[1] was
buzzing in my head, all about the savagery of the natives and the
unnatural crimes of the urban native. My rooms were far out at the end
of a wing, with a long window opening right on to the road. I had to
keep the thin curtains drawn all the time, or the eyes in the procession
of passing and peering black faces could survey the whole room. It
was half-past twelve at night and all had long been quiet when some
light footstep stopped at my window which was wide open. I heard
what might without much exaggeration, given time and place, be
described as a blood-curdling chuckle and a whispered conversation.
Silence followed. Then I heard a stealthy footstep coming down the
corridor. It stopped at my door and there was the sound of a hand
carefully feeling the door. I sprang out of bed and held the handle,
with my finger on the bolt ready to lock it if I could.

'Who's there?' I whispered fiercely.

'Night porter. Bring Missie pot of tea.'

'I don't want any tea. Go away.'

I shall never know if I wronged the night porter or if I was nearly
the victim of some thieving plot.

The sun woke me at six. When I came into breakfast I found some
rather unappetizing men at my table but a nice-looking couple beckoned me to sit at theirs.

The man turned out to be Captain Taylor, Chief of Police, so I
was able to salt my breakfast with criminal statistics, and found out
an immense amount between porridge and marmalade.

At 8.45 a.m. Mr. Barrett called for me in the Chief Magistrate's
car and we set out the forty miles to the Cowley Fathers' Mission.
I liked him very much and also the quiet, cold way he diagnosed the
situation and interpreted the countryside. We passed ox-waggons,
lashed off the road by screaming drivers, the big beasts looking half-

---

[1] Sorry! No time for the man from Leeds, a traveller in organs, who accosted
me in the lounge and spat the usual venom on the native question.

choked and getting their six or seven pairs into clumsy tangles at the crisis. We passed many natives in Balaclava helmets and curious clothes loping along on their little, ill-treated ponies. Minute, naked picca-ninnies herding cattle jumped and shrilled for glee as we passed. (Why ?) Once we forded a river and startled a girl kneeling on a rock who was washing bright coloured clothes, a picture of grace and beauty.

We saw a place where they were experimenting in checking soil erosion, the result of overstocking, a very serious problem in South Africa now. The terrible wound in the earth is fenced off, aloes and grass are planted and here and there a dam is built, so that the water will silt up the earth against the barrier and gradually fill the crack until it is no more than a deep but shallow depression through which the water will run gently.

Our way led through fold upon fold of rolling grasslands, with one horizon of hills after another. One gets that sense of the land being infinite of which Rhodes used to talk when he first came out and which seems peculiar to South Africa. Alas! for the Africans it is by no means infinite.

We came to St. Cuthbert's, the mission of the Cowley Fathers. These mission institutions are much the same in form, differing mainly in the range of their activities—the elementary, the secondary school, the training for teachers, the church, the workshops, perhaps the printing press. But they differ widely in spirit. Just as Lovedale stems from Edinburgh, Aberdeen and the kirk, so St. Cuthbert's is based on Oxford and High Church. White-clad fathers with white sun helmets and silver crosses, dazzling in the African sun, on their breasts; white sisters from Wantage: and in the school the teacher, Miss Wallace, from my old college, St. Hugh's. Most characteristic of all was the weaving school, where African girls were bending over looms weaving the skirt-lengths and scarves beloved and worn by Oxford women dons (like myself) and rectors' wives. Everywhere the Oxford accent, with Oxford taste in pictures and church furnishings, very familiar after the bric-à-brac of the German Catholics at Marian-hill, or the apparent indifference or ignorance in such matters at Lovedale. Not that I think these variations make much difference to the native: presumably the essential message is the same with the sincerity, devotion and patience through which it is communicated.

Miss Wallace had made the girls' 'common rooms' very pleasant indeed, with changing, well-chosen pictures from the illustrated press and a long chart of history through the ages circling right round the circular mud walls. But she was ploughing in hard earth and confessed it. Father Calloway, head of the Mission, was away. It is he who wrote those sensitive books, *A Shepherd of the Veld*, and *The Fellowship of the Veld*, describing his work and life in these parts.

I really do not think I took in much about St. Cuthbert's. My visit was too hurried, and the two Fathers who are the life of the place were both away in Oxford. It seems almost insolent to pass any criticism upon the work of the missions. No one can travel about in South Africa without realizing how old, and how great in extent, is the mission contact with the African, how late the State has come into the field of education and welfare work and still, to a large extent, limits itself to supervision and inadequate grants-in-aid. Yet, in trying to imagine a better future, it is impossible not to feel that the missionary too often gives just what is ready in his hand to give, without more careful adaptation to the needs of the native. At first sight, for instance, I was inclined to admire the weaving school. It looks so charming and equally charming pictures arise of native girls weaving away in their own homes to fulfil their own simple needs and even to sell the surplus. But, learning to distrust first impressions and getting down to hard economics, I discovered that the girls could never weave a blanket, or indeed, any other native necessity, at a price within the furthest reach of the native. His blanket, made in Germany or Japan, costs about 10s: theirs would be between £2 and £3. Well, then, it may be said, let them make for the European market. That is a small, capricious market, difficult to organize. 'Friends of the Mission' may buy enough to encourage the school of St. Cuthbert's and the work may be good for discipline and morale, but, from the questions I put to those in charge, I do not think they were looking much further than that. The best work is probably in the hospital where they train native nurses.

From St. Cuthbert's we drove to the magisterial station of Tsolo. Here I went into a Kaffir store and found the Russian Jew, a type which is percolating widely throughout South Africa, serving a host of native women. The interesting thing about the shop is that there was a barrier across the middle. On the one side were the 'raw reds', i.e. primitive heathens, who dress in ochre-stained clothes and blankets rubbed in fat, and on the other side the women known as 'dressed', 'school' or 'Christian' Kaffirs. It is a matter of convenience as well as social distinction for the dressed Kaffir generally needs different goods. I went behind the counter and looked at the goods—blankets, dress-lengths, suitcases, tin water-cans, boots and shoes, hats for men, braces cut out of old rubber tyres, patent medicines, European groceries done up in minute packets (tea by the ounce), sweets and cooking vessels. The inventories of the traders are the index of what we call civilization, and the index has been moving slowly up during the last twenty years. Outside, perhaps most interesting of all, were small ploughs and cultivators, and other farm instruments, all—alas!—coming from America or from Germany.

With some difficulty I persuaded a heathen girl to stand still in front of the Court House for her photograph. She had a beaded dress and bracelets and anklets of goat-hair and was clearly one of the beauties of the village.

Leaving the little trading centre we drove on to the Farm School. This is one of two schools that have been put up by the Bunga (the Transkei Council) to teach the people agriculture. It is a very interesting experiment and both the head of the school and his wife were intelligent people, earnestly devoted to their work.

The strange thing about this agricultural school is that it was thought of so late in time and need. If the native is to be taught a subject related to his life what could be nearer to him than that of farming which was, and within the native areas, still is, his whole life? Yet the missionaries for a hundred years have put literary and academic training first. This they should have done if ever African leadership is to develop but should not have left the other undone. They have given industrial training in some missions, as at Lovedale. In both cases they fit their pupils for a profession, to go out as wage-earners, not for the home. Too often they have merely been giving their students keys to doors which are bolted against them from the inside. But improved agriculture would mean improved standards of life throughout the native lands, the raising of the whole community. Above all, it might teach the native to think, for instead of learning, parrot-fashion, as he does too often, an alien jargon, he would be learning something which could be applied, with results potentially almost miraculous, by his own hands to his own life. And if he could be taught to reason about something so fundamental to himself there might be an end of the witch-doctor and all the superstition that torments his society.

The boys at the school must first have passed Standard V and they stay two years. They live a strenuous day, working from sunrise to sunset. Four hours of this is taken up with lectures. The Principal, Mr. Butler, is careful not to make the farm a kind of paradise, remote from reality. He does all he can to make it just one step higher than the native standard, a first step they can take: the second will come. His cattle are Lincoln Shorthorns whose merit is that they cross well with Kaffir cattle and so raise the general standard. The calves are even allowed to continue taking a little milk from them, again so as not to make too great a breach with native methods. Native crops have priority—Kaffir corn and mealies. They are coaxed towards fruit and vegetables.

I came in unawares upon some of the students while they were milking. They were washing hands and arms with great elaboration; each beast had its udders washed; the sore ones were vaselined; the shed was absolutely clean. No one was in charge of their operations. In the equally spotless dairy, with all its machinery shining as if fresh from America, a student, a little out of date, was singing lustily 'Rule, Britannia'. I was told this was the favourite song upon the farm.

We walked in the beautiful valley. The same willows I had seen in Australasia were beside the stream but not so bright or luxuriant: the bed of the stream was full of arum lilies and other flowers. All round us the slopes were thick with waving grass, showing what this soil can do when guarded and rested. Mrs. Butler and her two charming children walked with me. She is South African, willing to give her life and the life of her children to serve the natives—her eldest girl is to be a doctor and is pledged to native work. Yet she is no sentimentalist. She is able to do her part at her stage of the work without the support of much optimism or missionary principles in the more limited sense. She is critical of missionaries. She is horified at talk of equality. She speaks Xosa and Sesuto fluently. She described Dr. Aggrey's[1] visit and how her servant staggered and nearly dropped the plates when she saw a black man sitting at the table. Also Hertzog's visit and of the impression it all made upon him, at least for the moment. (Can it be that Hertzog is impressionable?) Smuts, I believe, has never visited the territories, far less the school. But the most constant and enduring impression seems to be that made upon the Backveld farmers. One of them said to Mrs. Butler, after seeing St. Cuthbert's and the School: 'I never imagined such things were

[1] The Gold Coast African, one of the first of his race to become an international figure.

79

possible—all those girls in their white dresses—so modest and well behaved!'

I was so much attracted by the Farm School and Mr. Butler had so much to say that I knew would be valuable, that when they pressed Mr. Barrett to leave me behind with them, I agreed. I parted from my friend and instructor with warm thanks and mutual good wishes.

I had not so much as a comb with me but Mrs. Butler was ready to provide all, so I stayed. They had to go out at night in their car to Tsolo so now I am sitting all alone on their verandah, with the whole air vibrating with insect life and all the sky shaking with stars, so the sound and movement seem one. The sound, indeed, is beautiful enough to be the music of the spheres: when so many crickets cry all at once on different notes, the whole is blended into one harmony. And high singing notes come down from the trees where the Christmas beetles, hanging like grey-green leaves, pulsate their wings in a tremulous soprano. The frogs make the bass, a soft roar coming from the whole length of the river in the valley. In the sky I can trace the lines of Orion's belt, the throbbing group of the Seven Sisters, and a lovely constellation, shaped like a coronet of even gems, whose name I cannot learn. I do not know if there are ever wholly dark nights in South Africa: I have seen none and tonight I can trace the whole sweep of the hills, the tables and cones and sugar-loaves, not as a black outline, but in their own deep blue-violet colour.

This morning I got up early and went for a walk, trying to drink in the country so that it should not be obliterated by the many impressions that I shall be taking in. I looked at the wide rolling downs, at the mushroom-coloured huts and kraals fenced in with grey-green aloes. This is the main piece of South Africa left to the Africans, overcrowded and ill-used for all its delusive look of emptiness and stark beauty, a country which exports not its products but its men.

After breakfast I went round to meet some of the students. Most of them were shy and far more silent than those in the two academic institutions. The African boarding master, Mdji, was, however, more talkative. When alone with me he asked me searching questions. Then he said:

'Only three weeks in the country! You have indeed a lot to learn, Ma'am, a lot to learn. You want us to tell you what we think about this school. We think it is the beginning of a new thing for our people.

We see that we have had the wrong education for many years. We went to the schools and put on European clothes and we hoped that we might become like the white men. We saw that the white men never touched a spade, never did any manual work. So we said—that is poor work for low-class people. If we want to raise ourselves we must get away from spades and the land. So it became my ambition to teach and that of all my friends. When our Superintendent, Mr. Butler, came to this land and worked with his own hands it was like a miracle, it showed us a new way, and the real way, to raise ourselves. I was very sorry, then, that I had been trained for a teacher. Do you know, Miss, that if I go out into my garden here, even now, and work in it, natives who pass say—"Ho, ho, you, an educated man! You, a boarding master! And digging the soil! Ho! ho!" '

He went on, 'But the people already are changing in the sixteen years since the school was started. They come to the school for rams to improve their sheep and they buy implements and plant with a machine.

'But there are no women for our men to marry. The girl from the school is too grand to work on the land in the old way. So our young men marry a "red" woman and always sink to her level. We want to have our women also educated in the right way. Myself, I think education should begin with the women.

'What do they think about us in England, Ma'am? Do they still care about us as they used to do when they sent out all those fine men who worked for us? We send deputations to England and they come back and say "They would not hear us. They say they have nothing more to do with us." And we cannot believe it. Why, do you know, England is like God to us. How can she not have power to help us? It was to Queen Victoria that we gave the power over us. How is it that the Dutch now rule over us?'

I tried to explain that South Africa was like a young man who grows up and marries and sets up a kraal of his own and is no longer ruled over by his father. But they cannot understand. They have a sense of betrayal and yet they still cannot believe that England, powerful and just, has finally abandoned them.

We were called outside to see a student who had been looking after the bees and they had swarmed upon him. Everyone was much amused about it but he could have been in real danger.

Mr. Butler promised, if I would stay a little longer, to take me round and show me the inside of some kraals, both Christian and 'red'

F

(heathen). So we motored for miles, just taking our own course across the open veld. In the heathen kraals, here and there, we saw the beer-drinks going on. The men gather each week-end at different houses and sit in a circle, the women in another, some distance away. Then they soak and soak for an hour and a half on a beer they make for themselves out of grain. From this come rows and crime, perhaps starvation from the waste of meal. After it I could see them riding home, reeling in the saddle, bumping and coughing, while the poor little pony finds his own way back. Clearly, the old tribal disciplines have gone.

We visited a Christian kraal. The mud huts were clean, some even had windows. Inside one, belonging to two 'school' girls, was an iron bedstead with quite clean sheets and pillowcases; pictures from magazines were stuck to the clay wall; a frieze made of whitewash and blue bag; a cupboard with newspaper on the shelves and a sewing machine. In another an old woman lay reading a book in Xosa. She was a noted midwife who had enabled many women of the neighbourhood to achieve successful births in conditions which might have defeated a European doctor.

Very different was the heathen 'red' kraal. Here the women in their beautiful amber dresses, with heavy embroidery in black and white beads, pockets of catskin and bracelets of goats' manes, were brewing Kaffir beer. Their eyes met us, wild, shy and uncomprehending. Their huts were black as night inside, windowless, and soaked with smoke. They had no furniture, only cooking pots. One woman offered us a tin of the muddy beer. I smelt it; a heady whiff struck my nostrils. She grimaced at our bad taste, drank half herself, and poured the rest down the throat of her small naked baby. Miserable cats and lame dogs cringed round the kraal. The men were evidently all away at a beer-drink.

Back to Umtata where my last day was hectic with work and interviews. I had a long, final talk with the Chief Magistrate, who was very frank and confirmed most of the general views I had formed about the limited scope of the Transkei Bunga, or Council. He gave me plenty of blue-books to send home. I find it hard not to plunge into my talk with the Chief Magistrate but I think it better to keep it for the more serious writing of my notes.

I left Umtata at night. The 'poor white' who hangs about the hall, intercepting tips that should go to the natives, came down to the station with me. On the way he unbosomed himself to me. Natives were all swine, he said. Not one was to be trusted. I listened in silence. Argument was so obviously useless.

I was not too pleased to find the man from Leeds on my train. He hung around my carriage, anxious to give me all the advice and information he could. He declared himself vehemently against the the Boers. They were all 'slim'; they let you down sooner or later. Never in his experience had relations been worse. There was no social intercourse. It was no country for Britons. He meant to clear out when he could. At last I got rid of him and lay down thankfully on my hard bed. There are no real beds in South African trains. They turn down the seat and for 3s you get sheets and blankets. But the train rocks so on its narrow guage that it is hard to sleep. Also we were going through the unfenced lands again and half in sleep and half awake I heard the hoots and the brakes and shuddered to think what much greater slaughter of the innocents we could be making at night. I could only hope that most of them were safe in their kraals.

The train stopped at six for breakfast, and then at 9.30 a.m. threw me out upon a junction in the open veld where there was no sign of man or beast. Here I had three hours to wait. It was a desolate experience. Conscientiously I looked round to see what I might learn here. There seemed only one point of interest—the low grade of the white clerks and porters on the station: pasty, ill-developed, sullen, stupid, both Dutch and English. It made one understand the reason for the amount of ignorance and deterioration in much of the South African white stock. Those who are not concentrated in the few towns are sprinkled about this vast country, with its scanty communications, with little in the way of education or external contacts, employing people whose primitive background demands, what it can seldom get, the utmost restraint and understanding. It is not wonderful that the result in politics is what it is, especially as in the Parliament the country districts are heavily over-represented as against the towns.

As I had had no exercise for very long, I walked for two hours along the straight, muddy, rutty road that transects the railway line. I met no one except a native tramp or two. In this country tramps run, or rather, lope.

At last my train! I found myself in the carriage with a nurse, a Welsh woman who had been fifteen years in the country, a hard-faced gin-and-beer drinking woman, who was full of information.

No, she couldn't bear the natives. A nasty, dirty, untrustworthy lot! Would always steal behind your back. She had also had a lot of experience with Jews; had made much money out of them. She gloated over the leakage from their well-filled safes in the direction of the medical profession. She told me that Jews were much more afraid to die than other people and that they were terrified when ill; always insisted on two or three opinions, a caprice much smiled upon by the doctors who throve in Jewish areas. They always wanted medicine in very large bottles, so the doctors kept a special size for them and watered the stuff down at a high price. No, she could not bear the Dutch either. Now that she was able to pick and choose, she never nursed them. They were very dirty and dishonest. She had been to farms where the farmers were worth huge sums of money and lived in squalor, with sacks stuck into the holes in the windows. A dreary encounter, this!

All day long, running up on the line from East London to Bloemfontein, we were in rich country, rolling downs carrying immense quantities of good sheep and cattle. How different, after the native areas, were now the size and culture of the farms. The contrast was, indeed, almost shocking. After the crowded, huddling huts spotting every slope and crowning every hill, the slow train would run five or ten minutes through immense rolling grass and arable lands before the farmhouse would appear gleaming through a sudden clump of trees.

As we approached the Free State the country changed. It was no longer so grassy: we got back to the karoo again, stony flats with sheep nibbling at the dry, salt-bush clumps, or gingerly tackling the emerald foliage of the mimosa scrub, which is armed with terrible white thorns. The shapes the hills make on the skyline—mounds, cones and tables—are almost unbelievable. And here the immensity of the farms was such that I got tired of looking out of the window for that little clump of pencil-shaped poplars and the windmills that marked the farmhouses. This is the area of 'dry farming'. They may go for two or three years without rain but the salt bush, the mimosa and the sheep exist and all the farmers are said to be rich.

And the flowers! I realize now that it was no such strange Biblical hope that the desert should blossom like the rose. It does in truth so blossom, flowers nameless to me, their colours shimmering in the heat-haze, so that you can hardly tell flowers from what seem to be flying flowers, the millions of butterflies fluttering above them. Just as no drought seems able to stop the desert from flowering, so no poverty or hard measure can stop the African from smiling. Little gamins, reedy-limbed and pot-bellied, wave and laugh from every location and give back four-fold measure of response for any sign of greeting.

But there are other than desert flowers. Streams are choked with masses of arum lilies. Gladioli and red-hot pokers and many other flowers that are precious garden blooms to us embroider the railway embankment whilst a sort of crisp everlasting flower, bright violet, or yellow, grows profusely and patches the slope with its vividness.

From my train I saw both sunset and sunrise over the karoo. I *will* restrain myself, but indulge me for a moment—what a feast of colour and shape, what sculptured clouds flushing through all the range of colours, what weird kopjes playing with the light and what a thrilling afterglow! No more! I will leave to the imagination those revolving miracles with which nature compensates for the harshness of the plains —and of man!

Poor whites again! A sight such as could not, I am told, have been seen a year or two ago. A gang on the railway wielding shovels, first five natives, then three whites, four natives and two whites. The train, to their obvious embarrassment, halted beside them. The whites hung their heads and looked away. I thought they were divided between Dutch and English. The natives went on working after one look at the train. This is a very unusual sight, I understand. Generally, when the whites are employed on the railway now—the policy of the present government—they are employed in groups by themselves, and, of course, at a much higher wage than Africans. We passed some of the places where poor whites are bred, squatters' farms, '*bijowners*', miserable plots and houses from which the Dutch wife replenishes the earth with ignorant and landless sons.

Another night in the train, and then Bloemfontein at half-past five in the morning. One hardly appreciates a strange city when wandering about at that hour without breakfast. It is a small, squared, insignificant town. A war memorial testifies to the fact that the contingent sent from the heart of the Free State was 90 per cent British. The natives, in the hideous, cast-off and patched clothing with which they caricature their masters, were pouring out of the location to work into the city. The English paper contained the report of an eloquent plea from a well-known liberal writer, Dr. Loram, addressed to the City Council, to allow natives to trade in their own locations. He pointed out that they had all the disadvantages and none of the advantages of segregation. The white man will not allow them to live in his towns yet monopolizes their labour, their trade and their custom.

Basutoland

November 1929

I don't think I have explained what I was doing alighting in the Orange
Free State capital. I had always hoped that on this journey I would
somehow get to Basutoland. I had read the romantic history of this
mountain kingdom, now surrounded by white South Africa. But to
understand the drama of Basutoland's position I must insert a little
history.

Early in the nineteenth century a very remarkable African,
Moshesh, had gathered together the tribes broken by the bloody
Zulu tyranny and had welded them together into a miniature nation
backing upon these mountains. He had later been driven off his rich
lowlands by the encroaching Boers but from his dramatic table-shaped
stronghold of Thaba Bosiu he had called a halt to Boer invasion. Hearing that other tribes had been helped by white people called 'missionaries', he sent an agent with 200 cows to buy some of these
valuable beings. This man fell in with some French evangelical
missionaries and so began a most useful relationship and the process
of the early conversion and Western education of this rugged people.

Moshesh was a diplomat as well as a fighter. When he defeated an
English force, which left forty dead Lancers on the field, he charac-
teristically sent a message: 'You have shown your power, you have
chastened. Let it be enough!' What he most wanted, indeed, was
British annexation to save him from the Boers and in 1868 he got his
way. He said: 'I am glad that my people should be allowed to rest and
lie under the large folds of the flag of England before I am no more.'
And, in a letter to Queen Victoria: 'My country is your blanket, and
my people the lice in it.' But would the Queen and her successors hold
on to that rather distant blanket? The lice proved restive and in 1883
Britain handed over the difficult little state to Cape Colony. This
Government, in turn, found the Basuto difficult to govern and, after

86

failing to disarm them in the so-called Gun War, they handed the state back to Britain.

At the making of the South African Union in 1910 there was strong pressure from both British and Boer leaders to take over the three British-ruled native territories. Basutoland was wholly, and the others, Bechuanaland and Swaziland, mainly, surrounded by South African territory. A compromise was worked out laying down the conditions under which the three territories *might* be handed over to the Union. In 1924 the first fully nationalist Afrikaner Government won the election and began to impose its repressive policies on its Africans. It also made increasingly strong demands for the three territories. Although the poverty of Basutoland drove some half of their active males at any one time to work long stints in South Africa, the people were passionately against being handed over. Naturally I was keen to see these sturdy people and their dramatic scenery and also to find out how Britain ruled them.

In Capetown, while riding with the Imperial Secretary, I had confessed my desire to see Basutoland and, if possible, one other of these so-called British Protectorates. He had passed on my wish to Lord Athlone as Governor-General and so here I was alighting at the little terminus of Maseru a few miles into Basutoland.

I always have a sinking feeling when I first encounter a new enterprise, never knowing what sort of reception I shall get and what personalities I shall have to encounter and from whom I shall have to elicit help. I therefore looked anxiously along the modest platform at which I had alighted. There was only one occupant, a fair, slender man, over six feet high, dressed in an immaculate whipcord suit of rather military cut. He introduced himself as the Assistant Commissioner of Maseru district (that is Assistant to his chief, the Resident Commissioner of Basutoland), and therefore in charge of me. He drove me in his car to the local hotel. It was not at all attractive but he explained that his own house was full of his family and guests.

The day was still young after my morning run in from Bloemfontein. So I asked if I could start work in the afternoon. He put me in the court, a large, simple structure, with the bare requisites of justice, a platform, a table, a dock and a witness box. It led out of his office so that from the magisterial table where I am now sitting as I write up my diary-letter, I can call across to him for information and papers. I can already report that among all officials I have met he excels in unselfishness and courtesy. In fact, writing later, I can report that he has almost played the part of my secretary. I could not say he did more than the wonderful Mr. Barrett of the Transkei, but he did it in a different way, with the easy courtesy of the well-bred Englishman, dignified and impersonal. As, in addition, he is very tall, over 6 foot, handsome and elegant, I find him rather formidable. This kind of fact is an integral part of my narrative because the whole success of each enterprise depended upon my reception at the hands of the responsible official. It was the personal factor at Fiji that made by visit there partially a failure; here in Basutoland it looks like making it a success— or I hope so, for I am only at the beginning of it.

At four o'clock on the first day, the A.C. (as I shall now call him) dashed me back to the hotel to change for tennis at the Residency and then took me there. As it poured with rain I played bridge with the Resident Commissioner, his wife and the A.C.

The R.C. is a good man. That is the first impression he gives and, I must confess, it is a surprising one. One does not expect, nor generally find, saints at the head of an administration and the R.C. seems to be almost that. Quiet, modest, simple, earnest, sympathetic, thoughtful—I have chosen all the adjectives carefully and they ought all to be superlatives. To be beloved and respected, as he seems to be, by the whole of a small society like this in Maseru is a rare tribute when one remembers how these official groups are often beset by jealousies and the friction of personalities. He was charming to me. He said the A.C., who had been there much longer than himself, knew far more about the working of the administration and the Basuto than he did himself. He would therefore hand me over entirely to him. Yet he would see me at any time and do all he could to help. He would not think of allowing me to leave after a week. I *must* stay at least a fortnight. He apologized for not entertaining me at the Residency: his wife had just had a motor accident and was still rather badly shaken. And the A.C.'s house was full of visitors. So I went back to my hotel and a good evening's work on the official literature. I feel that I am in for a very satisfactory visit.

I spent most of this morning with the R.C. He was Secretary in Uganda and after twenty years in that country he finds he has left his heart there and that it is difficult in four years to get to understand such different people and circumstances as he finds in Basutoland.

I can now see why Basutoland, high up in its mountains, is called the Switzerland of Africa. The boundaries of the Orange Free State, Natal and the Cape radiate from Basutoland like spokes from a hub. So Moshesh held a very important strategic position. I can see vividly how the Dutch stole all the flats, some of the best farming land in South Africa, and why the Basuto thought themselves justified in cattle-lifting from this *terra irridenta*. They have been so indulgently handled by the British that they forget what they owe to us and in their famous national Council, ignoring later events, they always refer back to Moshesh's original agreement by which the chieftainship and customs were to be kept intact. The Paramount Chief and the lesser chiefs have a great deal of power and a wide jurisdiction and the exact powers of the Government are rather hard to define. The Union, and especially the Dutch, resent this island within their boundaries and itch to take it over from the British. Hence a stream of protesting Basuto delegations to Britain.

The Basuto border is an obvious economic border. Outside it are wide European farms, railways, natives in their serf-like position, working for their masters, governed by a hundred restrictions. Inside the railways stop, the mountains begin, and in Maseru, only just within the country, the natives fill the town, strolling around with their heads held high, every look and movement proclaiming that they are in their own country. They wear great flopping hats and are robed, toga-fashion, in blankets of striking designs and glowing colours. Maseru is the city of galloping hoofs. As I sit now writing in the Court House I can hear the rapid, light tattoo of the little ponies and past the windows I can see the Basuto dashing full-tilt up and down the town. There is no etiquette about speed; here, you ride quietly across country, but in the town you ride like cowboys in a wild west film. Rows of ponies, fifty deep, are tethered to rails. By contrast the bowed oxen plod, step by step, four, seven, even nine pairs, with the great waggons, which are so much a part of South African history, moving climsily after them. They bring in grain, but mostly wool and bales of the long, silky, curly Angora hair which grows so well in the mountains.

In the evening I went a long ride on one of the A.C.'s ponies which, my being very out of condition, I had a great battle to hold. A girl staying at the A.C.'s house and another official came with us and we wound up a precipitous pass on to one of the stone tables that the Basuto made impregnable. It was down this very pass that they tumbled a body of British Lancers, not one of whom escaped alive.

From the top we could see inland magnificent ranges of mountains, not flat-topped but rising ever higher to jagged peaks. I felt how glorious it would be to penetrate them and leave the flat borderland far behind.

I dined at night at the A.C.'s house and found his wife a most charming woman, though very delicate. The terms for the Basutoland service are hard; leave is rare and passages to Britain are not paid so that those who enter the Service and have families are almost compelled to become South Africans. They have the further disadvantage of the high altitude which does not suit everyone and they live in a small white community. But they have great advantages which made me compare their lot with that of my sister's family in the Colonial Service. Here they can have their children with them, sending them to school in the Union; they have, at most times, I understand, a glorious climate, hot, sunny days and cold or cool nights. And plenty of ponies. And the country itself is most beautiful, though very few penetrate it as the stations are all on the border, and there are practically no interior roads, so that the whole mountainous interior was practically uninhabited until recent years when pressure of population has driven a growing number of natives to live where there used to be only summer cattle posts. As administration is indirect there is really little need for officials to go much into the interior.

This morning the A.C. held his Court under the pine trees outside the Court House. It was rather a striking scene. A few benches for the public were filled with natives lolling in their vivid blankets and big hats. Beyond them were many more all lining up to sign on for work at the mines in South Africa. I sat beside the A.C. A guarded prisoner stood in front of us, a fine, fiery individual, whose face looked quite impassive though on close inspection the movement of his neck muscles showed him less impassive than he seemed. On one side stood a white man, a slim, rather swagger young trader who was accusing the man of theft with violence at his store twenty miles out. On a bench in front were arranged the stolen goods which had been found hidden under rocks in the mountain. A goodly selection he had made—fifteen blankets, five pairs of trousers, pants and vests in bundles, bags of tobacco, cardigans, tea, candles and soap. It was all very informal: at the adjournment for morning tea the A.C. asked the trader into his office. I began to ask about the case but stopped myself, apologizing, as the matter was still *sub judice*. But that did not seem to matter and they talked it over together. Afterwards it transpired that the big crowds of natives who had rolled up, seeing a white woman there for the first time, thought a divorce case was coming on.

Today the A.C. motored me out to see Morija, the big mission institution which was begun nearly a hundred years ago by the Paris Evangelical Society, and which, but for a temporary expulsion by the Boers in the last century, has worked in Basutoland ever since. The missionaries were very hard hit by the war and the decline of the franc. Now, though they are still by far the biggest mission, they are losing every year to the Roman Catholics who have won over the Paramount Chief, at present a woman. It seems strange to find Latin Protestants and also to find them in a British colony. The head of this Paris mission is an Italian: his walls were hung with pictures of Mussolini. He was a little man, with a little wife and seven very diminutive children. The natives are being turned in considerable numbers into Paris Evangelical catechists and teachers to staff their village stations. One excellent thing they are doing is encouraging the Basuto to write stories and legends in their own language and they print them, having the biggest printing press of any mission I have seen. They seem on excellent terms with the Government as represented by the A.C. But they are in a state of gloom—because of lack of workers, and of funds, and they have lately been struck by a terrible scandal.

I spent the next few days meeting the various officials and working hard at education, police, health and agriculture. I thought that on the whole this Government has an able staff, working with a very good spirit. I did an all-day circular tour as far as the road runs and gazed longingly beyond this terminus towards the mountains. We had a Father White (Kenelm Order, Anglican) with us and he was very much against my taking a picture of a Mosuto lady bathing in the stream, but she did not mind. I was then taken to Roma, the Roman Catholic Mission, which is being handed over, rather surprisingly, to the French Canadians. (Is this because they will find it easier to understand—and surpass—the French Protestants?)

This is indeed a red-letter day entry in this diary-letter. Before I arrived here the A.C. had planned a two-week trek into the mountainous interior of his district. There are no roads so it means riding with

pack animals. The Resident Commissioner has now decided that I am
to go with him. It is an unbelievable opportunity and a very surprising
offer. The only trouble is that I am very much out of condition after
all this travelling around with no exercise and I can only hope that I
shall be able to stand it and not be a drag on the A.C. Those blue
ranges going up and up in height look pretty formidable.

I am writing my diary on the first night of the trek. Yesterday was a
great struggle to get ready. I had to pack off the few things I should
need on trek: these are to go off ahead with the horses in pigskin
saddle-bags. Then, last night, the Resident Commissioner gave a big
dinner-party at the Residency to give me a send-off. The whole small
official world, including the Assistant Commissioner's wife, was there.
We played bridge and danced. Everyone was much interested in the
coming trek. To me the evening was radiant with anticipation of the
adventure.

I write in haste. I must get this letter off at once. I will try to keep
some kind of a diary on trek. You can imagine how excited I am.

The A.C. called at 8.30 a.m. and we went off in his car as far as
the road would take us, a terrible road in which we bumped over
boulders, leaped spruits or churned through streams. We reached a
store and there found our fourteen ponies all waiting for us. We had
lunch under a cherry tree, loaded with fruit, and watched the natives
bringing their wool and grain on pack-oxen to sell to the trader.

Then we said good-bye to the car which was driven back by a
Mosuto, and set out at 12.30 p.m. on the first part of the trek. I chose
Stumpy to ride as one of my two horses and the one selected for the
Earl of Athlone, the Governor-General, when he was up here the
other day. My second mount is a grey, smaller, but more spirited. To
my surprise the pack-animals are all left running loose, the four
mounted police keeping them in order. It seemed so strange to see six
horses loaded with tents, beds and one's own personal luggage careering off, sometimes making a detour up a slope or strolling into a
mealie field to eat forbidden fruit from which the police chase them off
with long whips. But the horses seem to know their business and more
or less keep with you. They could not, however, be induced to form
up and pose for a picture of the start which was taken by the man who
was to drive back the car.

We set off at a trekking jog which reminded me of similar expeditions
in Somaliland. I had been warned not to talk to the A.C. on trek, as

he hated talking when riding, and had, so far, always trekked alone, making a positive rule of it. So when he made conversation I answered in monosyllables. In the end I had to explain why. But he said he would waive his rule as it was only 'babbling' that he could not stand. This means, I suppose, that I shall have to try to talk intelligently but not too intelligently.

I stopped once at the sound of singing and saw a line of men all hoeing in a field, raising their hoes in time with their song and very gay about it. I got a picture of them and they roared with laughter at me. 'Are you a man or a woman,' they yelled, so the interpreter said.

We rode steadily uphill all afternoon, until we suddenly found ourselves on the brink of a great fall of ground, with a valley cut by a tortuous stream at the foot. It was a most precipitous descent, with no proper path, and it was almost terrifying to see right below us our pack animals finding their own way down the rocks. I can't say I enjoyed it, sometimes scrambling and slipping down a rocky shelf with a long, sheer drop on one side. I got into trouble for holding my horse up; apparently, when mountaineering on horse-back, you have to give them all their head and let them make their own way. I was very thankful when we emerged on a grassy ledge and dismounted for a long rest. The valley still seemed far below but the mountains were a little nearer. Right underneath, wrapped in almost a circle of river, was the roof of the last trader's store on our route, shining out of a clump of trees. Here we were to spend two nights.

We dropped down, forded the river and climbed up to the store. The people who kept it were very nice and made us most welcome. The A.C. had arranged to introduce me everywhere to the natives as his sister but of course he did not attempt this with these people.

I spent a long time examining the store. Whereas in the old days nearly everything came from Britain, now only about 30 or 40 per cent does. The rest is from Germany, France, Japan, Czechoslovakia and America. Small ironmongery and prints (cloth) from Germany; cheap blankets from Austria and France; silk handkerchiefs and stockings from Japan; glass and jewellery from the Czechs; small ploughs from America. Things of the very best quality come from Britain, a sturdy £4 Paisley blanket as against thinner foreign ones, far better coloured, from 10s to 30s. The trader showed me a big spade which is delivered to him right away in the mountains for 3s 6d. German. I noticed its price-mark was 7s 6d. Not a bad profit? I saw a highly coloured, highly scented pomade in a glass jar roughly copying the white woman's cream jar, with gold label and screw-top. This is actually sold to the native women for 6d. It comes from France. The English do not seem to study their market, do not produce cheaply or push their goods when made. And Africa is going to be a huge, ever-growing market with a vast appetite for cheap ploughs and agricultural instruments and, ultimately, for sewing machines, gramophones and cheap motor cars.

I spent about an hour this evening working through this store. It is a most illuminating aspect from which to study the contact of black and white. For at the store you find out not only what the native needs, an index of his Europeanization, but what he produces, for he brings to the trader his produce—hides, wool, mohair and grain. The trader complains of the quality of the produce, grain dirty and broken by threshing on the earthen floor with oxen; mohair cut too short because the owners dared not wait lest thieves should cut it in the night; bad quality too because, in a land without fences, the angora has sometimes crossed with inferior goat. So the tale goes on. We say, 'Let the native develop on his own lines.' But if he does, and at his own pace, he cannot compete in the world's market. We may ask 'Why should he? He never used to.' He must because of the rising cost of the government and education we give him—and he now demands—and because, with the increasing pressure of population, the land as he uses it cannot support him. The agricultural and veterinary offices try to nag and regulate him into greater efficiency but the word is hardly yet in his vocabulary and theirs is uphill work. The indirect rule spells patience with abuse and inefficiency; and patience these days is a rare virtue in public administration and business. We might be a *little* patient. But the paces are so different, as if a motor car were to be hitched to an ox-waggon. To detribalize a native and then Europeanize him is easy; it has only taken about two hundred years in America and it is going on fairly quickly in the South African towns. But to raise a whole community in its own setting is a different matter: a little quicker in the towns and perhaps by more direct rule as in the Transkei, but still very slow. In Basutoland it will be slowest of all, as far as South Africa is concerned, as the state is largely cut off by mountains, by indulgent British rule, and by a long policy of crystallizing the power of the chiefs.

In the afternoon we went to see the natives dipping their sheep and goats in the very simple tanks that have been constructed all though the country. This is because the Union won't stand contact with the scabby sheep of Basutoland and threatens to retaliate all ways, including shooting them across the border fence. The operation has been reduced to its simplest terms; it is also rather amusing, except for the sheep. Eight sheep are caught with the help of tiny boys who struggle and drag at one leg to haul the terrified creature to the stinking green vat in which it will be submerged to its eyes and nose. The sheep are all held sitting up like a row of grannies, with the most varied expressions of misery and resignation. A little sand-glass is turned to mark the five minutes, and the sheep are flung in, to splash wildly in the dip, held under part of the time by long prongs.

At night I interviewed some local worthies in the stifling shed behind the store where the store-guard sleeps. There was one Frederic who told me some reasons why he considered the morality of the Basuto had degenerated. I will spare you, though he did not spare me and the inadequacy of the store-hand as an interpreter made it worse. We sat on store goods, crouched together, the three of us, the old man talking Sesuto, and his meaning flickering vividly over his keen, black face while, with a great range of intonation and apt gesture, he discoursed upon the old sex-discipline of the tribe, and how with clothes and school the old, strong, rigid fabric has collapsed.

Then came a chief, Mojela, dashing up on his gasping and beaten pony, much as the Somalis used to dash. A bad man, I thought at first sight, and was not surprised to learn he had just been concerned in a ritual murder, when he and one or two others (including the brother of my Basuto friend at Fort Hare) dashed an old man from the precipice, having a ritual use for parts of his flesh. But evidence against a chief is hard to obtain.[1]

---

[1] It will be realized from this reference that, for all the magnificence of the country and the attractiveness of its people, everything was not lovely in the Basutoland garden. Some of the chiefs were corrupt as well as conservative. Worse still, there was a taint of crime. Among the country's most valuable exports was the long, silky hair of the angora goat. As this reached its proper length—or perhaps before—thieves, or even neighbours, would creep out at night and shear the crop. But the worst crime of all was the secret ritual murder. A group of people would arrange to waylay at night a victim—man, woman or child—and cut off the genitals and other parts of the living body bit by bit to make magic medicine for chiefs, witch-doctors or others, and then throw what was left down a precipice. It was almost impossible to get evidence. The secrecy and the complicity of the chiefs meant that the full truth came out only in 1949 when an anthropological friend of mine at Cambridge, Dr. G. I. Jones, was sent out to inquire into this evil. He reported on nearly a hundred such murders committed over the past years. Convictions had been secured in only some twenty of these cases. (Footnote added in 1973)

Today I had to be packed up by eight o'clock in the morning. We have the most beautiful packs and pack saddles, all solid pigskin, provided by the Government. They cost about £20 each. I have one horse and two packs for my personal belongings, another carries the tents, another the beds, three others the kitchen things. Then we have an escort of four mounted police, fourteen horses all told, and generally a guide and local headmen in their gorgeous blankets join up by the way.

We dropped down the steep kopje on which the store stands, forded a river, passed a kloof where lately some wool-stealers were trapped at midnight by the owners and stoned to death. Then away, up a high ridge, and into the heart of the mountains.

I am writing my diary this first night of the real trek. This, the first long day, has been a wonderful, but rather hard experience. I am very soft with long lack of exercise and I was not fit when I started, so I have found the strain terrific. The natives were very vague about the distance and the A.C. could not verify it from the map. Moreover, the heights are so terrific that half the time the animals are climbing like cats and for the rest go slithering down in showers of stones and dust.

We rode four hours on end in these conditions and then off-saddled for lunch. It was impossible to eat; I don't believe one ever can eat much in mid-trek. The dirty old corporal, Bolani, with the vaguest ideas on cooking, and none about cleanliness, set to work on a sheep, one of three that our murderer friend Mojela had presented to us last night and which was promptly slaughtered in front of my face. The packs were off and all our goods strewed about when a storm broke. We packed up as quickly as possible and set out again in the pouring rain. The black loam turned to mud and was slippery as ice. The A.C. made me wear his huge military coat, so I kept dry while he was soaked. We went on and on for two to three hours up and down what can only be called stone precipices. We were just taking a rare patch of smooth slope at a canter when the A.C.'s saddle—which had had the wrong girths attached—slipped round and he fell on his head. His horse in a frenzy kicked and reared and got rid of the saddle, damaging it in the process, then bolted right back down the valley. I might have saved it if I had been quick, but I was dividing my attention between the A.C. and his horse and so did nothing to help either. He was rather shaken but recovered soon and then the whole outfit went dashing and yelling madly down the valley in search of the horse which was only retrieved after half an hour's hunt. I felt almost ashamed for him that it was he, and not I, who had suffered the first fall.

The next little incident was that a pack-horse went bucking and snorting past us, with all its bundle coming off by degrees and strewing behind him in the mud. The rain now turned into hail. We had been trekking for about seven hours and still no sign of the valley for which we were bound. The A.C. suddenly chucked it and decided to camp then and there on a particularly bleak ledge half-way up a hill. So we rounded up the pack-horses and in the soaking, dull evening stood about while the men fumbled with the packs and at last the tents went up and, in the mysterious manner of trek life, the hill was no longer bleak for there was 4 x 12 feet of home for each of us.

We had hardly changed when from all the little clusters of beehive huts spotting the hillsides, the young people began to trickle in and to lie prostrate in a circle gazing with wide eyes at us, following our every movement. Clearly our arrival on this grim hillside was a strange if not unique event.

Then dirty old Bolani got some dung from the nearest headman and with much trouble—though the rain had stopped—got a fire going. The smoke of a dung fire is just what you would expect it to be, and the fire being to windward, it eddied industriously into our tents. I tried to oversee the cooking but gave it up in despair. In the end we got chops cooked on a grill over the open fire with boiled onions and potatoes.

I was soaked through and utterly exhausted by the strains of the ride, being out of training and, in any case, unused to riding up and down slippery mountains. My other great trek was in Somaliland, mostly flat semi-desert. I was thankful to get to bed and slept like a log until the rising sun, taking advantage of an angle in the mountains, poked a finger into my tent and woke me. So I got up and worked for an hour or two, having brought some books on the country in my saddle-bag.

At nine o'clock we set out, leaving our large circle of admirers to glean what they could on the camping ground. I managed to get first up the hill that had daunted us so last night, but only by dint of dismounting here and there and dragging my horse over the sudden outcrops of stone that make such dangerous angles. As the A.C. and the pack clambered up I took a picture, but I do not know if it will come out or whether it will give any idea of the kind of country we have to cover.

We paid a surprise visit to a little Roman Catholic bush-school, where the children were crammed into a minute mud church, every nook blocked against the air. The atmosphere inside was so terrible that it was impossible to stay in it for more than a minute.

We were now getting really into the mountains which, from the heights that we so often mounted, could be seen rising in series, all green after the rains with a shifting blue dapple from the clouds over them. In the pit of the valley the strips of native cultivation maize, wheat and kaffir corn, stood out from the dun rock-strewn grazing of the slopes in brilliant little green rectangles and squares.

We descended a deep gorge and waded through the biggest river we had so far forded, the Senguingave. Then, steeply up again. By pushing hard we reached our intended camping ground by two o'clock. I was not sorry as I was feeling the strain of this very rough riding.

Our new site is in a dip between two low little hills crowned with two villages, quite an urban area after the wilds we had come through. It was pitilessly public. All the inhabitants of both villages at once crowned the rocks, their peering heads black against the flaming blue sky. Soon peering was not enough. They must come and sit round the tents and when I tied down my flap they lay flat down to peer in. But the A.C. did not seem to mind. He sat down in full view and enjoyed his lunch.

The headman was very superior, a young man of high birth, and he at once sent down three sheep. It took us half an hour to decide what to do with them, and how to get rid of two without offence. The A.C., in deference to my feelings, asked them not to kill the sheep right in front of us. They could not understand the reason for such squeamishness, so they dragged the poor suspecting brute past the camp and butchered it just out of sight and came back with the steaming remains.

The headman, Maana Lechesa, came to say that his people would like to give us a dance. I jumped at this and soon from over the brow of the hill came bursts of harsh singing thrown from the men to the women and back again. About sixty of the villagers, in red, maroon and blue checkered blankets came, step by step, on to the open place in front of our camp. In the lead were three figures, half-naked, with great tufts of horsehair and feathers on their heads and bunches of lambs' tails lashing behind them. They were armed with clubs and made prodigious leaps in unison, their ribs and muscles flowing under the dark purple and brown skin.

A big dog stood in the way, staring and grunting. One of the men in his dance struck it cruelly with his club, and sent it away injured and howling amid laughter.

But this dance gave way to one much older and more serious—the men's war dance, the 'Mokorotlo'—I hope I have got it right—by which the tribe always used to celebrate the return from battle. They danced the whole campaign in pantomime, with the song of praise to the chief and of joy at the victory. One movement was that of a down-stabbing spear, obviously killing the wounded. At intervals a single warrior would leap out and act again his triumph, brandishing his weapons, while the crescent of singing, stamping men would shout in deep, slow unison—'he—he', with the refrain, 'yes, thus, and thus he did it—we were there and we saw it.' The women on the wings were accompanying the rhythm with a shrill but ordered chittering which was most effective in exciting the nerves, and every now and then one of them would dance out and with songs and gestures of derision point out the coward who had turned back and offer to wield the spear herself.

Then one of our policemen, moved to frenzy, abandoned his tent-pegging and in uniform, mallet in hand, came whirling in front of the crowd to dance the exploits of the police, to the accompaniment of an impromptu song.

It was wonderful to see the utter unself-consciousness of these grown men and women as they pranced in front of us. And this included the chief who joined in violently but who, for all that, was in absolute and easy command of them all. It was a striking example of the Africans' use of the dance to express their feelings and preserve their history. It all ended with my distributing a box of sweets throwing handfuls in all directions to the struggling children. There was a short interval for tea and then the A.C. and I went up to pay our State call on the headman.

He really had a very nice little village, with the round houses built, not of mud, but of rough-blocked ironstone from the hillside and beautifully thatched. In one, sign of wealth and sophistication, was a double iron bedstead brought—heaven knows how—on pack oxen from Maseru. I noted two sewing machines—Singers too! The mud floor, polished with dung, was dark and shining. The grain was stored in enormous baskets, beautifully woven. The huts often led into a very sensible circular yard, about the same size as the hut, but walled neatly with a screen of reeds to keep away the wind and give privacy. Inside this the women can grind mealies between stones and do their cooking and keep an eye on half a dozen naked babies.

The A.C. helped me through a long interview with the headman in which we really tried to discover the exact position of his court and its relation to the higher native courts, a matter entirely their own concern and rather difficult to investigate, as they are suspicious lest their power and their revenue from justice should be diminished. However, by pressure of questions and by assuring him as far as we could that it was all entirely un-official, we managed to get a great deal out of him. He was so delighted, 'bucked to tears' as the A.C. put it, by the A.C.'s visit that he loaded us with food, three sheep, fowls, eggs and potatoes, and asked if he might accompany us part of the way on our journey.

It was bitterly cold at night, as so far it always has been. It is really extraordinary how the temperature varies. All through the middle of the day the sun is scorching like the tropics; and I can bear nothing but a silk, sleeveless shirt above my breeches. But when the sun goes in at night and there is heavy dew or frost, one must wrap up in all woollen clothes at hand. I have been thankful for the loan of six scarlet police-blankets on my bed, my rug and the A.C.'s thick military coat on top, not to speak of my battered old aluminium hot-water bottle. Even by day, if the sun goes in and you ride up over the saddle of a hill, a sudden wind cuts into you like a knife. Each night we have had to eat our dinner in a tent. I don't know whether it is a chill from the cold, or a stroke from the sun, or poison from old Bolani's veld kitchen, but something has made me very queer tonight. This is rather worrying as it would be heartbreaking to spoil, still more to abandon, this marvellous trek. And it would be very annoying for the A.C. I must keep it dark, unless I feel intolerably worse.

We have had a long talk on native policy tonight. He is very sound and almost over-modest. Defers too much to my opinion when I am all theory and he all practice. I am not sorry to finish these notes and get to bed.

After a farewell visit to the village this morning, we struck camp, a process that gets no shorter with practice, and set off over the near-by hills and then still further and higher into the mountains. I felt considerably worse. I have not eaten much since we started but today I have given up even trying. I rode my grey pony and to my horror found he had gone sick too, and after a few miles I had to transfer from him to Stumpy. There were no incidents on the road today. We passed a *letsima*, that is an occasion which, in return for unlimited Kaffir beer, a man invites all his neighbours to come and hoe his lands, which they do with much song and dance, ending in oblivion. I rode between Maana and Kaswell the interpreter, and Maana pointed out the various features of the magnificent landscape, there the paramount chief's grazing and cattle post, there a cairn of sticks and stones, medicine to keep the hail off the crops. The hills were so steep that the A.C. dismounted and walked a good deal of the way. Not so the natives, who are remorseless to their ponies, and sjambok them uphill and down in a way that is not only cruel but looks most reckless. I rode, too, though generally I am even more ready to walk than the A.C. as I don't like either going up or down these very steep inclines on horse-back.

We rode until two o'clock and then off-saddled on the slope of a hill. There was a little bush-school below us and the A.C. went down to look at it. I asked, remembering past experience, that the school should come out to us rather than we go in to the school, and this was done. The schoolmaster, rather a pathetic, amiable creature from Lovedale, was terribly excited. He did not know the A.C. who was paying his first visit to this remote district; he called him 'father' in a conciliatory tone of voice. They sang us a hideous song; we established the facts that the attendance was very bad and that the girls outnumbered the boys three or four to one. This is usual as the boys are always herding and it has deep and rather healthy social effects. He then brought out his wife, who was afflicted in the legs, in the hopeless hope that we could diagnose her case and, much to the A.C.'s horror, instructed her to lift up her long skirts. This she did and showed knees and thighs dreadfully swollen and scarred. We could only advise that she should be sent to Maseru to see the nearest doctor, rather impossible advice.

Off-saddling when you have so many animals, packs, and hangers-on is an untidy business, but the A.C. is very good-tempered. He knows how to push on when need be, but he also knows how to sprawl and eat his lunch in peace. I had still no interest in lunch.

We rode on past some glorious country. As we get higher the population is getting very sparse. The way the thin rivers have cut the rocky plateaux is most intricate, cutting the mountains into zig-zag patterns. Very often our path is a shaly ledge a few inches wide on a krans (precipice), and it continually amazes me to see our free-running herd of heavily laden pack-horses filing along entirely on their own responsibility, not to speak of our two spare mounts following on like dogs.

As I had objected to the very urban and public area of the last camp, I was allowed to choose this one. I rode on ahead with our guide, Maana, and I wanted to go on and on, as I saw the country getting wilder all the time.

Finally I chose a flat space half-circled by a river and completely surrounded on one side with precipitous hill-faces, a kind of natural theatre. The river ran below a face of sheer rock on one side, and from the tent door where I am now writing, I am looking out at that face which is tufted with rock plants, salmon pink cotyledons, wild myrtles and others I cannot name, while at intervals, the yellow and golden finks, weaving their hanging nests of pale green stems, look like mobile flowers themselves.

There was no keeping out of the water. We got into our bathing dresses and rushed in, mainly in order to have a good wash. I was still feeling too bad to bathe properly and was not encouraged by a crab seizing my toe in his pincers the moment I put it in. The name of the river was Meusugave, and the meaning of that is 'little black things'. We had wondered what this could mean. We soon learned. When the A.C. withdrew his foot it was covered with little black wriggling worms, which adhered firmly even when he put it back in the full force of the current. Wherever the water rushes hard, there the rock is covered with these objects, all drawn taut by the water, and holding on by a little string like a spider's web. Rather a tiring way of life.

This evening the A.C. and I had another long talk, poetry, history, life in general. His books are the *Chanson de Roland* and Bertrand Russell's last book of essays; mine are a history of the Basuto and Shakespeare's Sonnets. But somehow it is hard to settle down to read. The night was so glorious, with a half moon and the fascinating pattern of the southern stars, that we went for a walk along the river, which here sings a particularly good song, and saw the mountain mists shifting in the moonlight up and down the valley.

I woke up this morning feeling better, thank heaven! I got up soon after six and we went for a walk before breakfast. It had poured all night, and everything looked fresh and green and the rock-garden was radiant.

I cooked the A.C.'s breakfast and then, on the chance that Bolani's dirtiness accounted for my sickness, I restrained myself no longer but fell in my wrath upon the kitchen. I got the interpreter and made a speech on cleanliness, and then I had a big fire lighted beside the stream and all the pots and pans, plates, roasting grid, rags and tea-cloths brought out and boiled. I cleaned and washed hard and the police were so frightened that they sat for two hours slaving away in unreasoning imitation and polishing the outside of the pans, like the Pharisees. It was all very amusing, especially when the A.C. scalded out the milk bottles and boiled the tea-cloths. Still feeling domestic, I went and made a stew, the first in my life, I think, washing the chops in the stream and allowing none of the dirty Basuto to put a finger into it. Then we went off and bathed and sunbathed and bathed again and came back to a very good clean lunch.

It has rained all the afternoon and I now sit on the floor of my tent, while the A.C. sits in his, writing notes for me on various points in Basutoland. Tonight we shall sleep here in this glorious place and push on to the furthest limits of this mountainous district tomorrow.

A storm broke over the mountains last night and went lumbering round in circles among the hills, with tremendous echoes. Sleep was difficult with the rain blown like rifle fire on my taut tent. The forking of the lightning could be seen even through the canvas. I managed to get some sleep in spite of it and rose early to have a bathe in the stream. But the stream was now a young and lusty river, galloping over the stones and thick as coffee. It was icy cold too, and the flesh was weak. One had to risk the possibility of bright-eyed cattle-herds high up on the slopes of the mountains. There is cover from the camp for the water has cut a deep gorge, and great lines of pale reeds march along the banks. When I had finished, the A.C. who had decided against a plunge, had to go in to maintain his superiority and in the distance I heard muffled screams. It is cold and overcast now and all our retainers declare that for the moment further progress into the mountains is impossible.

I am not surprised as, after I finished writing yesterday, we went for a walk up the nearest spur and from it saw where the track led, a track for goats, it seemed to me, and not for horses. Moreover my grey horse is still sick. We could see our herd of about twenty spread out all over the valley, and my grey, as usual, standing without feeding, disconsolately swinging his tail.

At the top of the hill we found a cattle post, three or four youths living in a rough stone shelter. They had just kraaled the cattle and were milking them. The milk was for us. I did not look too hard at the battered biscuit tin with a horsehair cord through its holes, which was the milking pail, nor at the process of milking, done in violent competition with the calves. But I did ponder on the hard and lonely life of these boys, up alone in the mountains for several months of the year. Milking over, they mounted three young oxen and, lashing them with sjamboks, went careering down the hill. All the boys ride bullocks and the little ones ride calves and goats.

I have no luck about this sheep-killing. They brought us another sheep last night and as I came up from the stream I came upon the grisly business again. The A.C. was annoyed but his orders only meant that they stopped half-way for all I know and dragged the unresisting beast over the next rise. There is something so utterly resigned and helpless about a sheep when it is being killed.

I am rapidly learning to cook. After my success with the stew I boiled a fowl last night and made some bread sauce which the A.C. was kind enough to praise. After dinner it was very cold and we had to wrap ourselves up in many blankets and squat on the floor of a tent and read Edwin Smith's *Golden Stool* and discuss it. I borrowed it from the Resident Commissioner because I thought it would raise some general problems. It certainly does. The problems seem very different in the Basuto mountains, than in a study at Oxford.

We started again early this dull morning on some blue-books. But, thank heaven, the sun has appeared at last. The A.C. has decided to wait until one o'clock in the hope the track will dry in the sun. I rather doubt it and am a bit frightened of the next very mountainous stage. And I shall be very sorry to leave this camp. My tent is pitched in a bed of wild mint which fills the air with a lasting fragrance as I trample on it. When we were all in train to start I had to go back again at the last minute to fix in my memory the rock-garden growing up the wall of rock that rises perpendicularly from one bank of the Mansangave river; the clumps of wild myrtle clinging to the cracks in the rock; the flowers which formed brilliant purple stars in the cushions of moss; the tall coral and yellow cotyledons on red stalks rising out of a cluster of grey-green leaves; the yellow runnuculus, called by the Basuto the 'wet nose of the God'. There were branches of cherry-coloured candle-flower, drooping down to rise again in vivid points. The yellow finks were busy weaving their hanging nests, which tossed in the wind and were still green with the sap in the reeds.

The path certainly was very slippery. We started carefully down the slopes. The chief Maana, still helping us on our way, offered me his big white horse, which I could not refuse, so we changed mounts on a chute of black loam at an angle of about 60 degrees. Certainly the white was sure-footed, but his rough paces made me identify every item in my make-up.

We climbed a plateau, 9,000 feet up, the Ditsuming, and rode along the top, the sort of place that Rhodes would have called the roof of the world. The Basuto name of the ridge is 'the place where you wipe the crying eyes', and certainly the wind was like a lash and, in default of a cloak, one must drop the reins and fold arms across one's chest. But when I dared look up the view on both sides was awesome, such a wealth of hills of all sizes and shapes, with that glorious cloud-dappling on their slopes which seems a characteristic of this country and its climate.

We slithered off Ditsuming down into a deep gorge and followed all its zig-zags for an hour or more of quick riding. I had an anxious eye on my own pack-horse, which I had saddled and tied myself, as I had a bet on with the A.C. and one of the police that mine would not come loose. He was a forward devil of a horse and would canter to the van in a way that rattled the packs dangerously. However he got through to camp without mishap. One of the wretched pack-horses went lame, the white one with the beds, but we had to let the poor brute struggle on as there was nothing else to do. The spare riding horses would never submit to the humiliation of a pack.

We have found paradise for a camp. The A.C. said it was too wet but I asserted myself for once and we stayed. We are in a small, deep valley, with a narrow stream racing quickly down it, jumping from side to side among the rocks as it goes. Beside the stream are big cushions of grass; the stems spring and curve like fountains and fall in tassels of golden seed. In front of our tents is a level damp patch. If grass is ever a carpet, this is of the finest weaving, like the oldest Persian rugs. All is to a fairy scale. The groundwork is made of tiny, brilliant spade-shaped leaves: there are mossy patches set with countless white and yellow stars, no bigger than a baby's fingernail. There is a small clover, purple-pink, yellow cups like little celandine, and here and there, close within the weaving, but unable to hide its chalk-blue petals, is a lobelia. Sometimes a tiny knoll rises out of the plain, and the little flowers have grown richly all over it. Our carpet is bordered all round by great tussocks, golden where they are alive, silver where they have faded.

I went out late to wash in the stream. The moon was up. In the silence of the valley and the extra silence that night gives, there could be distinguished clearly the different songs sung by the stream as it slipped, shallow, over flat ledges of dolorite, or slid deeply round the curve of a pool, or rushed between boulders to pour like wine from a beaker. While it was still and in shadow its gleam was the black-green of a snake; where it was shaken it caught pale flakes of moonlight; where it was broken its foam was all silver-green under the moon. The stems of the reeds, soaked with dew, shone like steel. Clouds were driving across the sky and through them the clusters of the southern stars could sometimes be seen, Orion, Taurus, and here the Pleiades seeming to cut through the cloud like a lighted ship. I walked back, the frogs respectfully checking the brittle, cracking noise in their throats as I passed. From my bed the open tent door gave me a green triangle of moonlight to gaze at until I slept.

The next moment it was six o'clock in the morning. The dew on the carpet, each drop given full value by the very low sun, was white as frost, yet I could see the light just catching the blue petals of the lobelias. The low grass of the hill opposite was phosphorescent with the dew and the sun shining obliquely upon it struck the clumps of sedge and threw long shadow-lines behind them, drawn straight down the hill as if by a ruler. Some cattle passed slowly across, their square shapes aureoled. The herd-boy, all but naked, rode after them on a half-grown bullock.

I lay in bed gazing for long at this glorified slope and at the carpet which, drenched both in dew and sunlight, was having the most radiant moment of its day. Then I went down to bathe in the stream. A sharp turn in the falling ground sheltered me from all but the watching beasts and a lizard, rigid, jet-eyed, peeping sideways over a boulder. I stooped under water gushing from the rocks as if the nymph of the stream were pouring from a jug: the water, gathered from the mountain springs, was cold and tingling with life. I sat on a smooth shelf of rock and let it rush over me while I looked up at the deep blue sky above the rocky heights and gave thanks to God, Cecil Rhodes, Barbara Gwyer and the A.C.

Then my eye was caught by movement near the steep crest of one of the nearest hills. A huge vulture dropped, changing from black against the sky, to buff against the grass. Before I could count twenty there was a flurry of the great birds alighting and running to the same point, like dark-frocked elders to a meeting. Then the object, whatever it was, disintegrated and the meeting broke up into committees all over the hill to deal with the pieces. Always death in life!

Back to breakfast under a grilling sun, and the cooking of bacon and eggs over a fire made of dung, painfully collected about the veld by the police. For, of course, there is no wood. But dung should be manure. This is one of Basutoland's problems. After breakfast we walked down our little stream to where it joined another, and from there to a long incline of glassy ironstone over which the water was pouring in white swirls down into a deep brown pool at the bottom. Here we bathed and lay in the piercing sunlight and bathed again, lying right in the waterfall.

I wish that I were a botanist. The flowers in this valley are so lovely and all strange to me. The A.C. gathered twenty or thirty kinds in a few minutes. Along the waterside were big groups of yellow, sweet-smelling irises. There was another iris, a small creature, delicate as silk, pale purple blue, with an orange heart. There was the long, lily-shaped Afrikander rising out of the reeds; species of wild geranium, mauve or red-black like a pansy; forget-me-nots, not pale like ours, but deep sea-blue, in the banks of the stream. There was white crassila in the hinges of the rocks, clasped in its crimson calix; wild mallow, fragile and purple; slim white gladioli, and a dozen aromatic bushes and plants, wild myrtle, thyme, mint and sage. The garden was well planned to grow all varieties in close neighbourhood. There was the stream for all that grows on banks and in low wet hollows beside the banks and dry, grassy platforms, above a wall of broken yellow rock going up in tiers to the intense sky. Fortunately the A.C. is a botanist and is even putting together a book on the flowers of Basutoland. (But he is not to be made accountable for any botanic mistakes I have made.)

It was with deep regret and many backward glances that I clambered up the stony track out of that valley. But it was difficult to indulge regret. The steep road demanded all one's care, every hill we climbed opened out new valleys and further ranges. There were other gardens, too, by the way; slopes ablaze with red-hot pokers and rocky corners choked with arum lilies.

We met a string of staring pack-oxen, trailing poles for house-building—wood is scarce in this country. We passed a little Angora kid bleating and lost in a remote valley, but the A.C. was hard-hearted, and would not salvage it because he was afraid of being had up for stock-theft. I picked an arum-lily and a red-hot poker and put one on each side of my pony's head. He looked like the prizewinner at a horse show, all the more so when the A.C. presented me with a huge flower, shaped like a bouquet, which the Bushmen used to poison their arrows.

Soon after this we came to a little village packed high in the mountains, a very isolated position, for we are now very high. The small population with the goats and their curs clustered round us, a very farouche looking lot, without much civility to spare. Maana, who was still escorting us, was all impatience to push on and so were the police. So we began to drop again into the deep valley of the Singuangave river and to look for a place to cross. The river was deep in one part and full of the good earth it was carrying away from Basutoland to the Orange river and ultimately to the sea. My horse, Stumpy, rather lost his nerve in the mid-stream which was pretty wetting for me but he recovered and went on. I rode ahead with Maana so that I could get a snap of the A.C. piloting the caravan through the water but as it was five o'clock and sunless I do not expect a picture that will give any idea of the steepness of the gorge.

Up from the Singuangave, up the next mountain, from which we looked down at its tributary, the Jordan, executing the most amazing convolutions below us, first nearly meeting round a queer-shaped kopje and then indulging in twist after twist round interlocking hills. The police always push on as fast as they can, cracking their whips and shouting at the pack-horses when they attempt too impossible preci-pices or when they walk into the maize and grab a few mouthfuls. The A.C. and I were left far behind and we had with us a sorrowful little grey foal, a pathetic baby that, after the fashion of the country, has been trailing its mother for two days, the mare being ridden by one of our camp-followers. I thought we should have to pick the poor little thing up and carry it but it staggered on in great distress, desperately trying to keep mother in view.

Tonight, for the first time, we are camped right on top of a mountain. The name for the lofty platform of our camp means, I am told, 'in full view of the world', certainly a world foregetting and forgot. The air is very keen, and the mountains are like monstrous herds of cattle grazing in every direction. The floor of my tent is full of yellow everlasting flowers standing very erect in the grass, and rustling like paper at a touch. The A.C. calls them *heliciassus*. He may be right.

We are here to call upon a chief, Makhaobane a grandson of Moshesh. He is a member of the National Council and a supporter of the reforms of the Chiefs' Courts that have been suggested by the government and utterly refused by nearly all the other chiefs. As he was much impressed by the Resident Commissioner being an M.A., the A.C. is telling him that I am something even more wonderful, though whether the A.C.'s Sesuto will run to an interpretation of Fellow and Tutor, I don't know.

We had hardly halted, unharnessed the horses and turned them loose on the veld, than the Chief appeared, his men driving a great flock of sheep and goats down to our camp. The scene, like so much of life here, was very Biblical, with the shepherds in their flowing red blankets. A young sheep was selected from the herd and slaughtered. Cooking it was rather more difficult as there was little or no dung to be found and water was far below. So we had to wait until eight o'clock for our supper. However, we both find that we need very little to eat. Afterwards we wandered out to say goodbye to our guide, Chief Maana, who leaves early in the morning.

I slept late this morning and have just awoken to the glorious view that I see out of my tent. I have taken a picture of it, but it needs the deep blue cloud shadows and the lovely tints of the clouds themselves.

After breakfast, which I cooked, we went to pay our state call on the chief. We sat in the little round stone hut typical of the country. The floor had been newly smeared with fresh dung and the smell was strong. There was no window. Makhaobane had bought six stilted suburban chairs, which stood round the walls in almost ludicrous incongruity with their setting, not to speak of a sofa which had been carried fifty miles from the nearest track, tied on the back of an ox. It must have been a funny sight. There was a plush cloth on the table, two guns, a picture of the Prince of Wales, an appalling German lithograph of Jesus saying grace with a prim nineteenth-century family, and some spears. A rosary hung on a nail and on the table was a Christmas tree.

The A.C. made a speech about me, the chief made a speech to me, I made a speech to the chief, and then, with the loan of the A.C.'s interpreter, I began a long cross-examination. I went on for about two hours, and I could see that many of the questions I asked worried him as he did not like answering them in front of the A.C. He begged the A.C. to speak but he refused, saying this was my show. The chief protested that we had prepared our questions and he was all unready. I asked him about the mohair-stealing, about education, the courts, the position of the chiefs and many other things. It was all very interesting but I must record his answers elsewhere. He had been educated at Lovedale and his mind was a strange mixture of new and old, of a chief's conservatism and of a blind faith in 'education'. He protested about his people's backwardness and pointed out that it had taken many hundred years to produce me.

We came back, packed up lunch and bathing kit on a policeman's horse and rode for an hour, dropping down to the Jordan. Here we had a marvellous sun-bath among rocks and arum-lilies and then bathed where the force of the river spouted between rocks. We bathed, talked, dried and bathed again until 4 p.m. when we rode back to camp. We had arranged to call on the chief to see his cattle kraaled at night. He had some rather fine beasts. They are very docile. Even the great humpy bulls let little naked boys swarm up their tails and dance a tattoo on their backs without so much as blinking their great eyes.

After dinner we walked round our wonderful camping platform and looked from every side down to the valleys and outwards to the circular fresco of mountain shapes. Lightning was playing in and out of the clouds and a full moon had paled the stars, picked out the flowers in the grass and given our shadows a bright moon halo. Suddenly, in the utter silence, we heard a strange noise coming over the mountains. It was like the noise of a distant train and at first I heard it without thinking, then, suddenly, I stood still with the shock. The A.C. was still too. The noise, a dull and far-away roar, rose to an almost thunderous height and then died away. I felt cold all over. There was nothing, nothing at all, that could make that noise. It might have been the sudden roar of a river in spate rushing through a gorge but there had been no rain for two days. We listened, pondered, discussed in low voices, then went to the men's tents for help. They were all in bed but one said it was a sound that came two days before rain. With this impossible superstition we had to be satisfied and went into our tents. I confess I was shivering all over at this strange, inexplicable thing. Now, as I write this, I am thinking twice about sleeping out as I had intended. I write crouched on the floor, wrapped in blankets against the cold, having left the A.C. also crouched in blankets and reading the *Chanson de Roland*.

He woke up later last evening and we went out for another stroll. Then I made up my bed outside my tent and tried to keep awake so that I could appreciate the night. The moon was almost too bright to be looked at but from my pillow I could count the mountains and admire the blackness of the shadows between the silver cast by the moon. Then, again, I heard that extraordinary noise, rising from a faint murmur to a roar, very distant, but unmistakably a roar. Perhaps I wanted to be thrilled: at any rate I did not repress a shiver that came over me as I lay racking my brains for some natural explanation. The next thing I remember is the wind getting up and banging the tents: It could do nothing to me, lying in the open, but strike cold blows on one cheek and whip my hair about my eyes, extremely pleasant sensations. Next time I turned over, having forgotten where I was, I found myself staring in surprise at the moon-set over a castellated wall of mountain. But I did not see the sun rise: he was well up in a blue sky when I pushed out of the blankets into which I had retreated from him. What woke me was a stampede of cattle; the nervous, inquisitive beasts were all round me, advancing and backing with deep, apprehensive sniffs and staring at me as if I fascinated them. This woke the A.C. and he brought me a cup of boiling coffee and we chatted in the young sunlight, with all the golden chalices opening round us, and the morning world seemed very good.

The horses are late coming in; two rogues have strayed again. I unpack my bag and am doing a little writing while the men tug at girths and surcingles and make clove-hitches over the packs. The horses stand patiently; once caught, they let themselves be driven in like sheep. Only Robbie shows his superior breeding by restlessness; he walks off and generally acts with independence and thin little black boys with flapping blankets must run and hold him. I am to ride Robbie today and the A.C., of his unselfishness, is to ride my Stumpy. I tried to get out of it but he made it an order.

Here comes his chieftainship to set us on our way. He is in a purple reach-me-down and puts the A.C. to shame, for the A.C.'s shirt is slit and exposes the back-bone, and his shorts are patched à la Basuto. The chief's henchman is draped in a marvellous blanket, spotted like a leopard.

The last pack is up and we lead off with the chief. He is very apologetic about the path: I assure him it is nothing to some that we have come along.

We drop steeply down, down to that land so far below us, to those kopjes circled with glistening streams, all flat as a map seen from this height. Clumps of big irises, of the palest green-yellow and smelling sweetly, stand about on the slopes. The A.C. picks me some to carry and I inhale their beauty from time to time.

We ask the chief about the noise last night. He is very solemn:

'That, Morena, was the great snake.'

'What snake?'

'The snake that lives in the river. When it makes that noise rain will fall within two days.'

'How does it make the noise?'

'Morena, it holds up the water in the gorge and then suddenly lets it go.'

'Have you seen it?'

'I will tell you. One night we were riding along there and all of a sudden some big dogs that we had with us turned and came running back to us. They were shaking from head to foot. We could not hold them. They ran and ran right away. Then we saw it. We could not see it plainly because of the dark, but it was big and blue fire came out of it. I was so terrified that I stood trembling. Then I turned my horse and ran and ran until I could go no more. Whatever you do, don't camp near that place, Morena.' He pointed towards it.

I thought as much. I had felt that it was something supernatural. The A.C. said nothing would induce him to camp there.

The chief pointed out the cave where Setsi I, son of Moshesh, hid from the Boers in his war in 1873. The chief, having been at Lovedale for five years, wanted his son to be educated in England. Yet the boy lives up there in the mountains within hearing of the Great Snake of the River. Could the boy absorb such a life of contrasts?

Down and down until we are beside the stream, and have crossed it. The pack-horses go lolloping past us with heavy breathing and much squeaking of good pigskin. We cannot hurry. Each turn of this stream

1. Cape Town: Table Mountain and Table Bay

2. Basutoland: the author

3. Basutoland: the Assistant Commissioner breaking camp in the morning

4. Basutoland: the author and escort; a farewell picture taken in Maseru after the trek

5. A hut with reeded enclosure (p.120)

6. Katanga Province: labour camp hospital, maternity building

7. The official caption reads: 'From Native hut to European house. The African houseboy surprisingly soon finds his way about among all the mysteries of a European household.'

Photo South African Railways and Harbours

8. A Johannesburg slum

9. Pretoria: the Government buildings

11. Groote Schuur

11. Clements Kadalie and Allison Champion. From a hand-bill given to the author by Champion, dated 19th October 1929

12. Tshekedi Khama in 1930

13. Dr. Mottone

14. Cecil Rhodes's grave in the Matopos Hills

brings pictures that I want never to forget, that I must stamp upon my mind to last me all my life. Here I look back, and lifted against that radiant sky is a spur of tawny rocks, and in every earthy shelf are clumps of arum lilies with red cotyledons, burning like down-hanging lamps—a harmony of red and white, perfect association, planned by no gardener. Here is a waterfall, far-dropping water turning the grey rock black and in a scoop of ferny bank beside it a cloud of forget-me-nots of the richest, darkest blue. Then another perfect harmony—broken white water, black rock, blue flowers, green ferns and clumps of the golden fountain grass.

The valley steepens and narrows. We have been in higher, wilder places perhaps, but we never saw such mountain architecture as this. Towers, giant walls, domes, palaces and tombs of emperors, soaring vertical lines in black-brown rock, with wheeling vultures to give the sense of loneliness and the terror of height. And seen through every angle, on all sides, further multitudes of mountains, green, blue and paler blue to the last faint stencilling against the sky.

The path is rocky and steep and Robbie, still on loan to me from the A.C., goes at it with gasping desperation. For Robbie thinks we are lost because the pack train is away out of sight. Perhaps we are. But it does not matter: it would be no calamity to be lost here, not to have to say good-bye to flowery stream and painted valley and moun-tain majesty. We are over the saddle of the hill and beginning a long incline beside a deep-cut stream. Peering over the edge, as near as one dares, the water can be seen jumping from shelf to shelf, half-smothered in flowers and aromatic bushes. The rim of the gorge is bossed with buddleia, flowering soberly. Little mouse-coloured buntings call to us from the rocks and members of the versatile family of finks uncover their brilliant bodies as they fly, metallic scar-let, yellow or orange. Progress is slow: the horses, hunched against the slope, must step high over the rocks and sometimes slither back down chutes of stone. The A.C. remarks, fortunately at the bottom, that the Sesuto name of the path is Molimo-uthuse (as near as I can get it), which means 'God help me'. How bad it is, is proved by our meeting a native, leading his horse up, a thing I never saw before. He is gorgeously blanketed: a baby clings to his back, the wife follows with another. He has been working in the Free State. (But this is the real 'free state' for the Basuto!) The greeting is getting familiar, a lusty shout, throaty and long-drawn out, 'Eh—Morena.'

Far below us in the gorge is a mass of colour, a dozen lurid blankets spread out on the rocks and a woman, with a scarlet petticoat and a head-dress of cobalt blue, is kneeling in the wash of the stream. She rises to stare and shout a greeting. She is naked above the waist—a fine figure glistening. We yell the time of day to each other.

Further down. The A.C. wants to visit a chief who lives near here. His name is Dirahalibone and he suffers from dropsy. He will not go to see a doctor and so is stationary at his village. The A.C. asks the police where the village is. Just off the road, just over there, they say. So the packs are sent on and the A.C., Kaswell (the rather lethargic interpreter), and myself, go on. Well, the village may be 'just over there' as the crow flies, but then as the A.C. says, 'We are not damned crows.' And when to get from X to X you go across streams and kopjes it means five or six miles instead of two. We had already been riding, and riding rough, for four hours without a break and this disappearing village nearly finished me. For a little while everything went round me in a circle. But it was not a moment to ask for mercy. Being separated from the packs, we must keep going, for the packs are food and shelter. Moreover, some ugly clouds were beginning to peer at us from over the next range. So I decided to recover and we went on.

The village was worth an effort. Perched high, and planted, most unusually, with poplars, it was surrounded by a large population of glossy cattle. All the men were in a circle of trees and stones, having a Sunday chat, and a most vivid company they were, in blankets of scarlet and orange, with coloured head-gear and with a background of equally resplendent women. The chief, a sad mountain of flesh, managed to go one step outside his court, and there stood, his shape, but not his bulk, hidden in a dull tangerine toga. The women broke into the usual subdued arguments as to whether I was a man or a woman; the men complained about the sheep dying after dipping and demanded compensation; a disconsolate tax-gatherer held the A.C.'s stirrup and murmured about the difficulties he shares with his kind throughout the world, and we departed.

A dozen boys accompanied us down the hill waving branches and singing in parts, very effectively. I asked for several encores until their cheerful voices faded behind a turn of the hill.

Now to find our pack-horses! We skimmed the valley with our eyes and after long survey of a darkening landscape we at last distinguished them from various herds of cattle about two miles away. We chased along, forded a river, were defeated by a crag, made a detour, and joined forces after just on five almost unbroken hours in the saddle.

Our men had chosen the half-way point on the slope of a bleak hill, which was one side of a huge mountain theatre. A very comprehensive storm, with ugly deliberation, began to collect along the whole circle of summits. Before we could get at the food, the storm, thus massed, flung its attack. Continuous lightning, indifferently forked and sheet, several systems of thunder, each with a series of echoes, and then rain such as only tropics and sub-tropics know, weighty drops, close in tissue, strong in impulsion, and cutting you off as if you were blindfolded. We staggered about, doing what lay near at hand—a groundsheet over the saddles was my first thought, and the next the tents over the mattresses. When I hid against a shrub the size of a chair the A.C. flung a tarpaulin right over the shrub and me. Presently he joined me there, where we crouched and watched the water rush down the sheet on to our boots while the rain shifted about the valley, thinning and thickening alternately as it moved, but always voluminous. Old Bolani has his qualities after all: the way he stuck to the job of boiling eggs in the deluge was epic. Admittedly the deluge got into the egg and I had to wring it out like a sponge but that does not detract from his heroism.

The rain slackened. The A.C. decided to push up the next hill. It looked steep and, knowing what that meant after rain, my heart sank. We saddled up. The horses, frightened by the thunder, gave a good deal of trouble, and Robbie was quite hysterical. As I was first mounted I had to keep rounding up the strays and in the end half the pack rushed at the hill before the signal and went straggling up it any way and anywhere. The track, steep black loam, was like a diving chute, the horses dug and slipped and dug without making progress. Robbie became quite demoralized, shuddering and gasping and flinging his weight about. I began to lose my nerve, fearing I should never get him up without a crash. In the end he lost his balance, struggled convulsively, and went down on one knee. I slipped off in good order, and tried to lead him up, but neither of us could get any purchase in the mud, so there we remained, silly and helpless. The A.C. shouted orders and somehow we slid sideways and got a grip on a few pebbles and a lump of grass. I walked Robbie a bit and then mounted. But I hated it pretty badly and was not sorry when we reached a level platform just under the summit where the A.C. gave orders to unsaddle and make camp.

I write this crouched in my little tent. It is a pretty desolate hillside we are on. The storm keeps ambling round the walls of rock and seemingly can't get out. So thunder and pouring rain continue and it is so cold that even in a tightly shut tent the breath vapourizes on the air in clouds. The contrasts in this country are amazing. I can hardly realize that yesterday I lay in almost unbearable heat by the Jordan, though my limbs still tingle with the scorch, or that this morning we came through the valley of flowers with baking rocks beside us. Just as it has dashed the flowers the storm has wiped out the beauty of the past day or two. Cold desolation, grim mountains burdened with storm, dominate us. I cannot believe the sun can shine again. It is all the sadder as we have only one day left before we reach the plains.

And now I must stop writing and get to bed in the hope that I shall be able to sleep in spite of cold that numbs, wind that batters, and rain that beats on the canvas.

I slept fairly well in spite of the rain on the tent, whose music I find most disturbing and depressing, magnifying the rain and perpetually threatening to come in. It did come in on the ground and my floor was in pools when I woke. Dared by the A.C. I went down and had a bath in the stream which was jumping down the steep mountain in muddy, rain-fed torrents. It was an icy, thrilling bath, in driving rain, and I felt I earned all the congratulations I got when I struggled up the slope, my bare feet and legs blue with cold. I cooked the A.C.'s breakfast in the same downpour. All the eggs presented by the neighbouring village were bad, except two, which were merely stale and these I fried and handed to him without comment and he ate them—also without comment.

It took us over an hour to pack up. It was a grim business. I do not know which looked more wretched, the men or the horses, humped and drooping in the rain. Kaswell and Bolani were almost in tears and reduced to complete uselessness. I did what little I could, catching a mutinous horse here, tugging at greasy, sodden leather there. The A.C. always works with the men: he does not seem to consider it against prestige. The Basuto have little style; they are rather a slouching, dour lot, but they do eventually get things done. They seem to have no positive way of showing respect and yet it would be difficult to say that they are disrespectful. There is no saluting, no jumping up at the approach of the Sahib. They are mostly ugly, clumsy people too. Yet I admire the way that Tsaki, who looks after the packs, manages that loose herd as they struggle up and down precipices and plunge into streams. Riding a big horse and cracking a huge whip, he is everywhere at once and always shouting to the horses, scolding them for snatching at the crops, urging them on or warning them to go careful, soothing them with soft, whistling noise when they get excited.

They needed all of it this morning. We had to get over our last mountain pass, Bushman's Neck. It was not so bad going up, but the other side was steeper and longer. Rather than slither in mud we chose to go down the bed of a stream, an avalanche of stones with running water. It is the first time I had ridden down a waterfall, and I hope it will be last. I wanted to take a picture, but these moments are too desperate for camera work and, besides, the rain was driving hard and visibility nil. My spirits were low, too, for the view before us was leading us towards Maseru, some thirty miles over the hills in front and tomorrow is the last day of our trek.

I added one picture to my gallery: a reed bed, slender bright green stems and clinging to them a flock of scarlet finks, which cried and fluttered through the miniature forest as we passed.

The A.C. chose to camp beside a stream not far from the first store. The rain was relentless, the ground sodden, and putting up the tents rather a discouraging piece of work. We had an hour for lunch and rest and then rode off as hard as we could go to find some Bushmen's paintings near here.

The Bushmen chose their place well. Imagine a deep-cut stream, turning abruptly between overhanging walls of rock, the rock tawny but striped with bold, black tiger markings by the action of the weather. Under the lee of this rock is a smooth panel about 100 feet long and 12 feet high. This the little men had chosen for their frescoes and in one part it is thickly covered with them for about 50 feet. The patterns were faint and at first sight I was disappointed. But, under the A.C.'s instructions, Tsaki fetched water and splashed it all over the rock, and the paintings sprang at the splash into vigorous colour and outline. Many hands have been at work at different times, figuring different animals, at different angles, and to different scales. Sometimes one is superimposed upon another: in places the rock, exposed to all weather, has flaked away. But the sum and quality of what remains is amazing. The little men had a great sense of form, no less than of colour. Their elands and hartebeests are sketched with accuracy and care: their colours are different shades of red and ochre, with white. Their deer have always dark shaded backs and pale bellies,

pale faces, too, where the model demands it. Even the lighter markings
at the backs of the legs are noted. But it is the action that catches the
eye. The animals stand; they graze; they run and leap. The cranes
race with long necks extended; the men stoop or jump or draw arrows.
They even, most wonderful, turn their heads as it were towards the
artist. There is another quality too, a sense of pattern. Here and
there are designs made of processions of men, advancing with the
same gesture, naked, with arrows stuck in their hair, or in tall slender
ranks, with long garments from head to foot. There are other marks,
not to be interpreted, magical perhaps, circles and crescents.

How hard to believe, gazing at this art of a vanished race, that the
contents of their life were so limited, their evolution arrested so low in
our scale of measurement, these men with eyes to see, hands to exe-
cute, skill to find pigment that withstands the long attacks of time and
weather. The A.C. chose the outline of a partridge, a bold, rapid
sketch in dark red, as his favourite; better than Thorburn, he said.
I chose an eland and two young, all stooping their long necks to graze.
Also a whiskered lion, evidently at bay, and beautifully maned.

The damp on the wall dried, the colour faded, and we found our
horses, crossed the stream, left the paintings panelling that lonely
gorge and went on at a gallop through a driving rain.

We called, as in duty bound, at the store, rather fearing entreaties
to stay the night instead of camping in this continuous rain. But the
trader was in bed with a very common and not lethal African com-
plaint. He was a simple soul, who called me lady, and insisted on my
coming into his bedroom where he lay dishevelled, in sordid surroundings, dropping a long day's sequence of cigarettes into a chamber and waited upon by his pale little boy of ten. It was not a very
happy re-introduction to civilization and we hurried back to our
soaking camp as fast as we could.

For the first time we had a camp-fire made with fuel from the store
and the A.C. cooked some soup with the remains of our last sheep.
Kaswell, huddled over the fire, remarked that the great snake had
spoken all too well. When I told him I had heard it a second time in
the night, he said that was unusual and clearly accounted for the
volume of rain. We went on to other things, led that way by an old
woman who hobbled up, having come fifty miles to see a native doctor.

Kaswell told me how the witch-doctors 'threw the bones': how,
if he consulted one, he would surely tell him that the Morena (the
A.C.) had bewitched him and would demand a beast in payment for a

cure. He would then give him little pegs greased with various medicines from the insides of animals, to put all round the A.C.'s house.

'That's all right, Kaswell,' said the A.C. 'If once I get after you,
my lad, no little pegs will do you any good.'

'Should all fail,' Kaswell continued, unmoved, 'then I shall pay to
get the Morena killed. I should choose to have him killed by lightning,
and for that I should have certain charms and these I should recite,
standing in the river on a cloudy night.'

Dinner over, and the horses all penned in a kraal, for they may not
run free here, the men all went off to the big neighbouring village.
We made ourselves as warm and dry as possible and discussed the
native problem in its economic aspect, the League of Nations, the
Boer War, and finished up with Shakespeare's Sonnets. I am now
very tired, and have a long last day in front of me tomorrow. Alas
and alas, for the end of the trek.

The A.C. brought me coffee at six, and we looked at the day with a
night of rain just dripping into a dull morning. He was very stern and
would not let me ride back to photograph the Bushmen's paintings,
as I had planned. I had a dip in the muddy river, too near the village
to risk a proper bath. Then I cooked an omelette for the A.C. with
seven eggs, and very difficult it was, as it burned underneath and was
cold on top. But it was not too bad and put some nourishment into
the man.

We left the packs and rode on hard with Kaswell. We had much to
do and, in this more populous part, many chiefs to visit. We cantered
away, sometimes practising riding each other off as at polo, until we
dropped into a big track, where the walls with the tiger markings rose
on all sides, and some women, cut off by the swollen river, cried piti-
fully to be taken across on our horses. The A.C. was hard-hearted and
I was not surprised. The river was high and rushing in muddy anger.
We plunged into it in faith and almost at once were waist deep in
water. The A.C., riding tall Robbie, was pretty well soaked, but my
grey slithered down a boulder into the deepest part of the race, and
went right under, head and all. I clung to the saddle at the risk of
drowning him, and fortunately he came up the next second, puffing
water and very excited. I seized hold of him and he towed me out.
We had to cross again half a mile later but there was no mishap this
time.

Soaked as I was, we called on a chief Jaccottet (named after a French missionary) who had a very nice stone village. One house was so beautifully reeded that I asked to see the owner and to go in. He explained that his mother had done it all. So I took her photo with a few grandchildren, and she stood very proudly in front of her handiwork, a noble-looking old woman.

It was now getting terribly hot. Our clothes dried on us as we rode on as hard as we could until the mountain Thaba Bosiu came into sight. This is the most famous mountain in the country. It is a completely flat table, rising at a sharp slope and then crowned by a sheer wall of rock. It is absolutely impregnable except for three places which can be, and once were, barricaded and defended. Moshesh chose this for his stronghold and more than once defeated the Zulus, and finally flung back the Boers in the determined effort they made to break his power. But for that stand Basutoland might not now be under the Imperial Government and the A.C. and I would not have been riding on this trek.

At the foot of the mountain was a large village where an important chief lived. We sent the interpreter ahead to announce our visit and slackened pace. By the time we reached the village the men were all out staring and the women, in their bright dresses, twittering. The rocky hillside looked, in the distance, like a garden full of purple, orange, and crimson flowers.

'Eh, Morena,' they yelled, deep in their throats, and then were at a loss how to address me. Then a woman decided I was one of her sex and in her excitement rolled back laughing on the ground. Yet it is difficult to believe that they had never seen a woman dressed in boots and breeches. The scrutiny was so intense that I became rather embarrassed, especially as Kaswell murmured his interpretations.

Finally out came old chief Khoabane, a powerful, fat man, with a clever, unscrupulous face, but looking thoroughly muzzy, as though we had awoken him from a drunken sleep. An important, able man, he is a byword for his laziness. His court is congested; he cuts the National Council, and, greatest joke to the Basuto, he is too lazy to marry more than one wife. One is quite enough trouble, he says.

He looked me up and down and asked who I was. The A.C. made his usual speech about me, which I knew by heart, even in Sesuto. I struck in.

'Greetings, Khoabane. I am happy to see what good rain you have had.'

The Basuto is nothing if not blunt. He looked at me pityingly and said they had had a drought until yesterday. The A.C. chipped in with the story of our wanderings. Their eyes grew wide, and the chief looked in horror at us, clicking his tongue in depreciation and looking from one to the other, of us as if we were mad. He made us repeat the names of the furthest places we had reached.

'Well, well, tch-tch, such journeys are not for me. I should be killed. I cannot go out at all. I cannot sit so long as that on a horse.'

'Do you good to get some exercise,' said the A.C., English fashion. 'Take off some of your fat and make a new man of you.'

Secret smiles from the retinue at this.

'And now, Khoabane,' I said, 'we mean to climb the mountain to find the grave of your father Moshesh and pay our respects to his memory.'

At this he nearly swooned in sympathy. He shook his big head slowly from side to side like a frog, though I saw that the eyes which gazed at us, for all their dullness, opened on a keen brain. He promised to provide an escort. He doubted if horses could ride up (it must indeed be bad going if a Mosuto says this) but he would send a guide ahead to choose a path.

'God be with you and bring you safely home (you poor fools),' he said the last with his eyes.

'God be with you, Khoabane, and give you good rains and large crops and healthy beasts.'

We mounted and rode away from the village, all the crowd staring at us until we were out of sight.

Now began our last steep ascent. Away from the kraal, piled mountain high with manure, which the women were working into little cakes for the fire, and then upwards painfully, between the showers of boulders which had fallen down one of the three possible ascents. We were not surprised to learn from our guide that not even the Zulus had chosen to storm on this side. Riding soon became impossible, so we dismounted and left our horses to climb after us alone as best they could. From running free with the pack they had become very clever at mountaineering.

At the top was a large, flat space, with ruined remains of old villages. We found among the grass two old cannon, small inefficient-looking objects, one of which had been broken by a Boer shell. We rode around among goats and aloes and came to an untidy muddle of stone mounds. This was the royal cemetery of Basutoland. The graves might have been placed there yesterday, so fresh do the yellow rocks keep under the sun and rain. Something resembling a headstone generally stood, or had fallen, at one end of the stone heaps and on this, scrawled crookedly as by a child, was the chief's name. The grave-stone of the great Moshesh was no better. The A.C. knelt down and tidied it; he picked up the headstone and re-erected it. But if the graves were insignificant and neglected, the site was magnificent. From our high level we looked down on the heads of the weird kopjes surrounding us: the furious noonday sun was baking all the yellow rocks of which they were built and behind, pale blue in the heat haze, was the line of the Maluti mountains from which we had come.

The old man who was our guide now led us to another vulnerable spot, a break in the circular precipice. It was here in 1865 that the Boers, under Wepener, tried to storm the hill. He showed us where their batteries and entrenchments had stood away below in the plain; from these had come the shell which broke the cannon. Here, our guide said, on this high, dome-shaped rock, the highest point on the mountain, Moshesh stood to direct his forces. There, nearly at the top of the cliff, the forces closed in hand-to-hand fighting, spear against bayonet and there was no more sound of guns. Then Wepener, the gallant Boer leader, was killed, and the rest turned back, and went stumbling down. 'There!' The guide pointed to the rock-littered steep down which we had to go. The Basuto, wishing to partake of Wepener's bravery, cut out his heart and ate it but sent the body back to his men.

Now we must descend after the Boers. The old man led my horse, stopping every now and then to push the big stones out of his way. On the level at last and now a long canter towards the store where we were to have lunch and make our re-entry into civilization. I was as sorry to see the kind, white face of our hostess as I had been glad to wave good-bye to the last storekeeper we had seen some two weeks ago.

The car sent for us had not been able to reach the store as the river was in flood, but half-way through lunch a note arrived to say that a car was waiting on the other side. The trader offered to drive us the four miles to the river. It was difficult to refuse but I explained that I could not miss one mile of the last ride. And though we had been riding hard for four hours I was now so gloriously fit that I felt fresh as paint.

We rode rather sadly to the river. It was turgid and running fast.

On the other side the car—a new saloon—was glittering with metal and navy panels and seemed to belong to another world. We plunged in, the muddy water racing past us above the knee and emerged the other side, to dismount, greet the A.C.'s two young sons—very nice-looking boys, too—and a woman, a guest at the A.C.'s house. We said good-bye to the horses and the police for they must jog along the fifteen miles behind us to Maseru.

Hotel dinner alone, a stuffy evening's work, and a stuffy, hot bed. The descent from the mountains to the plain, from a tent to a stuffy hotel, was sudden and adaptation difficult.

A letter from the Chief Native Commissioner in Pretoria, scolding me for not being in Zululand and telling me to get there as quickly as possible. How can I go off to Zululand at a moment's notice, knowing no one, and just at Christmas time? However, I must get out of Basutoland. Clearly, in apportioning my time in South Africa, I have been here too long. I think I had better go to Johannesburg. The mines and the miners can't shut down even for Christmas.

A long day's work at the office, 8.45 a.m.–5 p.m., with a quick lunch in the middle. The A.C. pushed aside all his arrears of work, and turned himself into my secretary, looking up facts and having stuff typed for me.

I interviewed the Rev. Motsamar, a native parson of the French Protestant Church, and a government nominee on the Basuto Council. He was a cheery man and humble too. Quite convinced that in Church affairs they will not be able to do without the white man for a long time to come. Much grieved about the way the women run off to the Rand and become prostitutes round the mines.

In the evening the A.C. took me to see Fort Hare's cricket team play Maseru. It was all very sober and correct, and it seemed to me, having played the game at school and college, very good cricket. I was glad to see the Fort Hare people and they were much surprised when I met them on the field. One or two of my especial friends were there. The A.C. is extremely good with all the natives and always attends their functions. He was much intrigued by the way the students talked to me. 'It makes me feel I ought to ask them round to dinner.' But that, even in Basutoland, would be too much of a novelty.

I had a long wrestle, fighting against time, with the Basutoland official papers, 8.30 a.m.–5.15 p.m., with a half-hour lunch interval.

How the normal work of Maseru district gets on I can't imagine for everything is put so generously at my disposal, with police as messengers, the interpreter and the A.C. himself at my service, while several officials have sent in reports or figures on special points. The Resident Commissioner has gone away but he left a charming letter behind him. His heart is in Uganda where, I now learn, he was first tutor to the Kabaka, and then Colonial Secretary and I imagine that he has to be careful not to be referring the whole time to Uganda. At any rate, at our meetings, he apologized to me each time he did. And he confessed to me that he was longing to be able to open out his heart to me upon the subject when I got back. So his going away is a great blow. However, he has written to the Kabaka about me so I am sure of a welcome at the hands of black majesty if I ever reach Uganda.

I have had another long day's work up to 5 p.m. Then we visited the leper settlement. We went in pouring rain, and splashed about in muddy yards, with the lepers all huddled in wet blankets or lying in their rooms.

Leprosy is terrible in Basutoland, though old missionaries say there was not a case sixty years ago. It is hard to believe that it has spread contagiously in that time. It is maintained that clothing has had much to do with it. Nakedness in sunlight is hygienic but when women, having had the toilette of Queen Victoria once vividly impressed upon their minds, emulate her contour by strata of petticoats and count wealth and importance by their number, leprosy, a disease of dirt, has every chance to spread. (We saw one woman strip six skirts from her body to cross a stream, and she still had a few left.)

There were about five hundred people in the settlement, in all stages of the disease, from those whose extremities were dropping away from them, or who had the repulsive nodular type, to comely young people who showed no visible signs of rottenness and yet who were doomed in spite of their youth. It was a shock to learn this. The children looked so jolly compared with the older patients that I could hardly believe it when, in response to my cheerful comment, the matron said 'Hardly one of those will be alive in a few years.'

I must not lacerate your feelings by describing the horrors of the advanced cases nor of the children born into the doomed place. It is the custom in this country, when a child is born, to draw out one of the reeds in the thatch, so that it extends over the door. For a time no man may enter that hut except the husband. Here, having corrugated iron, they had extended a piece of rope on a rod, to mark this unhappy event.

They think little here of the new oil which is injected, and about which I had heard so much that was hopeful. 'I think it helps,' was all I could get from the matron. They do not even make the injections compulsory—they can come or not for it as they like. The process is painful and they do not want to harass the people. They discharge a few every year, some as hopeless but no longer contagious, a few who are cured, or are hoped to be. These last are not necessarily ones who have had injections. They believe that cleanliness and good food are the only cure, and these the leper can seldom get in the village, where semi-starvation, if not brutality, is the treatment for the useless member of society.

The A.C. was evidently a popular visitor. He talked to them all very cheerily. And reproved me for my silence. 'Have you forgotten your Sesuto?' I realized that I was not even greeting the lepers: I was looking at them as at things—cases—not people, absorbed in my own horror, rather than giving real sympathy. I tried my best after this and the attempts to respond through those dulled eyes and perished faces showed that humanity was still alight in them. The A.C. made his little set speech explaining me; some of them asked questions and made complimentary speeches though speech was sometimes distorted and almost unrecognizable.

The settlement is a terrible drain on a small country, costing £20,000 a year, and with no hope, it seems, of diminution.

All the people here have seemed pleased to see us back. The A.C.'s wife gave a dinner party for me this evening. Afterwards we went to the Council Chamber to patronize a concert given by the Fort Hare students to help pay for their travelling expenses. We waited almost longer than prestige allowed, until, half an hour late, the captain of the team, the little Zulu, Vinikulu, burst in to say they had had a motor accident and were all in hospital. (It was Vinikulu who had an affection for eighteenth-century literature and especially Pope.) So we went back and played bridge at the A.C.'s house.

This is my last day in Basutoland. I worked the usual hours, which included taking down full notes of a long interview between the A.C. and the chief Jaccottet, heir to Koabane, the chief of Thabe Bosiu, who is going to hold a Pitso (a general meeting of the people) to advocate the new reforms of native government which were turned down by the National Council. It was fascinating, though I hardly knew how to stop myself from intervening.

In the evening I went for a long—and last—ride with the A.C. It was really rather funny that having come through rivers and over precipices for two weeks unharmed, I nearly did for myself hacking quietly round Maseru. We were riding along near the edge of a steep cliff. The A.C. was riding Robbie; I was on a nervous mare lent by the Chief of Police. Robbie struck a patch of wet sand and went in deeply. He became, as usual, hysterical and flung his weight about, snorting. My horse reared, and backed towards the edge of the gorge, a sheer drop. There seems no way of stopping a horse which is quite determined to go backwards. One is quite helpless. The more I kicked and hit his haunches with my hand, the more he backed. It was all like a scene in a magazine story. I felt one of his back legs go through the crust at the edge, and the other falter. The A.C. having reduced Robbie to order, looked back and saw me apparently going over. He went white, and said 'Oh, my God!' My horse, with a sort of convulsion, saved herself, and the A.C. in a great state, came across and gripped my hand, saying 'You were nearly killed.' It had all been so quick that I had had no time to get really frightened. I had been much more frightened once or twice going up places in the mountains and then the A.C. had not seemed very sympathetic. But this upset him badly and we turned and rode soberly home.

After dinner the A.C. and his wife called and we all went to the postponed Fort Hare concert. Though we arrived a little late, there was no sign of anyone. No preparations seemed to have been made. The A.C.'s wife argued that it was bad for prestige to wait for them like that so she went home. But the A.C. and the rest of us decided to wait.

They turned up in the end, a comi-tragic crew, some limping, some bandaged round the brow, two with faces stitched up, and one with a face so battered that I did not recognize him. Heaven knows how they were able to sing—one confessed to me afterwards that it was agony— but sing they did. Vinikulu, the captain, conducted: they had no piano, they stood all huddled together, with a dim lamp throwing a transverse light on their shining, dark faces. Absolutely motionless, seemingly mesmerized by the conductor—'Svengali', whispered the A.C.—they sang. It was marvellous. They sang, in parts, the most ambitious songs, English and African, and some Negro spirituals. I do not think that any European cricket team, chosen for cricket and not for voices, could have touched them least of all after a motor accident. It was not only the richness and variety of the voices and the perfect tune and time into which they had trained themselves but also the restraint and feeling with which they sang. 'Stealing Away to Jesus' and 'One More River' were most poignant. You feel that when they sing they are speaking your language more than when they talk; a universal language of art and emotion which they speak as well or better than ourselves. Better, certainly. The educated African is going to be a great musician, the race will make rich gifts to the world's stock in this field and it could be the music of a whole community, loving and expressing music with a passion unknown to us. It is thrilling—I must use that word—to recognize the achievements of this despised people, to meet those who can meet you on something like equal terms and to foresee the possibilities of the future. I cannot understand how it is that so few South Africans can see the romance of this and can turn their backs upon Africans in fear or anger instead of stretching out their hands to welcome the few who have fought their way up to those standards which we have presented to them. But it is easy for a passing traveller to be liberal.

I was glad to see that the A.C. was much impressed by the Fort Hare men. He went up after and talked to them and subscribed to their expenses, and, on the way back, we wrestled with the problems of higher education for Africans.

Having packed at night, I was free to put in a long last morning at the office. The police, to whom I had promised largesse, turned up, and we had a photograph. I grouped them together, the polite young policeman; the dashing Tsaki and the rather lethargic interpreter, Kaswell. All these men had become so familiar to me on trek. The dirty old ruffian, Bolani, could not be found, so I put in his place the ablest Mosuto I have met, David, the chief interpreter, who had been a great help to me during my work in Maseru. He is a Lovedale product, as were the Chiefs, Jaccottet and Makabalo.

At two o'clock the A.C. called to motor me the eighteen miles to Marseilles in the Free State, there to pick up the train to Bloemfontein.

The contrast as you cross the Basuto border struck me forcibly. No more mushroom clusters of huts, no more wavering little strips of agriculture. Instead, vast level areas of grazing, with tall, rich grass and with great fat, square Friesians browsing; fences, which stand for efficiency, if not for the very life of the veld. And not a human habitation to be seen, except once or twice, wreathed in poplars and gums, the solid farm of the prosperous Boer owner. This is the land they took from the Basuto.

Our train, as is not uncommon in this country, was fifty minutes late, so we climbed a low kopje and sat on some stones in the blazing heat with the lizards. Below us was a small enclosure, to which successive generations of the Stoffberg family had been carried in coffins from their farm-house to this hillside. Over them had been placed white marble scrolls and urns standing on pedestals, with pious Afrikaans inscriptions. I never saw respectability look more ridiculous than these prim erections on the baked kopje, all the more ridiculous when we learned that the last Stoffberg had died as a result of hitting a native: he cut his own hand open striking the man on the mouth and got blood poisoning. One way in which the weak of the earth can confound the strong! I don't know whether or not the native was condemned for culpable homicide.

The train crawled up at last. I need not say that it was hard to say good-bye to the A.C. who had been such a good trek-comrade as well as an expert informant upon Basutoland. As soon as I boarded the train I went on to the swaying platform between the two carriages of which the train was composed. I was determined to see the last of the territory. In spite of a scattered hill or two cropping up alongside the railway there was no difficulty in seeing Basutoland. Right along the eastern horizon stood its magnificent wall of mountains growing more blue with each decline of the sun's light. Some of them I could still pick out as old friends—the two like a woman's breasts; the one like a devil's head, above all Machachne, the mighty one. Only a few days ago I had been among them, right up on their shoulders, sleeping between their knees, bathing in their cold streams. Because I knew that I should almost certainly never see them again I was forced to watch them as long as the light and the distance allowed. Of course I was thinking not only of the mountains but of the man with whom I had shared them. On such a journey you either make a friend of your fellow-traveller or something very near the opposite. I had meant to remain the detached academic observer on this tour. And now having committed my affections in Samoa to a few South Sea islanders I must needs go and fall in love with a range of mountains.

As I watched, the slowly rising shoulders of the near-by veldt cut into the substance of the Maluti range until I could see only the very summits, faint domes and spires pencilled against the fading sky. Then these sank and there was nothing but the Free State, rocks, grass, wheat, stubble all turning from gold to grey. That, I thought, really is the end. But as I still stood swaying on the platform to the motions of the rather elementary mechanics of this train, the land suddenly sloped downwards, as if to inflict upon me a final wound and I saw the whole Maluti range reappear so far away now and so pale a blue against a sky itself so pale that the distant vision hardly seemed to belong to the rose-gold on our sunset side of the world.

As I went back to my empty carriage in this almost empty little train I was possessed of a fierce hope that this little mountain-state, embedded in the Union of South Africa, should be saved from the threatened grip of the Afrikaner Government which is pressing for its incorporation. The Basuto are not angels but in spite of their dependence upon the Union's labour market, they have a spirit of freedom long crushed out of many of the tribes within South Africa. I can only hope that the issue will not be settled before I get home and that I may be able to throw what small influence I can wield on behalf of the Basuto.[1]

---

[1] I was able to join in the controversy after my return to England and I wrote articles upon it for *The Times*. I clashed with a formidable antagonist, Mr. Lionel Curtis. He wrote three articles in *The Times* during May 1935 urging acceptance of the South African demand. I therefore wrote a further article for *The Times* published on 16 May to controvert his views and remind the public of the history of Basutoland and of the other two Protectorates, Bechuanaland and Swaziland. Mr. Curtis proposed that our articles should be published in a single book and generously allowed me to have both the first and last words in the ensuing publication, *The Protectorates of South Africa* (Oxford University Press, 1935). As what I have written applies equally to the Bechuanaland Protectorate, which was also demanded by the South African Government, I have repeated this information at the end of the chapter on Bechuanaland (p. 210).

The Rand

December 1929

<hr>

Dinner at dreary Bloemfontein, then a wretched night in the train and I woke in the Transvaal—good veld and big farms and the famous Reef in the distance. It wasn't much fun, after leaving Basutoland, to arrive in Johannesburg at six-thirty in the morning and find I had booked at a vile hotel.

I hate this city. I know this is a hasty and stupid attitude, very improper in a student of affairs in the subcontinent, only to be confessed in this diary-letter and to be mastered as soon as possible. But, to begin with, it is hideous. Right along the reef are piled the entrails of the earth, higher than anything to be seen round English mines and of various sickly colours, ochre, grey, but mostly a pale sulphur. I had been led to expect something rather showy and glittering in the town itself but here, too, I was disappointed. It has still the marks of a town run up in a few months, marble-fronted and brick-backed, with one or two solid erections in the shape of law courts, town hall, etc. The European suburbs are much the same as suburbs all over the Empire but once you leave the few principal roads a sordid tangle of intermediate areas meets you—not yet slums, nor locations, but mean-looking shops and houses, inhabited by Indians, Lithuanian Jews, Cape Coloured, Greek or Chinese, all the intermediate races which tend to be parasites upon the native. I admit to a jaundiced outlook: I suppose my suspicion of all that the town stood and stands for colours my eyes when I look at it.

This morning I renewed a very interesting and valuable contact. This was with Margaret Hodgson, a South African woman whom I had known at Oxford when we went together with our weekly essays to Grant Robertson at All Souls College. She is now on the staff of the University here as a history lecturer. She holds very liberal views upon native affairs and it was both exciting and instructive to meet

130

her again in her own setting. Her chief at the University here is Professor W. M. Macmillan whose writings upon nineteenth-century South African history have vindicated the work and ideas of the early missionaries who have long been condemned in some quarters as sentimental and unrealistic on native questions. Margaret means to write herself on native affairs. It was an immense encouragement to meet an able young South African academic with such a vigorous and well-informed liberalism.

She confirmed views about South Africa that have been gradually forming in my mind; of the low standard of intelligence among many of the scattered and agricultural Dutch; of the decline of the British tradition; of the near impossibility of influencing Dutch opinion. She fights the temptation, which I have found in so many people here who have sensibility, to get out of the country.

She took me over the University. It appears that the students take little or no interest in the natives. They seem, on the whole, very materialist in outlook. They have fine buildings, beautiful sports-grounds and enjoy a very good time. She has tried, unsuccessfully, to start a circle for study of native problems. I looked at the lists of names on the boards, a good half of them Dutch and, among the rest, many eastern Jews. The registrar told me that these able people almost monopolize medicine and the law and are taking to engineering. They land from Poland or Lithuania, are met by their own people, start with a barrow or a second-hand clothes shop and in ten or twelve years have a car and send their children to the University. What a wonderful ability this ancient race has preserved!

In the afternoon Margaret and I went a long trek down to the Western Native Township and Sophiatown. The former is a new municipal location, very neat and well spaced, but dreary beyond description, hundreds of tiny, mud-coloured, two-roomed hutments— I cannot call them cottages. Even they cannot be leased at an economic rent with native wages what they are so the municipality subsidizes them and the employer keeps down the wages.

We went into a great barn-like hall, built as a speculation by a Jewish contractor. We were the only Europeans in the audience at what was advertised as a monster meeting for agitation on various points. The natives, much surprised at our appearance, felt it was improper for us to sit down among them in the audience and, after several urgent requests that we should go on to the platform, we agreed. I doubted if that were wise as it might identify us too much with the speakers. Indeed, this was done at once by one of the Africans who came up and pinned small green badges upon us.

Presently another European arrived, a youngish man, looking rather harassed behind his high-powered glasses. This was the famous (or, in most South African eyes, infamous) Mr. Ballinger, who has recently come out from England with British trade union support to try and develop the nascent trade unionism among the natives and to save their own Industrial and Commercial Union which is threatened not only by the Boer authorities but also by inexperience and by tribal fissures.[1]

The meeting was billed for 2.30 p.m. but at 2.45 a message came from the chief speaker, Professor Jabavu, that, knowing his people and their unpunctuality, he always waited until the meeting had fully gathered and had sent for him. This was rather annoying but then I don't suppose that he expected any Europeans to attend. We were handed a printed programme of speakers the length of which appalled me. But even this was not complete for it omitted to mention two lectures by Mr. Ballinger, one on wages and one on the pass laws. The programme showed the extraordinary mixed grill that is served to an African urban audience and the extent of their appetite. Hymns are mixed with an agitation which is full of dangers for them.

Professor Jabavu gave a speech that rather disgusted me. It was of the real Mark Antony technique, one designed to raise the maximum amount of racial-feeling with the minimum amount of indiscretion on his own part. He is the leading African intellectual, at least in reputation; a Professor at Fort Hare, where I had met him.[2] The natives, who worship academic qualifications, seem to regard him almost as a god. He certainly spoke very well as far as technique was concerned; gestures and delivery were most effective. But the longer he spoke the

---

[1] I must insert a note here about the subsequent history of Margaret Hodgson and Mr. W. Ballinger. In 1936, after a long struggle, the Afrikaner Government succeeded in abolishing the Cape native franchise, which they hated less for its political effectiveness than for the principle of racial equality upon which it was based. A new measure allowed for the election by Africans of three white members of Parliament for the Cape. Margaret Hodgson was one of these. She married Mr. Ballinger, who himself became a representative of the Africans in the Senate. In 1960 all representation of the Africans in both houses was abolished by an Afrikaner Government determined to rid white rule of any element of African participation, however indirect. The story of her able and devoted political life in relation to the whole grim record of Afrikaner imposition of political and social *apartheid* is told in her book *From Union to Apartheid*, Capetown 1969.

[2] See above, p. 53.

more I felt that it was a positive danger to have a man of his character exalted as a leader. Like Smuts on the other side, he is almost too clever at manipulating his own liberalism.

He began by defending himself against charges of timidity, of speaking softly. His defence was curious.

'In the old days, when we Bantu went to hunt the lion, we chose some young men to go out and find him and chase him. Then others, older men, waited in the thicket with their spears until the right moment came. You who work with Mr. Ballinger are the young men: I and others are waiting.' He might have given as an explanation that a Professor's job is to teach and write and not direct political agitation. He went on:

'I see you have some Europeans here. I am glad to see that. When we Bantu hunted the elephant we used to use tame, decoy elephants, so that the wild ones said—"You see, those creatures are not so dangerous. They have some of our own kind with them".'

He urged them to resist oppression, to collect money, to unite, to fight. But to fight with the pen and the brain, not the spear. But the audience, who were by now utterly carried away and who had groaned and sighed and called 'Shame' and who now called 'Let us fight' had, many of them, no pen and little political knowledge with which to fight.

He worked through some of the laws, especially with regard to land. I am sure that most of what he said was true. But some was exaggerated. It was all a subtle piece of suggestion. 'The white man has taken 80 per cent of your land and is now going to defraud you of the rest.' But this is a percentage based on the whole Union and the Bantu never advanced into a large proportion of its present area. And it must be said that much of the land, especially the Transkei, is very good land, whereas his figures embrace huge areas of karoo or desert of little good to anyone, except for the most extensive farming. Heaven knows the counts against the white man are many and heavy enough; there is no need to distort them. Moreover I saw how utterly a man of his education can impose himself upon the bewildered ignorance of his people. He had in his hand the blue-book he was discussing and he shook it at them. 'I speak by the book. I don't give you opinions. I give you the facts.'

Then Ballinger, with two interpreters, into Xosa and Sesuto, took over. 'Do you know that your labour is worth twice what you are being paid for it? The average wage is £3 5s a month. You must ask for a minimum of £7. There is nothing peculiar about your situation. The same thing happened to us in Britain. Our people were forced off the land and into the towns and paid inadequate wages, until they united to secure better conditions. Your greatest enemy is your own disunity.'

More hymns, more speeches, votes of thanks, interruptions, ever increasing heat and smell, and below us all those rows of sweating black faces from every part of South Africa, cut off from their tribes and lands; herded in dreary locations and compounds; hedged round by restrictive laws and customs; all advance checked by a colour bar; educational facilities practically nil—a bewildered, amiable people, just learning to resent their exploitation. It takes more than one meeting to make a revolution but meetings will increase yearly and some day the amiable, bewildered African giant may learn his own strength and use it.

We came out through the dreary municipal location, mile upon mile of tiny uniform brick huts, a model location, I am told. And though the natives pay rates they get neither light nor water in their huts. (This is still true of most locations though not of all.) They cannot pay an economic rent for their huts so they pay less and thus the big employers are subsidized out of the rates. Transport to and from town is admittedly dear and inadequate. But the locations are a model beside the real slums where entrepreneurs buy small plots of land, run up shelters of tin and charge 25s a month for them. Like the rabbit to the stoat the native is the natural prey of the adventurer and every kind of sharper—Jew, Indian, poor white, Dutch, English and African. With gambling, illicit liquor, drugs, rack-renting and prostitution, they all help to relieve him of the money paid into his loose grasp. I was told that at one station, from which large numbers go back from the mines to the reserves, the clerks would open the ticket office at the very last moment, when the natives were terrified of the train going and were mobbing round the window, and then sell tickets at great speed and give wrong change. The ignorant natives, hustled, hardly able to count money, and probably not knowing what the fare should be, would dash on to the train without questioning their change. I am told there were some men who boasted of making fortunes in this way. But such stories are legion. I saw a confidential report detailing the tricks of traders in the reserves—the cork under the weighing machine, the false arithmetic, etc. One native was cute enough to bring his own Ready Reckoner and when the trader quoted the wrong price, he produced his book. 'Oh, that,' said the trader, contemptuously, 'that is last year's.'

The subject hardly needs illustration. When you have ignorant, illiterate millions, into whose hands (as a whole, certainly not as individuals) enormous sums are being paid and when you have beside them a population of poor whites (estimated at one-tenth of the whole white population) desperately struggling to keep themselves from slipping down to the level of the blacks whom they hate and fear, and very well endowed to exploit them, the result is inevitable. Poor whites do not realise that their own safety in the long run lies in allowing the black to rise, so that there is no longer so deep a gulf into which to fall. Also to understand that if the whites' wages are kept at an artificially high level which so many whites cannot earn, some will earn nothing. In other words—let the economic situation adjust itself as it would if it were not distorted by law and custom so that, for having a white skin, you get paid ten or fifteen times as much as for having a black one.

I pottered about all day and had the great joy of finding at the post office many letters, and among them some from all those to whom this diary is sent.

At night I had dinner with Margaret Hodgson and Mr. Ballinger, and was able to find out a great deal about the I.C.U. (The new black Trade Union).[1] The original I.C.U. run by Clements Kadalie, a Nyasaland native, caught on like wild fire. It was a new and hopeful idea. Money poured in and at one time they had as much as £10,000 a year income. But Kadalie was, not surprisingly, financially inexperienced, and the money evaporated, partly by inefficiency, partly by sheer dishonesty. When Ballinger came out he was appalled by the mess he found but he set to work to clear it up. It might have seemed better for him to cut adrift from such an unpromising past and adopt a new name but then he would have lost such claims as the I.C.U. had on its monies and also for compensation for injuries such as that for the destruction of their office by whites in Durban. Also it was a

---

[1] Upon this, as upon other matters, I was, of course, doing all I could in the time allowed, to collect literature and take notes of interviews. In this diary, written for my family and a few friends, I could not deal fully with such a subject as trade unionism. However, as this matter was so important to me, not only in Johannesburg but also later in Durban, it may be useful to mention here a book describing events in this context by a man who was active at this time on more extreme lines than those followed by Mr. Ballinger. This was Edward Roux whose retrospective book, *Time Longer than Rope*, London 1948.

bad principle to run away from obligations. So Ballinger shouldered the whole burden, issued an honest and damaging report and introduced auditing and proper business methods. But though organization had come the funds had gone. Branches had broken away; discredited native officials developed rival shows; the disillusioned natives refused to go on giving. In Durban the second prominent leader, Champion, a Zulu, has defected from Kadalie and is, I understand, organizing his own union. I should like to meet him. I think that now Ballinger can hardly raise more than £1,500 a year income, and for himself gets nothing. Heaven knows how he lives! I imagine white friends here and in Britain keep him going. He is certainly a dedicated man.

I questioned him closely.

'What is your object? Have you come here to develop native trade unionism?'

'There will never be trade unionism in the real sense. The African native has missed that stage, all the more because it is harder to teach him skilled trades than it is with the European.'

'You mean that it is a case of organization of unskilled workers?'

'Yes, for African industry will be that of mass-production. Their organization will be more like that of the transport and dockers unions.'

'I heard you speak last night and I did not enjoy it very much. Do you not feel that you are rousing in these people a discontent that has no hope of satisfaction?'

'It must be satisfied. What you have said might have been said of Britain at one time. And the Africans are already discontented. The industrialized native in every town—I do not refer to the special case of the contract labourers from the reserves living in huge compounds—is everywhere underpaid, overcrowded and over-taxed. Do you realize that whereas Durban has accommodation for only 18,000 natives there are 40,000 there?'

Ballinger ran through many instances of bad conditions. He told me that in that gang I saw working on the railway bank, shovelling earth, the whites would be getting five or six times as much a day as the blacks. His main job is to draw up cases for increase of pay for presentation to the wage-boards. Then the employers come and contest his claims. In his opinion the employers are hopeless. They cannot even begin to put up a case and merely look foolish and get angry under his cross-examination. He has produced little practical result so far. The wage-boards draw a distinction between what should be paid to 'civilized' and 'uncivilized' labour: the skilled or semi-skilled native falls between the two. In some cases employers, to avoid the action of the law, pay the skilled native skilled rates and then, in secret, make him pay half or more back to them.

'You are a Labour man', I said 'and there is a Labour Party in this country. What are your relations with them ?'

'None at all. They have no link with Labour at home, and not the faintest resemblance to it. The only men I could have dealings with are the Communists and then only with half a dozen of them.'

'Is it true that Russian money is being distributed to the natives ?'

'Yes, a certain amount. It comes irregularly as it is difficult to get it in. Mostly through certain Jews. Russian money was used this month to finance Dingaan's Day celebrations.[1] Any native who cared to come to the Reef was to have his expenses paid for the week-end. Hundreds came. But it produces no political result.'

I asked about his relations with the police. He said he was at first allowed entry for three months and is now here only on sufferance. He is perpetually under police supervision and now knows well by sight the detectives who dog him. He has no fear. He knows the law well now and he defies them to dare deport him. He does not mind how much they attend his meetings. But they don't play the game. When Mr. Patrick Duncan[2] asked in Parliament why he had only been let in for three months and why he was allowed to stay only on sufferance, the Minister of Justice (a misleading title in this country), the famous Pirow, whom the Africans lately burned in effigy, said there were reasons which he would prefer to tell the hon. gentleman in private, implying that Mr. Ballinger's reputation was almost scandalous. He promised to bring to me all the documents he found it safe to keep and which had not yet been taken by the police. This is an example of the methods to which the Afrikaner leaders can resort in their attempts to silence an effective, and well-informed and courageous critic of their repressive policies.

[1] Dingaan's Day was kept by the Dutch in commemoration of their defeat of the Zulus on 16 December 1888. The natives would keep a counter-demonstration. A few days before I arrived in Johannesburg they had celebrated from 10 a.m. to 4 p.m. while on the same day in Capetown they had burned effigies of Smuts and Pirow, the Minister for Justice. In 1973 these African activities seem almost incredible.

[2] Patrick Duncan was one of the young Oxford men who worked with Lord Milner and were known as his kindergarten. He became the last British Governor-General in 1937–43.

Today (24 December) I went to lunch with Professor Macmillan, the historian protagonist of the native races of South Africa, the apologist for the old 'sentimental' missionary and the academic hammer of the Dutch. A red-headed Scot, South African born, he dragged himself up from the MSS of his third book—on the present 'native' problem—and we began without ceremony on that subject.

He is bitter. How a man can bear to live in this country, feeling as he does, with his working hours filled with the grim history of native policy and his leisure with its present injustices, I do not know. In a long, and to me, deeply interesting talk, we came to the following conclusions.

The Dutch were originally emigrants of mainly low class. As a result of their long isolation from Europe and the more complete isolation of the veld far in the interior away from government, they have developed a kind of permanent inaccessibility to ideas and are all but invulnerable to outside opinion. The majority of them are, at a certain low level, born politicians and quite unscrupulous. They have not and they will not alter their attitude to the native as being the eternal inferior. Deprived of the system of slavery, they are elaborating a system of legalized serfdom to meet their needs.

I cannot help thinking, myself, that the British are guilty of a betrayal of the native, a moral, in some cases, almost a legal, guilt. In the first half of the nineteenth century we sponsored the native, recognizing his potential equality and, in the Cape, granting him the franchise and at least theoretical equality before the law. Our support of the native was one reason for Britain's conflict with the Boer, with all the resulting disturbance of the middle and late nineteenth century. With the growth of imperialism, with Disraeli, and then Chamberlain, a change came over our hostility towards the Boers; the native began to fade out of the foreground. After the Boer War, the Liberals came in, full of ardent generosity towards the defeated Dutch enemy; all the more so as some of them had doubts about the justifiability of the Boer War. So, in a series of handshakes, progressively warmer, the breach was apparently healed and the Union achieved. But as it is difficult, if not impossible, for us to be liberal towards Boer and native at the same time, the native now tended to get left. We allowed the Boer states to come into the Union still maintaining the complete exclusion of the native from citizenship and, with the single and (as it seems today) hazardous safeguard of demanding a two-thirds majority vote before the Cape native franchise could be abolished, we handed over the native races to this new South African Parliament. We even, in the Schedule to the Act, contemplated the time when they might take over the territories, Swaziland, Basutoland and Bechuanaland. (Whereupon, as I may have mentioned, there followed deep perturbation in the latter country, helpless indignation and a deputation to London. So far Britain has not given in on this issue and the fight is still on and I hope to take some small hand in it when I get back to England.)

I suppose—and men who played a part in creating the Union have confirmed this to me—that the British felt very secure of their position. Our attitude to the Dutch was rather patronizing and also rather sentimental. It is partly based upon our vanity about our own fair-play and liberalism that makes us so indulgent towards our enemies. Not a bad trait but in this case unfortunate. I suppose that few in Britain foresaw that the Dutch might rise again and swamp the British, using, instead of the rifles of 1900, the political weapons of the majority which we had put into their hands.

Now it has happened. Well may the bewildered, frightened native rub his eyes. 'But,' he says—some have said this to me—'I don't understand. These people were your enemies and our enemies. We accepted your rule, in some cases we voluntarily handed ourselves over to you, in order to get your protection against them. You taught us an unbounded confidence in your strength and justice. You fought them again in the Boer War and we showed you our loyalty and prayed for your victory. And now—here are the Dutch ruling us, threatening us with new laws and even to take away what you gave us, what we value as the clear symbol of our potential equality—the Cape Franchise. And when we turn to you, you shake your heads and look away, and say—"We can do nothing but advise you to submit".'

The Dutch are indeed in the saddle and the English-speaking people here everywhere troubled and hesitant. Hardly a day passes but I hear evidence of the Dutch quietly 'cleansing' the Civil Service of English-speaking officials and substituting Dutch, or deflecting promotion towards their own people, away from the English. The favourite method is bilingualism. The English are always bad at languages and are, I am afraid, a bit contemptuous of Afrikaans as the bastard dialect of less than a million people and almost without a literature. So the English have not seen their way towards learning it or, at least, learning it well. Whereas to the Dutchman English was vital if he were to pass beyond his farm and hold his own, to get any higher education or to travel. Now the British can be refused appointment or promotion on this linguistic ground. I heard of an obvious candidate for a big post, the second-in-command, being pushed aside for some Dutch official from a small dorp. The case was so bad that the rejected man went himself to protest to the minister concerned.

'You are not bilingual,' was the reported answer. The man protested: he showed his certificates. 'No Englishman', he was told, 'is ever truly bilingual. And no Englishman can understand the Dutch, whereas all Dutchmen understand the English.'

Of course we are largely to blame. We little thought, or we had chosen to forget, how much bitterness and repression was stored in the hearts of the Dutch; how much sense of inferiority there is that only the most blatant of nationalisms can cure. They have waited, have endured our superiorities, have smarted under their sense of being slandered about native policy. And now, having won their nationalist majority, their time has come. They mean to make the most of it and they mean to perpetuate it. There are various ways of doing that.

The most disquieting fact as regards native policy is the position of the British. Even if some may have feared that the Dutch might be beyond assimilation, surely none feared that many of the British would be influenced by the Dutch. But the South African Party now has little or no policy: it is divided between the old stalwarts of the Cape and those, especially from Natal, who would vote with the Dutch on the native question. British liberal traditions have worn thin; fear is catching and the poor white, who is sometimes British and who has a vote, is the greatest enemy of the native. No wonder the South African Party hesitates to declare a policy and calls vaguely for a Convention. Few dare to blow on the trumpet the old battle cries of justice and liberalism; even Rhodes' dictum 'Equal rights for every civilized man south of the Zambesi' is forgotten, for white 'civilization' is now seen as a racial possession, not a communicable state of being.

Well, I may modify these opinions as I inquire further. I certainly think I must try to understand the Dutch better. At present I meet only those who dislike and fear them.

On Christmas Eve Mr. Ballinger and an ex-Sinn Feiner, Beckett, called on me and had dinner with me in this hotel. Afterwards we went out into the native quarter and called at the Bantu Social Centre, erected by one of the great friends of the African here, Mr. Howard Pim, an old friend of Rhodes and of Jameson, much bound up with the history of the Transvaal. Here we met Thema, an African intellectual, who has just written an article in the *Round Table*. I saw, framed with her photograph, a vigorous letter from Sybil Thorndike on the artistic capacity of the Bantu and the scandal of excluding him from society. So there are some direct links, however few and slender, between Africans here and intelligent British liberals.

We went on to a native dance-hall and then back to the centre of the town. Here was pandemonium. From the whole forty miles of the Reef the whites had come in to celebrate the birth of Christ by letting off steam. The streets were impassable. Thousands of hooligans, 50 per cent of them drunk, all wearing paper caps, and some with painted clown faces, were eddying about, letting off crackers and fireworks, blowing on tin trumpets, and wielding flails or 'flickers' of coloured paper. With these they were hitting the faces of the girls as they passed and indulging in violent horseplay. All my latent respectability came out; I felt almost as though I could have turned a machine-gun on to them. It took Beckett and Ballinger all their time, fighting inch by inch, to get me through them and back to the hotel. Wild looking girls, in low-cut dresses, were screaming and struggling, or being chased through the crowd by lurching admirers. I could not help relating it to my main subject—all these leering, drunken, degenerate looking people, to claim such absolute and eternal right over the native and to have the power to enforce their claim! These are the people with whom a native (teacher or doctor he may be) may not ride in the same tram-car. These are the kind of people who went out and shot up an orderly native meeting the other day and when one native died of wounds, after such suffering, and the killer was arrested for murder, went and demonstrated against his arrest. They cowed the authorities into giving him bail and the Mayor put up the money. These men have the vote.

No sleep tonight. The orgy in the streets still goes on. (They broke into the restaurant next door to my hotel, smashed and looted it, in spite of the defence put up by the native servants.)

Johannesburg on Christmas Day was so beastly that I stayed in and worked all day.

Today, Boxing Day, Mr Howard Pim took me on a very interesting drive right along the Reef. The whole chain is strewn with its entrails and sickly looking they are, too. The rock, crushed to powder in the stamps and soaked with chemicals to extract the last particle of gold, is dead stuff, so dead that I believe it is thirty years before the first feeble grasses begin to patch it. The dry powder is piled into enormous, steep hills, pale sulphur colour, which run like a range along the forty miles of the Reef. The part that is called 'slime' is run over plates of mercury to extract the last vestiges of gold and over corduroy velvet to extract the platinum. It is then poured out and, hardening as it pours, builds up an erection of absolutely straight, horizontal lines, mounting in tiers. The 'slime' then cracks as it dries and makes regular vertical flutings. As the slime is coloured brilliant yellow and orange, with shadows of deep purple, the weird Satanic beauty of these dumps can be imagined. And all rising out of the green veld against a brilliant blue sky, often reflected in pools about their bases. The story goes that a Johannesburg Jewess, waking as the train ran into a wintry Switzerland on her first visit to Europe, woke her husband to say 'Look, Abey, at these big dumps. Doesn't it make you feel at home ?'

Mr. Howard Pim came out to work with Rhodes and knew him well. He regards Rhodes and Botha as the two big men of South Africa. He never heard Rhodes laugh. There was, occasionally, an abrupt guffaw but no real laughter. Also he never argued. He would simply state his view or his wants. If you countered him he would say 'I'm not arguing. I'm telling you.' There was a look in his eye as though he were always thinking of something beyond the immediate point under discussion—the next, or perhaps, the ultimate step. Howard Pim was in Johannesburg at the time of the Jameson Raid. He realizes now that it was a great crime and the real cause of war. But at the time he backed it. The Uitlanders got a large consignment of Lee Metford rifles just beforehand and did not know how to use them. He did, so his job was to instruct them. He took me out to Doornkop and showed me where Jameson, trying to cross a marshy spruit, was held up by the Dutch, who lay behind some boulders, the only cover they could have found in the whole region. He maintains that Jameson was so sick that he was hardly responsible for his actions and that Botha pleaded all night to have him shot. But Kruger refused.

I went to see Mr. Alfred Palmer, an artist who has come out to paint the natives. It is rather interesting that, parallel with all the new anthropological appreciation of the native, there has gone an artistic interpretation. They are closely linked. I felt that when I saw Aletta Lewis painting in Samoa: she painted the Samoans well because she loved and understood them. The same with Mr. Palmer. He came out as a middle-aged man. He found a new field of work and regrets that his whole life was not given to it. His drawings and bronzes of Zulu chiefs reveal all the wisdom of the tribal patriarch, their dignity and courage, and his black madonnas are marvels of feeling. Being a modern he delights in the colours of African bodies in different lights: struck by sunshine or shadowed under forest, he finds them changing from brown to purple and even to a deep cobalt blue. I think the Zulu achieved perfection in savage dress or undress, metal wire circling his fine limbs, armlets and anklets of feathery fur, plumed head and leopard cloak and the bold pattern of his skin shield. To paint them Mr. Palmer lives with them, eating and sleeping in their kraals, until his models become his friends.

I went down at midday to Ektuleni, the House of the Peacemakers, where Miss Maude works, the daughter of the Bishop of Kensington. (I know Barbara Gwyer will be interested in this, as we read the literature about this place at college and wondered if I would ever get there.) Ektuleni, when reached after a dreary journey through the slums of Sophiatown, looks very clean and modern, standing on top of the stony outcrop of a little kopje, which gives it a sense of light and space in those oppressive surroundings. Inside it is Oxford-English to the last bit of china, with gay London Underground posters, homespun curtains and Medici prints. A cheerful crowd of women in bright linen aprons were preparing a Sunday School party, calling out to each other by their Christian names, all very happy and united. After lunch we all went out to the baking bit of hillside which their fence encloses. At the various gates we let in the crowds of black children who were able to produce a ticket to show they had attended Sunday School. They were dressed much as any crowd of slum-children in England would be dressed because their poor mothers had slaved to turn them out presentably. I shall not forget one family of three small boys, all in blue blazers with yellow braid and yachting caps. There were even some in shoes and stockings .Where, I fear, they may have differed from an English crowd is that no sooner had the buns and pink lemonade been doled out than there was a rush back to the railings to share lavishly with those shut out of Paradise.

Meanwhile they were divided into groups, each of which was coaxed by some perspiring white into playing a European game of some kind—tip-and-run or hunt the slipper. In most groups they seemed docile but rather bored. One, Canon Parker, and a young Dutch Communist whom he had converted, were sweating as they organized races. I approached a group of boys who were lazily rocking on a see-saw.

'Now, boys, why don't you go and run races over there as you were asked to do?'

'Why?' asked one of the boys. 'Do *you* run races when sun hot on your heads?'

Why indeed? I wondered. A perfect answer from a sensible African to a silly European, myself.

Miss Maude, the head of this mission, is well known and beloved in her district. She took me out afterwards and the passage of her car was hailed by one long scream of greeting from waving children. She drove me into the Western Native Township which I had passed before and where little two-roomed brick houses are built in endless rows; enough to hold—or reckoned to be enough to hold—14,000 natives. The shacks exhibit the most pathetic attempts at decency and civilization. The tiny margin round each one embraces flowers and even trees that choke the hut. Some tenants have put up pretentious-looking railings and gates. We called on one old woman who speaks English, Dutch, and three native languages. She takes in all the stray children she can find and supports them by washing from morning till night. She had just added to her responsibilities a little child to save him from going with his mother to the Reformatory; also a young Zulu woman deserted by her husband. No trained investigator can understand how these people live on their wages. I have seen dozens of specimen family budgets drawn up, all showing, even on the most modest estimate of expenses, that the expense must largely exceed the income. The impossible is made possible by nearly all the women doing washing or charring or brewing illicit native beer but also by the unquestioning way in which they all help each other. It must be remembered that native wages are low, based on the idea that the standards are primitive, and yet the urban native is on almost the same footing as the white who earns seven or eight times the wage—that is, he must pay almost as much for transport (perhaps more where he is pushed miles outside the town), also for food, and, indeed, for all that he buys in shops. He and his family must wear European clothes. Yet his wages are kept down artificially. This is partly because the colour bar prevents a natural advancement and partly because of the system of buying cheap labour on contract to the Union. The men are assumed to be partly dependent upon the produce of the reserves from which they are brought and so can afford to accept low wages, especially where they are housed and fed in compounds. But the eroded land and inefficient farming of the reserves offer them and their families at home very exiguous support.

The Howard Pims came to fetch me up to the luxurious suburbs where they live and where I am to spend the week-end. It lies over the edge of a ridge so that the whole of the Reef and the chain of dumps are entirely hidden and the house peers out through a wooded slope on to the flats and low hills of the Transvaal.

We went down at night to a very interesting meeting, one largely run by Howard Pim, which met in the Bantu Men's Social Centre. It is the Joint Council, European and Bantu, started a year or two ago as an unofficial body, in which the races can meet to discuss the burning problems of their contact. The native members are doctors, teachers, even political agitators; the whites are clergy, lawyers, university staff, etc.—the 'Negrophil' people, abhorrent to the Dutch Nationalists.

They discussed a new bill dealing with land and farm service, designed, it would seem, to restore the more complete serfdom that existed before the 1828 'Emancipation' of the Hottentot. The farmer can establish a native on his land and the native pays by ninety days of service. But the farmer has complete discretion as to how to distribute the periods of service and can thus prevent the man from ever going away to earn wages elsewhere. Nor can the man leave without a written permission. The farmer also has a claim on the labour of the man's children. Such redress as the native can ask for is likely to be small in outlying districts, with country magistrates in control. But the bill is not only iniquitous; it is also silly. Legally, it is a tissue of mistakes and clashes with other legislation. The Joint Council decided to expose the minister in charge as a fool rather than as a knave and to attack the absurdity of the draughtsmanship.

I think this Joint Council—there are two others in Durban and the Cape, but they are not so active—is one of the most hopeful things in South Africa. It gets a lot of its stuff into the English half of the

K   145

Press and is a wonderful education and stimulus to its own members. The worst of it is that the Dutch Press is practically untouched. The English do not study it, never read it and thus, with little social contact, the two sections go their own ways with the minimum of understanding.

After the Joint Council I went to a native dance-hall with Ballinger. There was a curious mixture of costumes and styles of dancing, one native being in a swallow-tail and white tie. I soon picked out some very familiar faces and saw that the Fort Hare team was there. I went and talked to them and then persuaded the proprietor, a native, to hold up the dance while the Fort Hare men sang to us. They did not sing so well as before and I thought the ardent dancers were not too pleased to have their dancing interrupted, especially at the dictation of white intruders. I had to drink poisonous lemonade out of a bottle with a straw: I wanted to refuse but Ballinger, with finer feelings, insisted that I must hurt myself rather than the proprietor's feelings.

Early this morning, Saturday, I was called for by Mr. Ray Phillips. He is the head of the American Board of Missions on the Reef, and is one of the outstanding personalities here. And, of course, officially distrusted. His great aim is to provide wholesome recreation for the workers during their stay in the mines, known as the 'University of Crime'. He has put into his work all the vigour and efficiency of his nation. He has won over solid financial and administrative support from the Chamber of Mines and he runs an open-air cinema in each mine once a week. He also organizes games and classes of all kinds with, of course, religious services and evangelization.

There are always, at any one moment, about 180,000 natives on the Reef and as they are here on contracts from seven to nineteen months it is clear that enormous numbers are passing through. You may remember that I saw them coming and going from the kraals in the Transkei and also in Basutoland. They are mostly 'blanket Kaffirs', young and utterly raw, but there are other old-timers with whom they mix. They remain underground about nine or ten hours a day. For the rest of the time they are loafing about in the huge compounds except when they get passes to go into the city, which is eagerly awaiting them and the chance to get hold of their exiguous cash by every lure known to the scum, white, brown and black, male and female, of a dozen races which preys upon them. It really requires very little imagination to guess all that happens under these conditions.

I went to at least a dozen mines, walked round the compounds, and into the sleeping rooms and kitchens. In most—not all—mines the conditions are reasonably good in a material sense. This is to be expected in view of the enormous economic importance of the mines and their essential foundation of native labour. The food is abundant and varied: the yards are tolerably clean: there are dispensaries, hospitals, and showers. Only the independent, struggling mines outside the big companies were filthy, crowded and badly equipped.

Perhaps what most impresses is the beauty of the men. In the afternoon, Saturday, they were lying about resting, many dressed only in their blankets. Most of them could be called primitive tribesmen with the peculiar beauty and fascination of their kind. It is hard to describe this beauty: it is partly in the carriage of the body, generally a fine body, and carried unselfconsciously, with the grace of an animal, which a very little sophistication can destroy. There is the expression of the eyes which, whether defiant, sad or happy, seem to express a different system of thought from ours. Then there are all the trappings of savagery, fantastic earrings, wrists and ankles loaded with metal, hair flowing long or cut into weird patterns on the scalp.

These men, beautiful, dangerous children, are taken from about a quarter of a big continent, away from the discipline of tribal conditions and village life and are flung together to do strange work, in unnatural conditions, deep underground, with Johannesburg at the doors of the compound. The picture is not all dark; money goes back to help, in so far as money can, the exhausted reserves; much that is good may be learned. But the mixed tribesmen tend to unlearn their own social disciplines and develop a new common life on a lower level. Add to that the prostitution and disease waiting at the door of the compound and the vice within, and remember that nearly every man goes back to his tribe in some measure a changed man and at worst may become a centre of demoralization and indiscipline in his own community.

But it is too late to regret. The mines are there: South Africa is largely dependent upon them. Along the Reef, beside the black miners, a large European population lives, with another black urban population to do all the manual work of a chain of towns. From the South African point of view, the mines *must* be kept going yet profits seem to demand that the black labour should be underpaid, since the white labour is overpaid. White labour can claim almost what it wants, and it demands a ratio of one white to ten blacks in order that it may retain its level of employment. A high official in the Chamber of Mines, who would not dare have his name attached to this statement, told me that this white labour could be reduced by 50 to 60 per cent; that where one man looks after a gang of ten, he could look after a gang of fifty. (On one occasion when the whites struck, the blacks went down, under a handful of managers and clerks and it is said that they sent up *much more* rock than the average.) Whereas the whites get £1 a day the blacks begin at 1s 8d, and the average wage is 2s 2d, the same as it was thirty years ago, though the cost of blankets and other necessities and the demands of the natives have increased several times over. Of course, in assessing these figures, it must be remembered that the native gets his keep and the white does not, but the white gets all sorts of advantages such as free education, high compensation for accidents, etc. Thus the inflated pay of the white worker keeps down the pay of the black miner in spite of the fact, admitted privately to me by some Europeans, that in the thirty years of the mines the black has tended to advance, and the white to decline, in skill. The price of serf-labour is the lethargy of the employer. The senior official of whom I spoke agreed with me, of course in confidence that the position was economically farcical.

Now the mines, though they abstract dangerous percentages of men out of some of the African reserves, are short of black labour. They are crying out for at least 20,000 more. This does not, as in normal conditions it would, lead them to offer more wages. Instead they ask that the law forbidding them to recruit north of latitude 22 degrees be repealed. It was because the health of the natives from the further north suffered in the mines that the ban was laid. Now the mines declare they can meet the health danger with better knowledge and equipment. Perhaps the growing value of the African will lead to his being less wastefully used and financial competition will do what humanity has failed to achieve. But we shall not deserve nor get any thanks from the African.

Mr. Phillips, my American missionary, was a hustler. I had to whip round those compounds at the double. They left me with a long series of pictures of stifling dormitories with layers of concrete bunks: bodies thrown in all attitudes of rest: groups squatting, gambling, drinking, or cooking; lumps of meat dangling from the ceiling, and piles of the tawdry gilded tin, or painted wooden boxes which each miner takes back in pride to his kraal.

After the mines with their compounds came the city with its slums. I begged Mr. Phillips to show me the worst as well as the best. The people here must be sharply distinguished from the miners: these are a permanent, largely detribalized crowd, in many ways similar to the poor of any big city, but in worse condition owing to the sudden transition from primitive tribalism and also to official neglect or worse. They can take over little or nothing from tribal experience of use to them in their new life, while they have far less resistance to the demoralization of city life than the European and no power to obtain redress, nor voice to cry their grievances, even if they could analyse their own sad position.

I have already spoken of the new municipal locations, or townships. They represent the best. The worst are the places where the natives have ensconced themselves a stone's throw from the stately squares in the centre of the town, teeming warrens in old warehouses or backyards. These are another form of exploitation: here the owners have run up rows of tiny tin hovels, about 8 x 5 feet and let them for 25s a month. 'No worse than the slums in England,' says the South African in defence. I have seen the worst slums of Sheffield and some other towns and I found these in Johannesburg bad beyond all comparison, beyond imagination. The yards between these one-room dwellings were almost invisible for the crowds of people, native, Indian, mixtures of all kinds, with here and there a poor white. What happens when these people try to lie down in their hovels, I cannot imagine. By day there is hardly standing room. Some of the people were obviously idiots; others are obviously criminal; half of the women live by professional prostitution or by brewing illicit liquor which was fermenting in petrol tins on slow fires; some were busy burying their illegal product in underground 'hides'. The ground was littered with children of all ages. Some were looking surprisingly healthy. Perhaps a death rate of between six and eight hundred in the thousand means that the survivors must be very fit. Add to the crowd innumerable chickens. The sanitary arrangements and the stench I can leave to your imagination. Of course, in any other country plague would soon advertise the conditions and make a national or an international scandal. But here the sun, coming at midday pretty nearly vertically into the courts, apparently saves by sterilisation. Mr. Grimshaw, of the International Labour Office, when he was here, said that these yards were worse than Hell's Hole in Bombay, hitherto reputed rock-bottom in slums. And next door to one of them is the huge sports field,

Ellis Park. The University is spending vast sums on artistic altera-
tions, plus £13,000 on a little pavilion and many thousands on a
swimming bath. The city is full of swimming baths and not one for the
natives who have not even domestic baths. I suppose sharp social
contrasts exist in some degree in England but to me it seems more
wicked and static to keep people in such conditions on the ground
that their skin is black.

When I got back we motored out to the Country Club, parked our
car in a glistening row of other aristocratic machines and had drinks in
luxurious premises, surrounded by exquisite gardens. Then on to the
open-air swimming pool. The Country Club is a growing feature of
colonial and American life. This one is very exclusive and costly. No
Jews admitted, no retail traders. This is one of the prizes for which
men strive, with a car good enough to hold its own in the car-park,
with beautiful frocks for wife and daughter so that they can sit in
confidence upon the flowery terrace to drink their cocktails. And the
whole elegant superstructure is built on black labour; men and women
from those seething yards work in white houses and hotels and even
take the washing back home. There was hardly a hovel without its
bending black woman and a pile of ironing. I wondered how many
owners of those silk vests and pillow-cases had any notion where they
would be washed and where hung to dry. How the washerwomen keep
them clean I cannot imagine. These extremes of luxury and wretched-
ness strike the imagination like a blow. Perhaps most of the natives are
too unsophisticated to rationalize their conditions while the majority
of the whites have immunized their consciences. I hated the Country
Club, and yet I felt it was easy for a passing observer to cast a stone
and claim to be 'without sin' in South Africa. At the least we must
search for ways of using such influences as are left to us in Britain.

Worked nearly all day. Called on Bishop Karney, said to be marked
out as the next archbishop. A nice, ugly man. He used the gravest
words I had heard about the general situation, and very strong words
—for a bishop—about the Afrikaners. He sees no hope anywhere. As
the Government refuses even to begin to collect information on which
to base their projected native policy, a necessity urged by every body
and commission that has sat the last ten years, the leaders of the
churches intend to do it themselves. But they have to ask the Government for facilities in their task. The Bishop has to go to Pretoria to

try to persuade Hertzog to receive the deputation. It is doubtful if he will. He has already refused many weighty deputations. The Bishop's wife feared the acquisition of a South African accent for her children and will struggle to send them home to school. Though personally very charming, I imagine she is the sort of Englishwoman who alienates the Dutch.

Dined with Professor Macmillan and he told me how the Government sent him to make a report on a certain native area and when he told them that the area was overcrowded, exhausted and neglected, they simply suppressed the report. He is now going to publish it in his new book. He, too, is very despondent. We worked out with maps and figures the proportion of land held by the natives, the vast majority of the population. It worked out, I think, at about one-thirteenth. Though some of the reserves are fairly good, the proportion is balanced by including a stretch of Namaqualand, which is largely barren. He tells me that when the British Government originally took over Swaziland it asked the white concessionnaires to present their claims. They claimed three times the total area! Like so many people here, he loathes and distrusts Smuts. He and his wife would both leave the country if they could.[1]

I went on to Ray Phillips to see the film he has produced and shown throughout America. It is a marvellous film, representing the highest American efficiency and energy. He dashed all over South Africa to get it. He first shows native life: dances, schools, witch doctors—life at its simplest and most 'bush'. Then comes the recruiter, the journey to the mine, the mine and the compound, drinking and gambling, then the work of the Mission. The poor man has shown it a hundred times. It was typical of his kindness to run it over again for me. It takes one and a half hours, with him darting from the gramophone to the projector and delivering his lecture at the same time. I kept a long silence at the end and then Macmillan, who had come to motor me back, said:

'Phillips, I've never seen the sky without any break at all in it until now.'

'Nor I,' said Phillips, sombrely.

The verdict of these two expert and devoted men struck me like a physical blow. They told us how they went to see Jansen, the Native

[1] Professor Macmillan detached himself from South Africa during the thirties and continued his distinguished career as historian and teacher in British universities, travelling widely and writing books on Africa.

Affairs Minister, and how he did at least allow them to talk as long as they liked. But at the end he said:

'Gentlemen, there is one road for the white and another for the black and they never meet. Segregation.'

Yet the whole point of what they had said was that segregation was impossible, had already been abandoned for the convenience of the white man. He at once needs and resents the black in his town; he draws the men in for labour and tries to keep the wives away. He pushes the workers miles outside in some location, which means heavy transport expenses to bring them back daily: he refuses to regard them as permanent citizens, and, then, suddenly deciding there are too many, pushes a number out. The female house-servants he keeps in back premises where they are the victim of any illicit vagrant who waits until the lights are out, the willing victims perhaps where life is so unnatural. No black man or woman is allowed to be out after 9 p.m. without a special pass—to be applied for each time. Contraventions of the pass-laws are criminal offences, it must be remembered, and huge numbers of natives find their first contact with prison through them. A native may have to be carrying four or five documents at once—contract of service, permission to be out after 9 p.m., permission to be in the urban area where he works, receipt for payment of tax, special pass for a woman to be residing in a white area. There are others I cannot remember.

The refusal to regard the native as an integral part of the township for which he works is all part of the bluff about segregation. Regard him as temporary and you can neglect his interests as a ratepayer, deny him light and water and deny him also any political power, municipal or national. You can neglect him if he is ill or starving. And you can also go on talking about the native developing 'along his own lines'. I should like to ask these Dutchmen what *is* his line in the Johannesburg slums. Having got him there, broken or weakened his contact with his own tribal area, the white man affects not to see him. I saw the advertisement of a little watering place near East London—whose location I visited—saying—'Come to bright, clean X. All white area. No native locations.' I wonder how long that will last and whether the workers live underground.

Rather a long but most interesting day. I went out shopping early and called at 10 a.m. at the imposing Chamber of Mines. Here I had an appointment with the great Mr. Taberer, who gave up government work for a princely salary under the Chamber and is in charge of all the native labour on the Reef. He is also Chairman of the Native Labour Committee of the International Labour Office at Geneva. He is reputed to know fluently ten native languages.

A broad, short, stout, Henry VIII sort of man, forceful and egotistical. He was furious that I had come only on the last day to see him and went quite purple over Kerr and Lionel Curtis not having given me an introduction to him. He had only an hour to spare. That was not enough. I was leaving tonight, was I? Well, tomorrow early would be just as good as he would send me early to Pretoria in his own car. So he rang up my hosts, the Howard Pims, and said that, owing to the fact that I was dining with him that night, they would have to put me up till tomorrow.

Well, one can accept this sort of bullying once, especially when you really want what is on offer. Taberer soon had the whole office buzzing, as Napoleon might have done had he commanded a row of bell-pushers and an army of typists. I was loaded with reports and typescript. 'Anything you ask for, girl—we have nothing to hide.'

From the Chamber of Mines to that of Horrors—the C.I.D. Here I met the two heads of the Johannesburg section. They had all the facts and figures ready for me. One man, newly appointed, was very nervous; the other, just retiring, was outspoken, Colonel Quirk by name. He thundered against the slums as breeders of vice and crime. The 1928 figures showed, among other things, that the native population of 138,000, provided in 1928 more than 73,000 criminal cases and, though under total prohibition, provides 85 per cent of the arrests for drunkenness. (I saw a drunken white reeling about to his own and other people's danger, with natives sniggering at him, and a policeman, after a look, turned and walked the other way.)

Then I asked to visit the Native Court. Colonel Quirk begged me not to go. No lady could go into it, never did go. Apart from the nature of the cases, the place was filthy and verminous. It was a disgrace to the city. It certainly was. There were no whites at all except the officials. The place stank and was half-dark. It was crowded with natives. The magistrate looked as if he did not mean to put up with me; the poor man was in the last stages of gloom and weariness. But I managed to stay.

First Case. One, David, whispers in the ears of the disillusioned white interpreter his accusation against Brunie in the dock.

'Brunie stole 10s from me on Saturday night, when I was asleep. Sisha saw him do it.'

'Where were you?'

'At the house of a woman.'

'What woman?'

'I don't know. She was not there. We were all sleeping in a room, seven men and three girls, and after we were asleep Brunie got up and took 10s out of my pocket.'

'You were sleeping in your clothes.'

'Yes.'

'Who were the girls?'

'I don't know.'

'You were drunk?'

'No, we had just had a little dancing and singing.'

'You people don't dance and sing unless you're drunk.' (Not true, that.)

The weary magistrate discharges them.

Second case. A drunken, half-insane woman—remanded.

Third. A native at the Maypole Dairy, accused of keeping money paid in by customers. A nice-looking boy. Pleads guilty but tells how his employers had compounded his crime by making him pay the money back, and work for nothing until all was paid off and only after that they pounced.

Fourth. A man-and-woman brawl in a yard. He is accusing her of tearing the flesh off him with her nails. She accuses him of pouring boiling water down her chest and flogging her with a stick. This is quite simple. Strip them both. Some apprehension about me but the magistrate orders the police to proceed. No female wardress for the woman: the interpreter deals with her. The examination proves 50-50 injuries, and after more revelations about their relations, the magistrate, in the final stage of pre-lunch exhaustion, drives them both away. I went on to meet two black detectives and the head of the Pass Office but I have not the heart to record all that grim stuff.

At night I went down, as agreed, to the great Mr. Taberer's house.

I found it was dinner *à deux*, though the champagne almost took the place of a third presence, such was its importance after a hard, hot day.

I cannot imagine more romantic possibilities than there are in this man's job. (This opinion is not the result of the champagne.) Here he is on this seething gold reef, in charge of the social and material condition of 200,000 raw natives from all over South and South East Africa. He is given wide scope and a good deal of money by the Chamber of Mines who must go a certain distance in keeping the crude, essential labour force contented and healthy. He co-operates with and subsidizes missionaries, especially Mr. Ray Phillips. He is sent at a moment's notice to any mine where trouble threatens and goes in alone, perhaps to reduce thousands of hysterical tribesmen to reason by his influence and knowledge of the languages. Sometimes he goes on tour to the native territories and holds huge meetings at which he addresses them on the advantages of mine work.

In the partnership of Mr. Taberer and the Chamber of Mines, mammon seems to have struck a compromise with God. (I was reminded of the last act of *Major Barbara*.) Mr. Taberer, a missionary's son, trained at Keble College for a parson, must have mortgaged at least part of his conscience. And yet, I suppose, it is well that he should be there. Of course he would not agree that the drawing of men from the reserves is bad. He defended the mines as the salvation of the overcrowded reserves (but two wrongs do not make a right); as an education (but that is just the question); as the basis of South African prosperity which is as necessary to white as to black (but how is that prosperity shared out?). He insisted that the natives came because they wanted to come; came huge distances, sometimes walking, and this in spite of their fear of working underground, in spite of low wages, drawn by the glamour of Johannesburg and the fair dealing of the mines.

Even on the question of the propagation of vice he was ready with defence—already these vices were known to the native in his own life—they were not so bad as painted—strenuous efforts on his part to check them.

But when we switched to general politics, there was a change. He owes no allegiance to the Dutch. They have no part nor lot in the Chamber of Mines, are not even shareholders, though they provide 75 per cent of the 'supervisors' below ground, a class he condemned roundly. He spoke very freely about the nationalists.

'Every Dutchman is a brute where the native is concerned. The Dutch were too clever for us at the Union. Now they have us at their mercy. And the native too. When the native says we have betrayed him, he is right. But (as I told Mr. Amery) Great Britain need not imagine she is finished with us yet. If she allows the Dutch to take away the Cape Franchise she will have to repair her mistake. We are drifting towards war again, war on both Imperial and native issues. And if only for the sake of the native, and the reputation of Queen Victoria, the home government will have to step in.'

I queried his prophecy of war but he stuck to it. I guess that the old Uitlander-on-the-Reef attitude that produced the Jameson Raid and largely, the Boer War, still exists and expresses itself in him. For the huge British interests here feel again, as they did in the nineties, but now on a subcontinental scale, the grip of the Dutchman, taxing them and resenting them. They feel, too, very bitterly, as the shafts sink lower and the galleries spread wider, the increase of working costs, and these cannot be cut down unless they can reduce the expensive white labour. They dare not reduce this white labour because its Parliamentary Labour Party is now in the saddle with the nationalists. The old issues of South African history are all there in new guises. But organized white labour is a new appearance and, from the native and English aspect, a deadly one.

Back at 11.30 p.m. and had a long talk with the Pim girls. They are delightful, keen and jolly, but full of good works. How splendidly tenacious is the Quaker element, how distinctive in its attitude, and how widespread its permeation!

Pretoria

December 1929

Mr. Taberer was as good as his word. A beautiful Packard with white chauffeur came after breakfast and we swept down off the Reef at fifty miles an hour and then across dullish veld and farmland, an hour's run north to the old capital of the Transvaal, now the administrative capital of the Union and so the centre of government activity when Parliament is not sitting in Capetown.

Soon after my arrival at the Residentia, a Dutch hotel, the Imperial Secretary dashed in. It is to him that the Colonial Office have entrusted me while in South Africa so it was a great blow to find that he was just off to Johannesburg and the Cape. I had relied on him to help me here as he had helped me to visit Basutoland and the Transkei. However, he was by way of being late for his train, so I could not keep him. He was much interested about my trek and spoke very highly of the A.C.

Then they rang up from Government House where the Governor-General is now in residence and Princess Alice asked if I would come up to lunch. As it was about noon I thought this a good effort in informality for Government House—and royalty, too.

I taxied out and passed the square with the huge, ornate buildings which old Kruger and the burgers built with the gold looted from the Uitlanders on the Reef. It's not a style I would choose myself but the sunset-coloured stone with which it is faced almost excuses it.

Running up and out of town, Sir Herbert Baker's Union buildings suddenly burst into view from their glorious station half way up a long steep kopje. All the way round from England I have looked forward to seeing them. Above the buildings the hill throws two rounded crests, studded with golden stone and planted with pine and cypress. They are long and low, retiring in a bold half circle in the middle, bound by an unbroken roof of red tiles, and carrying, well apart, two lofty cupolas. The substance is the stone of which I spoke, the stone of

157

which South Africa is largely made, which lies just below a skin of earth and jags out of all the hills or rises in great bastions to catch the sunset. It almost seems as though perpetual dipping in that marvellous light had dyed it the colour it is, a rosy gold. For building it is a perfect stone, soft, variegated, and the very substance of the countryside. And what a stage Africa gives an architect, with a back curtain of such constant and intense blue, such a high, wide platform, decorated with pines, cypress and silvery gums! Baker has cut the hill below into a series of terraces, with stairs, statues and gardens all patterned to lead up to the long, low pile above.

Government House is big, pure white, owing something to domestic Dutch architecture but with a classical touch to give it more grandeur. I was the only visitor, though there was a large house-party there, mostly familiar English titled names. All was done in state. We waited until the double doors were thrown open and H.E. (Earl of Athlone), Princess Alice and her daughter, Lady May Cambridge, came in. I really forget exactly who Princess Alice is, being bad at royalties, but she seems to have a slight resemblance to Queen Victoria and the Prince of Wales, though she is pretty and well dressed. I was very shabby, being just as I was from my journey, but I have (almost) got over worrying about that sort of thing. I had to sit next to H.E. at lunch. He is a tall man, with a little turned-up white moustache and rather a varnished expression. I had, of course, had talks with him in Capetown.

'So I hear you have been in Basutoland?'

'Yes, your Excellency. Do you remember Stumpy?'

'I don't understand you—stumped—'

'Stumpy—a horse. He carried you in Basutoland.'

'Ah—ha, so he did. An excellent, steady pony.'

I told him I had ridden him and he asked about my trek.

'Ah, Captain Ashton. I think he is quite remarkable. Such knowledge of the country and so pleasant and charming. And it seemed to me he had great command of the language—the native language.'

'Yes, indeed. I was deeply impressed by his ability. He was very kind to me.'

'So *he* took you into the interior. Who made up the party?'

'It wasn't exactly a party, your Excellency. There were just the two of us.'

I hoped this would not cancel out the good qualities of the A.C. in his mind, for I was trying to make up my own that he might be in for promotion. But H.E. went off on to the chiefs and said very hard things about them. I ventured to protest and even to offer my own interpretation for it will be too silly if, after indulging them all these years, the Government suddenly allow themselves to get exasperated and that is what I think I see coming. But the G.G. clearly did not like this and when I raised the question of future policy he said 'Ah, we shall see—we shall see,' meaning 'I am being discreet and shall conclude this subject.'

It may be that I am getting egotistical and like the sound of my own voice recounting my travels but it does seem rather silly to ask a person where she has been and then to deliver on each region a little speech full of very generalized information.

After lunch Lady Swaythling gave us an exhibition of her pet chameleon catching flies, rolling his eyes on his victims after the manner of Felix the cat. Then I had a long talk with Princess Alice, who delivered herself of her views on the native question. She showed me over the house and the glorious gardens and then we went to the G.G.'s study and had another talk. He delivered himself forcibly of his opinion of the South African Prime Minister. (Was I to take the indiscretion as a compliment which made up for our recent lack of contact?) H.E. was also very down on the educated native, and criticized Lovedale and Fort Hare. I realized that the views of both the Governor-General and the Princess were very conventional but I soon saw it would be silly to attempt an argument. So I heard them out and then walked off to have a close-up of the Union buildings. I really did appreciate the Athlones' kindness very much in asking me up at a moment's notice and treating me as a guest of honour. Perhaps it was silly of me to have expected so much more and to be depressed about the views held at this high level. I expect it would be dangerous politically for more liberal views to be declared at Government House. After all Athlone is governor not only of the British.

I walked away from Government House through rows of modern, pillared houses, whose rock-gardens were formed by the outcropping stone of what were bare kopjes not long ago; along roads hewn out of purple and orange rock, under avenues of young jacarandas, soon to burst into the purple blossoms for which Pretoria is famous. I had a close-up of the Union Buildings and admired the detail of woodwork and sculptured stone, court yards with cloisters supported on rosy marble pillars. It is a building that makes you catch your breath. I think it is the finest modern building I have seen, though the

Washington Railway Station, and the Lincoln Memorial are also, to me, in the first class.

Communications in Pretoria are appalling and taxis extortionate. Trams go once in half an hour and the distances are immense for the town is spread widely in its trough between the hills. The result was that I walked four miles in the afternoon heat in my best tight shoes before reaching the Union Department for Native Affairs.

I did not know whether to laugh or to cry when I saw it. It is absurd. Everyone admits the native to be *the* problem in South Africa, everyone who thinks; he is four and a half to one in numbers. But his affairs for the whole Union are housed in a makeshift office, a small, dark, dilapidated private house. The land-bank, a few doors away, is two or three times the size, and brand new. The Dutch Secretary for Native Affairs, Major Herbst, to whom I had a letter, was away, so I asked for the Under-Secretary, not knowing his name, but praying he would not be a Dutchman. He was one Allison, and very Scots, and the poor man was just leaving the office for home as it was half-past four. However, he saw me, and talked until five, and gave me the texts of five native Acts to read. He was rather nervously discreet as are all Native Affairs officials, especially English-speaking ones, under this Government.

Next day being 1 January and a public holiday—they do themselves well here—I had all day in which to digest the rather heavy stuff I had collected. The day after—another public holiday for some reason, except for government officials—I spent the morning with the Under-Secretary. Considering he did not know anything about me he was extraordinarily kind and without his patient explanations and administrative experience I never could have understood the terribly complicated machinery of the Union system. I was only sorry that my old friend, the inscrutable Mr. Barrett of the Transkei, who has just been promoted to third in the department, does not turn up until Monday. Mr. Allison is doing his work, his own, and Major Herbst's, yet he is ready to see me at any time without appointment and for as long as I like. Such kindness is quite overwhelming, all the more as I was very stupid about the laws and he had to talk to me as to a child.

In the afternoon I went down to the local Native Affairs Office for Pretoria and district and called on Mr. Hook, Native Commissioner.

He allowed me to do what I wanted, which was just to watch him at work and see what sort of contact of white and black he has to handle. In one corner of his enclosure, lying patiently on the ground, were the raw natives from the country, trying to get into the towns. They were to be examined by the doctor and turned back or sent to hospital if diseased. If admitted, they go the municipal compound, have their clothes sterilized and are bathed. There they get a six-day permit to look for work, and start on their rounds—on foot, because they are not allowed on the trams and no special trams are run for them. This must make for great hardship, as distances are great and the location far out, especially for natives who have to be in early for work. One Pretoria citizen, a woman, to whom I commented on this, said 'They can hire taxis.' I thought of the famous reply of Marie Antoinette when they told her the people had no bread. (But I believe that history has vindicated her, and that cake had a different meaning then.) It is just these small inconveniences that mount up to such a sum in the life of the native and which, in his unrepresented state, he has no hope of redressing. His treatment on the railways is very bad, and, as far as I can see, much of his life in towns is spent hanging round Pass Offices or in jail as a result of contravening the Pass and Liquor Laws, both very elaborate and hard to keep.

What was most interesting was to sit in the room while farmers brought complaints about the squatters on their farms. A tough-looking Dutchman came in sputtering about a 'boy' he had found on a farm he had just bought. He told him to clear off his land but the fellow would not budge.

'How long has he been there?'

'I dun know.'

'What was the arrangement with the last farmer.' Same answer. 'Perhaps his crops are just about to ripen.' Silence.

There are other cases, the reverse of this, where the farmer takes over the serfs with the land, as in feudal days, and compels them to remain, even against their will.

As I watched I became increasingly sorry for Mr. Hook. He was a badly paid, hard-driven official, working in a sordid office—everything to do with natives is sordid if provided by the Government—and vainly trying to hold the scales even between black and white, with little support, I expect, from the Afrikaner authorities above, much unpopularity from white employers and incomprehension from the people below, the natives.

The next day he took me out on an all-day drive to visit some native reserves. But first we went to the native location of Pretoria. The Superintendent took us round. It was certainly better than some I have seen but that is not saying much. The Superintendent, however, was very proud of the enormous improvements he claimed to have made and proudly showed us his star houses. Certainly some of these were very good. I marvelled again at the earnest way in which so many natives struggle towards European standards of decency with their clean beds, counterpanes, pillow-cases, sideboards with cloths and scissor-patterned newspaper on the shelves. We found a Chinaman with a regular factory for the brewing of beer. To brew beer is not an offence but to sell it, or for a native to be in possession of it, is an offence. So there is an assumption of official ignorance of what happens to the large output! Something is wrong either with the law or its administration. We went on into the country, across miles and miles of flat land. Huge farms, each with its huts for native squatters, lay between two running lines of kopjes. About thirty-five miles out we struck the first native lands, one of the areas where natives may buy. There are not many and the buying is not an easy operation. Members of a tribe subscribe: their finances get muddled or corrupt: the white farmer in this proclaimed area sits tight and asks two or three times what the land is worth. If the natives appeal to the Native Department they may get help on the business side but often they are too suspicious and embittered to ask help and come to grief on the rocks of loans and mortgages.

We called on one group which has added field to field with the guidance of the Native Department. Very different was the atmosphere in this place from Basutoland. The paramount chief, a dull, frog-eyed person, evidently knew his 'place', a very special one in the Transvaal. We sat on three rickety chairs in a clean yard of red clay. Two comely girl-wives hovered about us and a fine young nephew stood on one leg and smiled. The interview lasted an hour but I cannot remember anything worth recording as my companion had not much of a 'way' with natives and evidently thought most of the chief's replies were not worth translating. But something of the old native coutesy still clung to this depressed household. The chief gave me ten eggs and his wife contributed two really beautiful pots that she had made herself out of red clay and patterned black and white. The next day, upon advice, I despatched to the kraal a packet of cheap jewellery that haunts my artistic conscience. We skirted other locations. Mr. Hook talked hard. One, two, three o'clock passed without lunch, and my interest in native affairs waned. We passed the famous Hartebeeste Dam built at the cost of over £1,000,000, partly to provide labour for poor whites, partly to irrigate (white) farms in the valley.

Upon my return I called again at the Native Affairs Department with some hesitation as it was after four. It was as well I did. The Under-Secretary was waiting for me, with a batch of blue-books, and a plan to meet his wife and go out to the Country Club. She proved charming. We drove out and I had the chance to see again the glorious gardens and views that the British have out here and that makes one realize how reluctant they are to go home to the congested, cloudy little country of England.

Mr. Taberer came over from Johannesburg to see me, bringing more literature about the mines. (I shall have more excess to pay, plus excessive congestion of the brain!) He promised to show me all kinds of things if I would only come back to Johannesburg and I half agreed to break my journey and stay with him.

At night I found at my hotel table a youngish woman in pink perrls and cheap black satin who had missed her train back to Lichtenburg. She gave an appalling picture of life on the open diamond diggings there, the starvation and crime. The worst whites and the worst blacks have rushed there and are now starving together. 'The natives are *awful*,' she said. 'We've given up calling in the police: the police simply take their part, so our men keep order themselves, and if they catch a native prowling near our huts—' she broke off with a baleful look.

Early morning—eight o'clock—I boarded the 'Union' express that carries officials and politicians from Pretoria, administrative capital, to Capetown, legislative capital, one of the clumsy arrangements necessitated by provincial patriotism. For all the supplementary fare it is inevitably a sad contrast to the 'Congress Ltd.', the train which runs from New York to Washington. But I carry a letter from the General Manager of Railways. This works like magic and I always get a two-seater carriage to myself. We ran south through the dull Transvaal to the sudden monstrosity of the Reef.

At lunch, after the proper interval, and some exchange of salt and pepper, I said to the young man at my table:

'Rather uninteresting country this, isn't it ?' I referred to the immediate view. But he was a Dutchman, and, taking it as a general insult, he replied icily.

'Not to those who onderstand it.' After that there was silence.

We ran through a vast stretch of karroo, heart-breaking by day, a lake of colours in the evening. It was still light when we stopped at Kimberley and I looked out eagerly at the blue earth. This was the place which was the scene of Rhodes' first dreams and first success and out of which the money that had brought me here had come. The earth is not so blue as Rhodes' graphic biographers had led me to expect but a sort of soft slate-grey. None of the wealth in the earth has left any traces around; the whole place is grim and desolate, stuck on the karroo like a ring of mole-hills. Certainly none of the wealth has benefited the natives; their location is as tattered and tumbledown as the worst I have seen. The black miners, of course, are in closed compounds, in which they spend the whole period of their contract and only depart after keen search and a strong purgative to discover gems secreted in their stomachs.

As we passed Kimberley a man who had been hanging about the corridor came in and asked if he might talk to me. He was a big farmer in the Transvaal and had had some agricultural training in America. Drawn, of course, on the native question he said:

'I never have any trouble with my natives. I have about two hundred of them. If you are hard on natives they never give trouble. Hard and just. I don't let them get mixed up with law and the courts. I hold a court myself and give sentence. I sentence them to so much labour on the farm, without wages, and they always accept my sentences.' And so on, to generalizations that exposed ignorance of the most elementary facts. When I at last disclosed my own views his enthusiasm to make my acquaintance flagged and I made a mental note that my opinions were quite a useful defence, when needed. I have been told more than once that ten or twenty years' residence in South Africa is not enough to fit a man to understand its problems and yet the very speakers have not known how many natives there are, where and how they live, have never entered a reserve and hardly heard of Fort Hare and Lovedale. It almost seems as though the majority of South Africans have a subconscious inhibition against any real confrontation with the native problem.

It was time for sleep, so the coloured man—always coloured bedmakers—brought in my blankets and pillows, made the bed and collected the very reasonable 3s fee. Morning found us out of the karoo and approaching noble mountains, with heads of bare, tilted slate. Their lower flanks were coloured by a remarkable shrub I have never seen elsewhere, bearing withes of lacquer red on a stump of green-gold, as metallic as that gold paint we used to buy in nursery days to paint stars and crowns. We circled round these hills at a steep gradient and dropped down to the rich fruit and vine valley where lie Huguenot, Paarl and Worcester, whence come the wine and peaches, and then on across the white sand of the Cape Flats.

Second Visit to Capetown

January 1930

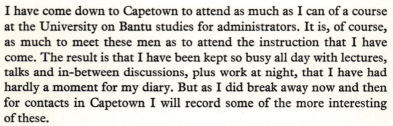

I have come down to Capetown to attend as much as I can of a course
at the University on Bantu studies for administrators. It is, of course,
as much to meet these men as to attend the instruction that I have
come. The result is that I have been kept so busy all day with lectures,
talks and in-between discussions, plus work at night, that I have had
hardly a moment for my diary. But as I did break away now and then
for contacts in Capetown I will record some of the more interesting
of these.

Almost as soon as I arrived and had settled myself again with my
same kind Capetown hosts as before, I dined with the Imperial
Secretary—splendid title!—The honourable Bede Clifford. He is very
much at the hub of imperial interests as he concentrates especially
upon the work of the Governor-General in his rather separate capacity
as the High Commissioner for the three territories directly ruled by
Britain, Basutoland, Bechuanaland and Swaziland. This is a difficult
and now, in face of Afrikaners' claims for their cession, a very sensitive
task. He also assists Lord Athlone in relation to Southern Rhodesia.
It is a position with very delicate official responsibilities and also
demands a lot of social activity.

I had better confess in the secrecy of this diary-letter that I have
succumbed to a temptation which, when I set out, I had resolved to
resist, but to which I succumbed in New Zealand over the Samoan
crisis. I have been playing politics. I had no sooner got to Capetown
than I was followed by a very urgent letter from the A.C. in Basutoland to the intent that the High Commissioner, Lord Athlone, was
proposing to coerce the Basuto chiefs into accepting a limitation of
their jurisdiction and this in defiance of the Resident Commissioner's
promise to the chiefs. What I was told was, of course, strictly confidential and it was very important, if I did enter the fray, to appear to

be innocent of having received any special communication from Basutoland. (Not easy!) I felt certain that the new policy was wrong and arose from accumulated exasperation with the conservatism of the chiefs, and perhaps the dishonesty of some of them. But a policy of abrupt and sweeping reform could undermine the whole system and destroy the confidence of the people whose independence of the Union was already being threatened from South Africa. I even questioned, presumptuously perhaps, whether these officials living in the Union really understood the situation in Basutoland and the part played by the chieftainship, imperfect though it is, in holding the endangered little state together. That the paramount chief is at present a woman does not help the situation. There seemed to me a tendency here to take too seriously the criticisms of the chiefs by a few educated Basuto which has got into the papers here and to assume that this represents a deep general discontent. I am keeping in close touch by letter with the A.C. and have decided to meet all the people most directly concerned with the issue and to put to them my views on the territory, favouring gradual reform but bringing out how deeply pledged we are to the system of indirect rule, how much the abuses of the chiefs are exaggerated and the general contentment of the people in contrast with the South African natives. I thought they might give some weight to my views following my weeks of study and travel in the territory.

A further thought that worried me was that if the chiefs were mishandled and became disorderly in their opposition this would weaken Britain's defence of their semi-independence and play into the hands of Hertzog. Even if those in authority re-acted against my intervention some of my arguments might get lodged in their minds without their source being remembered.

The five people most concerned were, of course, Lord Athlone himself (who, just to remind you, is High Commissioner for the territories as well as Governor-General), Captain Clifford as Imperial Secretary and Captain Birch-Reynardson as His Excellency's secretary. There is also Mr. Patrick Duncan who is a judge in the High Court for the three territories and also leader of the South African Party in Parliament, while Smuts is away—lecturing in Oxford!— and lastly, Shirley Eales, head of the Basutoland Department in the High Commission Office here in Capetown.

I was fortunate enough to sit next to the Imperial Secretary at table when the Athlones, now back in Capetown, invited me to dinner I found, however that he could beat me at talking and as soon as I raised the subject in an abstract, tentative kind of way he engaged me so hard that—most improperly—I never even knew who was sitting on my other side. But I managed to get across enough of my views to excite his interest and after dinner he took me into a corner and we went at it until midnight when the Earl and the Princess brought the party to an end. Clifford is a thin, worn, nervy, highly intelligent man, rather cynical about native affairs, professing the utmost disillusionment, almost indifference, about the results of all we are doing now in the three territories. He has a glorious American wife and a very self-important mother-in-law who utters at intervals the most reactionary remarks about native affairs without correction from him.

Providence has favoured me with opportunities for my plans. Two days later Princess Alice asked me again to lunch at Government House to meet the Resident Commissioner of Bechuanaland so that I could arrange for a visit to his Protectorate which, of course, would also be affected by any change of policy. Captain Clifford was there again and he told me that Captain Birch-Reynardson had asked if he might sit next to me. So I found myself between Lord Athlone and his secretary.

The Governor-General and I picked up Basutoland where we had left it in Pretoria and I used all the eloquence I possess to put my views without awakening his suspicions—so I hope—that I knew all about the designs he and his advisers were developing against the chieftainship. He was much more patient this time in allowing me to disagree with him than he had been in Pretoria and even in the end admitted that there might be some truth in what I was saying. Concentrating on Athlone I had no chance of speaking to Birch-Reynardson but we arranged to meet some other time.

Afterwards I talked to the Resident-Commissioner of Bechuanaland, a rather taciturn, elderly man who, I afterwards learned, is reputed to allow Captain Clifford to run his immense dry Protectorate from Capetown. However he was very kind to me and promised to make all arrangements for my visit. I do hope I shall be able to get there.

Today Captain Birch-Reynardson called and took me out for a long drive in his car. I find him one of the most intelligent men I have met since I left home and, of course, as Lord Athlone's secretary, he is a key figure both in helping and in educating me. I had to hurry back to lunch with Mr. Patrick Duncan at the Parliament House where a new session is just beginning. Here is another of those extra-ordinary characters who, after the Boer War, were drawn from cool England into the fierce heat of South African politics and administration. He is one of Lord Milner's so-called kindergarten, Oxford and Balliol, a Scot and a distinguished classical scholar and writer, a student of Aristotle. From Oxford he went on to study law, entered Parliament here as a follower of Smuts, and became Minister for Health and Education, but of course lost office when the Nationalists took over in 1921.[1]

The idea was for us to talk about the position of the chiefs in the three Protectorates and he had invited the Resident Commissioner of Swaziland to make a third at lunch. So now I have met all three of the Protectorate Commissioners. I must confess that I did not have much success with Duncan. In fact we disagreed completely. As a lawyer he has no indulgence for the laxities of the chiefs. He can get no further than his instinctive horror at the vices which he sees inherent in the system, or rather lack of system. However, he did me the honour of putting all his cards on the table, all but the one which I knew he held about the current proposals for Basutoland.

I thought what poles apart his views were from those of our West African authorities, and notably, Sir Donald Cameron, and I speculated what it may mean for Africa in the future that the continent is being directed along such different and, indeed, opposing lines. How it will all end I do not know. The A.C. is fighting tooth and nail the ordinance which is proposed and doing all he can to push on with his form of indirect rule, pressing the chiefs to reform themselves from within. It is not reform that is mistaken but the speed and the spirit in which the High Commissioner's office is pushing reform and their tendency to over-rule the British officials on the spot. Unfortunately I shall shortly be leaving Capetown and, travelling around, I shall be out of touch with Basutoland's affairs for a month or more.

Sir William Solomon arranged a little luncheon party for me at a Muizenburg hotel. To meet me he asked the Chief Justice, Sir James Rose-Innes, and the Archbishop of Capetown. We had a most interesting talk but a very gloomy one. They are all Cape diehards who

---

[1] He returned to ministerial power with Smuts in 1933. In spite of strong liberal views he voted for Hertzog's abolition of the Cape native franchise. He became Governor-General of South Africa from 1937 to 1943, when he died. In his speech after Duncan's death Smuts said of him that 'if not a popular leader, he had in him the stuff which leads the leaders.'

in native affairs stand for the Cape Franchise based on the policy of identity against that of differentiation. But they were all sad and grave about present developments and the threat which the Afrikaner Government holds over the future.

I have also been seeing a good deal of Mr. B. K. Long, the editor of the *Cape Times*. He is reputed to be, and seems to me, to be one of the most intelligent men in South Africa. But can the editor of the leading newspaper be a wholly free agent? In fact he has abandoned defence of the Cape Native Franchise. He wanted me to write for him not only on Samoa but on the Basutoland issue. I have drafted the latter article but I do not dare to have it published as I fear that it might get the A.C. into trouble as all the powers-that-be here know that I worked and trekked with him and might think I was merely reflecting his views. Indeed, I greatly fear that his opposition to the new ordinance which is planned will not do much good to his career.

I lunched today with Mr. Houston Boswell who, like my friend Philip Nichols in Wellington, is one of the new bright Foreign Office representatives in the Dominions. And, like all these F.O. people, very clever and interesting to meet. But there was nearly a scene with the party at the luncheon table when I confessed to my friendship with Ballinger who, they asserted, was in Russian pay! Wherever I go I make a point of defending this brave man who I find is regarded as a sort of monster, a renegade to his country and his colour.

In this connection I have managed to persuade the conference which—on and off!—I am attending at the University to invite Ballinger to an after-dinner discussion. This, though composed mainly of officials, produced a most interesting exchange during which all hostility towards him faded away and many of the participants confessed to me afterwards that a man like Ballinger was a boon to the country. His honesty, moderation and good temper impressed them all and especially his unique knowledge of the urban native.

I met Ballinger again for a talk. We sat for two hours on a seat in some public gardens, it being difficult to find a *locus* for such a meeting. We were watched all the time by no less than three detectives. The same day they had stolen his bag, full of papers, from the railway cloakroom. I assumed that my meetings with him are all reported to

Major Herbst, Afrikaner head of the Native Affairs Department. Ballinger told me something of his privations and the times when he hardly had enough to eat. He has indeed had a grim time between the natives and the authorities, a lonely time, too, which only a man of his exceptional courage and resolution could have endured.

Today at the last possible moment I managed to get a ticket from Government House for the opening of Parliament and, dressed in my best, went down to the Parliament House. It was quite a dramatic show. Sailors and soldiers of the South African Defence Force lined the approaches. Inside, the Senate Chamber was packed. It was easy at a glance to distinguish the Dutch women, wives of the Nationalists who are now at last in power and so able to take the chief place at these imperial public functions. Mostly big, fat, red, hard women, they were bursting out of their party clothes and tight gloves. Their true dignity would be on the farm. They were waving and nodding to their husbands who marched in to hear the speech from the throne, farmers and lawyers from the Free State and Transvaal, big, lean, stringy men, some with shrewd but none with intellectual faces. One or two looked almost sub-normal. Or was it only to my prejudiced eyes! It was easy to pick out the Britons, mostly well dressed and gloomy.

The Governor-General and his wife looked magnificent. They came up the steps through a guard of blue-jackets. ('Why,' asked the Nationalist Press the next day, 'is the opening of Parliament attended by sailors belonging to a friendly but foreign power?') Princess Alice, all in hydrangea blue, smiled, but rather wanly. I could hardly recognize my friends, the members of the staff, sweltering and alert in epaulettes, scarlet, pipeclay and the rest.

The Governor-General read the speech well in English. Some of the Dutch M.P.s talked all through this. Then it was read in Afrikaans and they listened. The two interesting points were the appointment of Ministers Plenipotentiary to various countries—an expensive form of self-expression for young nationalism. Then, ominously, came the announcement of a joint sitting to deal with the native question. For Hertzog's anti-native bills have now reached parliamentary maturity. Racially, South Africa is now set on the downward path.

'God save the King' naturally aroused little response among one section of the audience, who, incidentally, are demanding a national anthem of their own. But it is even more difficult to manufacture a bi-national anthem than a flag. It needed very little imagination to recognize the atmosphere—the ceremony with all its British tradition and imperial pomp, and the men in power, still having to go through the ritual, some with indifference, some with contempt, some no doubt with active hatred.

As I watched I asked myself again. 'Did British liberalism misfire over the Dutch?' After the Boer War we gave everything, even the chance to lose power. Now the Boers have taken it and the British, and still more, the natives, are paying. It was only in a rush of typically British sentimentalism that we could have hoped that the Dutch would forgive and forget. They have been biding their time. Now it has come and the British, and the natives right through the Union, in a hundred ways, big and small, will be made to feel it. Perhaps, however, it is darkest before dawn. Expressed may be less dangerous than suppressed hostility, coupled, as it now is, with what we may hope will prove the sobering responsibility of power. (While I write these words as if they were a psychological necessity, I doubt their validity.)

A long morning's shopping in Capetown which left me impressed anew with the inefficiency prevalent in this country. Complaints about my camera were received with ignorance and hostility. Dresses altered were all wrong. The telephone system is the worst in the world. Hairdressers are expensive and bad. The wretch who did my hair said she thought it was a crime the way they were educating the natives. 'What do natives want with education? They get far too many privileges as it is. It makes you sick when you get on to a bus and a native sits next to you dressed as you are yourself.' (This custom is a relic of Cape liberalism. For how long?)

In the afternoon Sir William Solomon, who has just resigned the Chief Justiceship of South Africa, came to see me. Such a modest, simple man, one of the old Cape stalwarts, ready to die in the last ditch for the Cape Franchise, but recognizing it now as a lost cause. He was educated among natives at Lovedale. Quite a number of the most prominent and liberal men of his generation were at school there and are playing a great part in native questions. Such co-education has been prohibited now, unfortunately.

My friend, Captain Birch-Reynardson, the Imperial Secretary, came up at 5 p.m. in his splendid car and took me for a long drive.

We went to call on the Prime Minister first to write my name in his book. So I saw, for the first time, close-up, the lovely and historic house, Groote Schuur. There was only time for a glimpse but I got the impression of the simple fantasy of the Dutch gables. Certainly the Dutch gave something to the world in this unique style of domestic architecture which combines elegance, dignity and homeliness.

Afterwards we drove on to the famous old vineyard of Groote Constantia. This alone is almost worth a visit to South Africa. At the first glance the mind registers 'perfection'. Its backcloth is made of the lofty heights of the Table range; around it are the young vines; it is flanked by rows of old oak trees that catch the golden light and sprinkle it softly over paths and walls. The steep old thatch looks soft as grey fur. Solid teak doors and windows are flush with the wall in eighteenth-century fashion and the strange angles and curves of the gables are carried out with a sure touch with their white plaster cut clear against the brilliant sky. The great barn at the back is surmounted by a fresco of astonishing beauty. It is in deep relief work, and represents naked children gambolling among the vines. 1791 it is dated and it is a bold, clean piece of work of that period. Here and there a child's active limb pushes right out of the stonework and on the central panel a man is sitting upon a swooping eagle, caught in a swerve of its flight. I must try to get a picture of it. A work of art like that in this fine but raw country is water in the desert.

Meanwhile my companion was pouring information and state secrets into my ear and I learned something of the trials of being an English Governor-General in a restive dominion. The troubles of the Stonehavens, with whom I stayed in Australia, are as nothing to those of the Athlones though even in this intimate diary I don't like to write of them. The Imperial Secretary—you can see how this provocative title attracts me!—is in a unique position to judge this country for he must see everyone and know everything and act as eyes, ears and, perhaps, brain to the Governor-General. This man is very intelligent: he stands out as one of the four or five most intelligent men I have met since I began this tour in America. Perhaps it is simply that some minds are the complement of one's own, a kind of intellectual mating takes place and living and helpful ideas are born of it. It certainly is encouraging when I hold my conclusions up to such expert judgement to find that he is in general agreement with me. I wish I could see more of him but both his wife and the Prince of Wales arrive tomorrow in the *Kenilworth Castle*. He is in charge of the

Prince for ten days and he anticipates golf and picnics and being perpetually on duty.[1]

I wish I could do justice to these last few days but the trouble with these crowded periods is that there is hardly time or strength left to record them.

This day, 28 January, is my last day in Capetown, so I have had to get up very early to pack and write letters. Then I went off to the town where I had several interviews. One was with the Dutch Major Herbst, who has got quite cordial. It is difficult to make him out. He has a cherubic smile. He smiles and smiles at everything but it is hard to say if he is a villain or not. His English accent is bad but it is not that that makes you know you are with a foreigner. He is cautious. I cannot draw him. All darts are turned by his smile. When, for instance, I spoke of the infant mortality in the Rand towns, he smiled and spoke of the hordes of black children who spill out of every hovel and whether his smile was that of one who dotes on little black children or the grin of a potential Herod, I really don't know. He smiled when I told him of Basutoland. But he made very uncomplimentary remarks about my Basuto as labour: surly, it seems they are, and indisciplined. He even smiled as he spoke of the Jameson Raid about which he came to London to give evidence. Well, perhaps, one day I shall know, for he accepted (smiling) my invitation to Oxford and to my college when he comes to England next autumn and I trust my Principal, Miss Gwyer, to get to the back of any smile, even an Afrikaner's.

I had plenty of Dutchmen that morning but of another generation. It will hardly be credited that there exists in the Union only one set of fully accurate maps showing native areas and the meagre fragments now being released for native purchase. These maps are owned by the Native Affairs Department and are battered with much transit between Pretoria and Capetown and much thumbing by official Committees on Native Affairs. They are large, amateurish and inaccurate. I got permission to photograph them. Where, in what light, and with what exposure and focus were questions that soon collected the entire staff of the entire Native Administration Department out of their offices.

---

[1] I lost touch with him after this journey. In 1972 we suddenly decided to meet again and arranged a dinner party *à deux*. He said he must make a quick trip to South Africa to see it once again. So we fixed a date to follow this. Alas! he died while in South Africa.

(Men love to give technical advice to stupid women.) The Minister was away at a Cabinet meeting; the Secretary, Herbst, attending him. The Minister's private secretary, fair, red, and very Dutch, was the moving spirit. In the end we got the largest map out into the yard. A native boy, one Julius, climbed out of an upper window and, leaning perilously down, held the top; the Under-Secretary lay flat on his back in the yard and held it from below to prevent the wind blowing it: all the others yelled advice in Dutch and Dutch-English from windows and doorways. As the maps went up there were appropriate comments. The Orange Free State, which forbids natives to hold land, was nearly all white.

'Now Julius, hold up the Free State. Ah! this is the prize map. Don't smile, Julius, or it will be taken as evidence on the photograph that native opinion is satisfied with the allocation of land in the Free State.' A dour joke!

Suddenly Major Herbst appeared, looking for his lost secretary, and there was an embarrassed silence. But, once more, he only smiled. I backed out with many thanks and apologies.

'Not a bit. We like it. Come again.' I felt that the first step in a much-needed *entente* had been made. Or had it?

General Hertzog had promised to have a talk but as no message had come I had to give that up and go to Government House to make my official farewell. As I had the use of the Cartwrights' huge limousine I was able to do this in style and really felt very sorry that I should not see that sweet and lovely Princess Alice again.

Then to the Imperial Secretary, to Cooks, the bank, the railways, the *Cape Times*. Then I went to the Law Courts where Sir James Rose-Innes had arranged to have me taken round the various courts. In these I could see again how the machine of civilization catches the uncivilized. This was much worse than the court I had visited in Johannesburg for here they were in a tremendous hurry. Even I, sitting in front and understanding English, could not follow what was happening—mumble—bark—nod—gesture—a sort of secret rite. What of the poor, round-eyed Africans in the dock, with a weary interpreter whispering as much as he could catch—or bother with?

Here is a native prostitute, hair hideously frizzed, the signs of degradation visible even to our eyes which too often tend to see degradation on all African faces. A pasty Dutch policeman gives evidence of having arrested her for shouting obscene language at night in the main street. In his blurred English he explains how she kicked and fought him and brought out a razor with which she cut herself in her frenzy. The girl, who has enough shame to drag her coat collar half round her face, stares out above it with angry, frightened eyes. The policeman says she was not drunk. This rouses her. She cries out that she *was* drunk, as if it were a defence, and insists on having her companion, already in the cells, dragged out in order, seemingly, to say that she was drunk.

'Two months hard labour. Next!'

The next man's record of crime is so long that it takes nearly twenty minutes to read it. It would have been as quick to read the periods out of jail. He is a hardened criminal, helpless and hopeless. He pleads for a chance. He *will* work this time. The police laugh aloud: the magistrate is sarcastic.

'Six months hard labour, with a period of solitary confinement on reduced diet.'

The public prosecutor, next to me, whispers explanations in my ear. 'No, we have no Pass Laws yet in the Cape. I come from the Transvaal where we have them. They ought to be introduced here. They come in so handy. You can run them in for that when you can't run them in for anything else.'

I would not like to give a false impression here. Speaking generally I think—though this is not saying much—that the native gets a better deal in the law courts than elsewhere. (Perhaps this is rather a guess.) As far as English legal influence comes in (for South Africa is under Roman-Dutch law) the scrupulous treatment of the accused is in some measure extended to the native. But—and there are big exceptions—not the most patient judges and lawyers can cross the distance between their culture and that of the native and make him understand what they are doing with him. Nor, where language is a barrier, can interpretation really meet the case, as anyone who watches natives in the courts can see. There are other exceptions. The native commits, inevitably, a large number of technical offences which, if his skin were not black, would be civil and not criminal, or would not be offences at all. These are mostly offences under the Pass, and Masters and Servants, Acts, and I believe that seven-tenths of the natives in gaol at any one time are there for these technical faults. Prison is not for the native the disgrace it is for the white man but the people who say that he *likes* to go there because he is well-fed say that sort of thing to please themselves. It is one of a series of sayings that are used, unthinkingly no doubt, to blunt the edge of the social conscience with regard to natives. And the fact is that these boys (for they early fall victims to the many regulations under these Acts) consort in the prisons with real criminals who corrupt them in more ways than one and very often form criminal gangs to work together when they come out. They do worse than that. In their unnatural prison life, barbarism has full play. I have read an account by a magistrate in Johannesburg of how secret trials are held, and prisoners who will not fall in with the wishes of the 'judges' are condemned to torture. Here is one magistrate's story, told to me:

'I had a very fine Shangaan[1] messenger who disappeared one week-end and my efforts to trace him were unavailing. After three months he came back to the office and burst into tears, telling me that he had been imprisoned for two months for an alleged theft of some petty kind. He described revolting scenes in the prison of Johannesburg, the torture that was inflicted, the "trials" held by prisoners' organizations that had formed there and which later manifest themselves in those murder gangs which terrorize the native quarters of the Rand and other parts of the Union.'

The native, except perhaps in the High Court, certainly does not get equal justice with the white man. He is punished much more heavily for the same offences and in any case in which a white woman is concerned, anything may happen. This is especially true of the magistrates' courts. When it comes to murder, as in parts of America, the jury system becomes a danger. The murderer of the white man gets the rope every time; the murderer of the black man is unlucky if he gets a few years. The white jury does not trust the judge and so is more likely to acquit completely a white man. This occurred in a terrible case of the murder of a child a few years ago. The natives assure me with what truth I know not, that especially on farms and in rural areas there are many murders of natives that never come to light.

I have just read about an almost incredible case in which a white servant—there are not many of these—accused a black cook of hitting her because she threw the skin of a fish she was cutting up all over the floor for him to pick up. The prosecutor appealed for lashes as well as the hardest possible sentence—for the native of course!—on the grounds that he was a member of a subject race.

[1] From Portuguese territory.

Zululand

My time in South Africa will soon be running out. But it was obvious that I must take a look however brief, at the great and tragic Zulu people, the defeated warrior tribe, both in their scattered reserves and as 'labour' in the port of Durban.

So I have come from Capetown to Maritzburg, the capital of Natal. It has taken two days and three nights to get here from Capetown and once again I had to endure crawling round the north of beloved Basutoland and looking again at the marvellous panorama of those so well-remembered mountains and passing the junction for Maseru.

So, arriving in unknown Maritzburg at 5 a.m., I was not very joyful. However I found that Major Herbst had kept his word and I was expected. A certain Mr. Malcolm, an official with knowledge of Zululand, is to take me round that historic region and after that I am to have a look at Zulus in the port of Durban, my point of arrival in South Africa. Details had been arranged by the Chief Native Commissioner for Natal.

First I learned what I could in Maritzburg.

It is sad to find so many of the officials in the Native Department deeply frustrated by the policies of the Hertzog Government. Nearly all the officials I have so far met, except for a very few Afrikaners now at the top, are 'British' and had spent most of their lives working in a reasonably liberal atmosphere within the limits of racial division. But now, as Hertzog's Afrikaner Government fastens its grip, the whole spirit informing the native administration is changing.

The Chief Native Commissioner for Natal began by showing me housing for natives. The Superintendent of Native Locations motored me all over the town, showing me the best and the worst of the conditions there. The best were delightful little cottages he had just built, the best I had seen in the whole of South Africa, 17s 6d a month as against 25s in most places. They had electric light and tiny gardens which the Zulu inhabitants have cultivated delightfully. We went in to many of them and I was again amazed at the order and cleanliness inside. The rapidity with which, given a chance, the native adapts himself to a self-respecting urban existence is most impressive. I do not think that the argument used in Britain that it is no use building decent houses for slum dwellers for they will ruin them need be used in Africa. (It is certainly invalid for Britain, too.) Of course there is supervision, but supervision never made those gardens or the curtains, or the crochet, hand-done, on the pillow-cases; nor did it paint tins for flower-pots and vases, nor the simple coloured frescoes decorating the walls.

I went to the Native Affairs Department and met the Chief Native Commissioner for Natal. He provided me with numerous maps and documents and cursed heartily the policy of stagnation which had long held Zululand back.

Mr. Malcolm today arrived from Pietermaritzburg in his car and I got aboard. We left Durban in hot mist and rain and went through the hinterland of the city, over which the Indians have spread their sordid tin huts and messy-looking but, I believe, quite effective bits of farming. As in Fiji, these ex-indentured labourers flourish, and strike as strange a note among the Zulus as among the Fijians. The little, finely made, parchment-coloured old men sit in their doorways and the women, unveiled here, flash their crowded bangles and cerise saris in the sunlight.

As soon as you leave Durban you run into fields of sugar-cane running up and down the low rolling hills, the lissom, pale flags thrashing today in a high wind. But sugar palls, mile after mile of it, with here and there one of the dirty, ramshackle crushing mills that I remembered from Fiji, the hideous compounds for the labourers and the Indian villages at intervals. A bit of interest was imparted when we ran into some native-owned sugar plantations—all too few—and I learned that they were making a great success of them and banking large sums.

We drove without stopping from lunch until half past seven. The country grew a little wilder but even after we passed the Tugela river and were in Zululand proper we found white farms piercing the native reserve, which is made up of the now scattered bits and pieces of the old Zulu kingdom. The native parts were easily recognizable by their patches of measly crops and gaunt scrub cattle. After the round or square stone or mud huts of the Basuto the Zulu house is a very different affair, a beehive hut of grass, windowless and with a tiny door to be entered crawling. The Zulu is, however, far handsomer and more courtly in his bearing than the Mosuto. His salute is that of the Roman, hand and arm lifted above the head. He seems much more primitive: a sure sign of this was that even in this mixed area, the women are half naked, as are many of the young men.

Tonight we reached Eshowe which, in the days when Zululand was run as a unit, was the administrative headquarters but is now only the biggest village and the centre of a magistracy.

Up early and prepared a questionnaire for the local magistrate, and then went down to the Court at 9 a.m. He is the son of the man who did so much to make the success of the Transkei administration. He was most contemptuous of the contrast presented by Zululand, its stagnation and conservatism and the unprogressive attitude of the other magistrates. He at once tried to get at me to do some of his propaganda work, which he cannot do himself, in the South African Press. In fact he was raging at what he called the crime committed against the Zulu people. But all this was too dangerous for me. I have already done much to compromise my status as an impartial academic inquirer in getting mixed up with the high politics of Basutoland and then associating with Ballinger. In any case I can have no hope in this brief tour of getting anywhere near the bottom of Zulu politics or administration with their long and complex historical background. However, I hope I can learn and record something to interest readers of this diary-letter.

We got away at eleven and drove hard to the next district, Melmoth, where we caught the magistrate in his office at twenty to one, surrounded by five Zulu policemen. In complete contrast with the last man, he proved a real diehard of the peculiar Natal type. Here is the attitude as I should interpret it; 'We know the Zulu and no one else does. He is a fine, unspoiled creature in his natural state, very courtly and respectful to us, and we mean to keep him so. Therefore we shall not educate him nor shall we introduce this new-fangled system of native councils. As for the Zulu in the town, we will assume that he is there only on short leave from the kraal and that therefore he neither needs much pay nor need we regard him as a problem. If the agitators get to work among him and a few of the bad lots make a row, then strong measures will soon bring them to order. So out here in his own country' (the greater part of which has been filched from him!) 'we shall preserve the authority of the chief and the good old native laws and customs and thus live happily ever after. Damn those interfering men transferred from the Transkei to teach us our business. They don't know the Zulu and we do.'

That was his case, and in every second word he gave it away—the prevalence of witchcraft, the difficulty of enforcing cattle-dipping, the low standard of agriculture, etc. It was a picture of stagnation which left me contrasting the relative progress in Basutoland, where political conditions are somewhat the same—indirect rule and isolation. How much depends upon the traditions and character of the men in charge!

We asked our man to lunch and got more of his philosophy. It was useless even to argue with him. I went out after and inspected a store, always a revealing piece of evidence, with a suspicious little Jew shuffling after me. I saw that the plough demanded by the Zulu was cheaper and poorer than elsewhere and that the goods generally were limited in range and inferior in quality. But the Zulu still fancies himself as a military man and coats of martial cut, and even imitation officers' uniforms, are sold to him.

We took to the road at 2.30 p.m. and set out to call on a man who had been Chief Commissioner for Natal up to the South African Union. Inevitably diehard, he was a fine-looking, asthmatic, red-eyed old gentleman who rumbled on against the Dutch and, in native affairs, inveighed against any attempt to touch the established order. Wait another two or three generations, he said. And, of course, *he*, if any man, 'Knows the Zulu'. But wait what for? They have waited in Natal since the sixties. The love for the Zulu of men like this is the sort of love that kills. Lady X, his wife, quite a woman of the world, represented in shriller form and from a woman's point of view, the cherished Englishness of Natal. She was all denunciation of the Dutch, all talk of how in the days of the flag controversy she had covered the car with Union Jacks, and she rejoiced to record that 5,000 young Britons in Durban had prepared themselves for war. It was all the talk of a generation that has gone but is here preserved in an isolated corner of isolated Natal. I did not argue. Working and travelling at this rate, one is economical of argument and quick to know when it will be wasted.

We extricated ourselves at 5.30 p.m. The best thing we had got out of it was a glimpse of some of Alfred Palmer's remarkable Zulu paintings. (Palmer was the man I saw in Johannesburg who had so much impressed me. He, at least, understood the Zulu!)

Now we passed rapidly into wild, lonely country, sixty miles of it. Huge vistas of hills rolling up into mountains—not the sharp table mountains and pyramid-kopjes of so much of South Africa but shapes that are seen in other continents, rounded, crumpled heights. And trees! A miracle in South Africa, not only, everywhere, a spotting of thorn scrub, of euphorbia and *cactus ferox* in stiff spikes, but in each fold and even beside each stream, real trees, including the lovely ilala palm. We pushed our car through wide, shallow rivers and went through rich, deep, thorn-shaded veld. So wild in this country that koodoo and water-buck live here, though we did not see any. We passed the spot where Dingaan treacherously slew Piet Retief and his forty men in the vain hope of saving his land and his freedom.

The Zulu kraal is circular, with cattle in a stockade in the middle. Round each kraal you see the veld patched with the miserable, untidy bits of cultivation which is all this tribe seems capable of. In these two pictures that I took you can see clearly the layout of the kraal. In one you may get some idea of the glorious, rolling, spaciousness of Zululand, with trees like darker shadows in the crumples of the hills, every range a different blue. Below you see the beehive hut at close quarters. What a poor thing it is compared with other tribes' housing! I flatter myself that the middle picture is a good photograph. You can even see the cattle in the kraal.

We passed the battlefield of Ulundi and saw still standing the lone tree round which the British in July 1879 made their square and this time beat off the Zulu warriors, where Cetewayo, from a bare hill above, saw the power of his nation broken at last and fled in despair. But on the battlefield, pierced by many assegais, lay the body of France's young Prince Imperial who had insisted in joining the campaign.

It was icy cold and not even a glorious sunset over an immense basin among the mountains, with every range swimming in violet light, could make me sorry to see little Nongowa sitting on top of a high hill and to find a great log fire in the tiny hotel. I am half asleep as I write. Tomorrow we visit the chief's school, the main object of the tour, and meet the local magistrate.

We drove out early this morning through the dozen houses that make up Nongowa—the labour recruiter's, the veterinary officer's, the agricultural demonstrator's, the magistrate's clerks', etc., until we reached the Court House. I should guess there is a similarity about district commissioner's or magistrate's offices all over the Empire— a long, low building, with the doors of the different officials opening on to a verandah; the tree under whose shade crouch the suitors and hangers-on, mumbling all day to each other about their litigation; the native police, arrogant in their uniforms, lounging about the verandah pillars; the prisoners working on the grass and paths; the flag post; the tattered notice-board. Inside, the official, a little cross and thirsty, sits at his littered, dusty desk, and wrestles with forms and registers and licenses when he should be away out in his district, sitting under a tree and listening to the old men talking themselves out and so forging links of sympathy between black men and white rulers.

This man was born in Germany and is approaching retiring age, an unkempt, insignificant man to look at but from whom a few faint sparks of humour and interest could be struck. All his work had been with the Zulus. I gently suggested criticisms of stagnation and neglect against the administration. He smiled wearily. 'The Zulu has only one answer,' he said, when you suggest reforms to him. 'Who complains?' His favourite proverb is to be translated 'Tomorrow is also a day.' Progress and reform! 'Why? Why?' he asks. 'And have we any answer? For what future can Africans strive in this country?'

Being unable in my ignorance to question this well-informed fatalism, I asked leave to inspect his records of court cases. I examined his register and found, to my surprise, that the chiefs still recorded cases of witchcraft. But the majority of their litigation arose out of the custom of paying 'lobola', the cattle price for wives. I cannot here write down all the results of my inquiry at the office but they convinced me that there was very little control of the chiefs' jurisdiction and that South Africans had better attend to Zululand before criticizing the Imperial Government in Basutoland. (By the way, I have just seen a report of the Dominions Committees on inter-Imperial matters which modifies the King's veto. Suppose the Union Government advise the King of South Africa to hand over Basutoland and the British Ministry advise their King to refuse the cession?)

After about two and a half hours I left the magistracy and took a photograph of it before boarding the car. The people in the foreground fled as soon as they saw the evil eye in the black box but the police soon dragged them back and forced them to keep still. But it was significant of the wildness and shyness of these people.

We now went on to the school for sons of chiefs, and reached it just before lunch.

This school was begun ten years ago. About that time, Solomon, the son of the Zulu king Cetewayo, was allowed to go back among his people. The Government, however, refused to recognize him as paramount chief as they still dreaded a recrudescence of the prestige of his formidable militarist dynasty which over the years had cost Britain millions of pounds and hundreds of lives. But to the people he *was* paramount chief. It was thought that, under these difficult circumstances, something should be done to keep him quiet, and it was suggested that an agent, half-official, half-missionary, should be attached to his kraal, to be a kind of court chaplain and to run a school for the royal sons. As Solomon had set to work to build up a set of about thirty wives there was no doubt the school would be well supplied. The man chosen, an Anglican parson, Oscroft by name, advised, however, that it would be better to have a school for sons of all chiefs and to establish it near the royal kraal. This was agreed and that is why the school is in such a remote place.

Mr. Oscroft had plunged into his task with no precedents, no experience and very little money. He worked under suspicious Native Affairs officials who were half afraid of what they had let themselves in for and who, though they did not know how to handle education, yet refused to lose their grasp of the school and to allow the Native Education Department to control it.

Mr. Oscroft had as many obstacles on the other side. The chiefs did not want the school. They are almost entirely illiterate and very conservative about their few lingering powers and suspicious of all change. He began with two pupils the first year and four in the second. They were not boys but men, uncles of Solomon, big, stupid, illiterate men, with wives and affairs to distract their attention. With these he must start to build his school, literally build it. So he worked as foreman and put up his own house, the schoolhouse and the school-room. He made a road to the school and when a native saw the son of Cetewayo labouring on it he cried out to heaven to witness the downfall of the race. But I cannot recount all the history. There are now sixty sons of chiefs in the school, drawn from all over Natal and Zulu-land and they are between the ages of fourteen and twenty-five.

I went in to see them at their classes, taught by three native teachers. Geography and arithmetic were in progress but I wanted to try to test their general intelligence and outlook as far as one can without knowing their language, and allowing for all the devious ways by which truth gets lost on its way out of their minds into English words. So Mr. Oscroft called the whole school together, sixty black, shining faces with alert but suspicious eyes. Some were very fine looking, almost beautiful, ranging to types which we find repulsive. Most were sons of chiefs, some were commoners sent to attend their chiefs.

I started a kind of debate with the boys in order to find out what their attitude was in the points that matter most for chiefs. Here are some of my questions and some of their answers.

Q. What do you think should be the penalty for witchcraft? (I knew if I asked them if they believed in witchcraft they would think I wanted them to say no.) I got three answers.

1. Prison. *2.* The witch should be chased out of the tribe. *3.* All witches should be killed. They should be hung up in trees until they are dead. (Some applause greeted this last.)

Q. What is a chief's most important duty to his people? This produced a great variety of answers which were mostly conventional. It was too difficult to get them to grade duties in order of importance, so I gave that up.

Q. Ought native law and custom to be changed, or is it still good for the people? This, too, was misunderstood, and the only answers to be got were attacks on Union native law, especially the Pass Laws.

Q. Is the country overstocked with cattle? (I do not know if I have at any time made it clear that this is the curse of natives' territory. They increase their cattle until the country is exhausted and the cattle are so miserable that they are worthless. They count wealth in quantity of cattle, not quality, especially as they buy wives with cattle. I might also add that until the government introduced dipping, the cattle were intermittently swept off by disease. Now they have doubled in ten years.)

1. No, we have no cattle left and not enough land. *2.* The Government kill our cattle by dipping them. *3.* All the grass is going because the dip on the cattle burns out the grass.

Q. Would you rather have ten small beasts or five big ones that produce good milk. The vote was universally for the ten even when the difference was further explained.

In the afternoon Mr. Oscroft took me for a long walk and we visited the kraals around and went into them and talked to the people. The Zulu hut is a beehive with a round roof of straw to the ground, and a tiny little entrance made small with the object of security. It is a sign of their conservatism that they keep huts like these long after there is any need for security. It would be difficult to imagine any entry more difficult and undignified than crawling on your hands and knees into a Zulu hut. I show a picture to indicate this and also to illustrate the beauty that some of the women have. (The picture was taken by an R.C. missionary.)

The inside of the Zulu huts was dark and rather unsavoury. Straps of buckskin supported assegais and knob-kerries: long beaded strands and baldrics of cats' tails, which they wear for ceremony, hung on the wall. Civilization was scantily represented in most by a bit of tinware and a second-hand army tunic or shirt. The roof was black with smoke and the floor littered with crumpled calfskins. One of the strangest things to me about these Africans is the way in which Christian and heathen live side by side in apparent amity. For the difference here is not one between two theological ideas but between two ways of life and even two modes of dress. You may remember I noticed this in the Transkei. But here in the same kraal you see the Christian woman in her long print petticoat and bodice and her tur-banned head and also the heathen in skins, and beads, with her hair drawn up into a shape that suggests that there may be something in the Egyptian origin of these people. The man who owned this hut had been for five years a rickshaw-puller at Durban but he had relapsed so completely into tribal life that we knew this only from the tin-plate number nailed to the pillar of his house. But then rickshaw-pulling cannot be a very educative profession. On top of this house was the witch-doctor's little erection of teeth and sticks to charm away the lightning.

We saw the kraal of the dethroned paramount chief, Solomon Dinizulu, a semi-European house on a high hill. Unfortunately he was not there or Mr. Oscroft, who is a sort of unofficial agent supposed to watch the unfortunate man, would have taken me there. But he told me a great deal about him and his efforts, within the many limitations set about him by the Union Government, to build up some semblance of the old Zulu nationalism. He now holds yearly meetings at his kraal of representatives from all over Natal and Zululand. Mr. Oscroft goes and spies upon the meeting for the Government and he showed me his confidential reports. It seems that the Government cannot altogether conquer its fear of a recrudescence of Zulu militancy. Fear of the Zulu sank deep into the mind alike of both British Natalian and Boer, so great was the military power and aggressiveness of the Zulu kingdom against black and white alike. But Dinizulu's annual meeting is at present a tame affair. The representatives pay £5 for the privilege of coming. This goes into the Zulu National Fund and such is their faith in their chief that no one has ever asked what becomes of it. Solomon does what he likes with it as he does with the fines from his court. He probably makes several thousands a year.

They all loathe the Dutch like poison. In the nineties, when there was a division within the reigning family, Botha and some other young men offered to help one section against the other in return for some land. The Zulu story is that when the final claim was made it turned out to be for an immense tract of Zululand and now the Zulus gaze at this great wedge, some of the best land in their country, as bitterly as do the Basuto at the abundant flats of the Orange Free State. The point came up at once when I met the school. With all their apparent submission the Zulu have a long and bitter memory for injustice.

We wandered back through a valley beside which the little herd-boys were watering the cattle before driving them into the kraal. It is difficult not to sympathize with the native in his love of cattle. They may not be much good as beef or milkers but they *look* very fine, so big and glossy, and the great bulls, with a half-hump and huge spread of horn, look creatures one would be proud to possess.

At night, after dinner, with pen and notebook, I interviewed Mr. Oscroft, and learned much about his school and about the tragedy of the Zulu, past and present. The Basuto never won such great battles against white men and were never crushed so deeply as the Zulu: their great leader Moshesh knew not only how to fight but how to come to terms with reality. It was twelve o'clock before we got to bed and I am afraid I left both my host and his wife quite exhausted—not to speak of myself and my kind friend and guide, Mr. Malcolm.

We got up this morning at 5.30 a.m. and were away by six. We had two hundred miles of appalling roads in front of us. I had by now got to know Mr. Malcolm quite well. He is an earnest, experienced man, a world away from his countrymen in his point of view, as nearly all Native Department officials are or should be; a passionate believer in native rights and political equality. All day we talked deeply, confirming each other enthusiastically in our liberalism. Heaven knows what we said! I sometimes marvel at the many, many hours I have spent in intense discussion with experts and cannot afterwards remember one definable point we reached or one basic fact they gave me. I can only hope that it all packs in as a sort of general background to one's more vivid impressions.

I remember that at one point he humoured me by a detour which would allow me to dip into the fringe of indigenous forest for, as I think I have explained before, you get by that a manifastation of the life of the country that nothing else seems to give. I have found on this trip that trees come next to men in importance and how often and bitterly do I bewail my ignorance of botany.

We plunged in through deep grass soaked with dew. Then, out of the intense light, we passed into evening. It is a deep, dark forest, full of pits choked with vegetation and with the octopus-like tree, the monkey rope, climbing and clinging everywhere. The trees had small dark, shining leaves, except the fever tree, which is paler with its leprous yellow trunk. Millions of trees, twisted and interlocking in a never-ending mutual struggle and all nameless to me! Even in this hot land, no fire ever ruins this forest; it is so matted with damp. This is the Ngome forest where the Zulus, had they not been people who preferred to attack and fight in the open, might have lurked to prolong their resistance.

We had seen very little erosion so far, for the veld carries here a thick protective skin but as we turned in a loop westwards out of Zululand and into Natal we met it again. We stopped in a drift and I photographed Mr. Malcolm and our gallant Chevrolet against a background of erosion, and then he took a picture of me for a souvenir. Presently we came to erosion that was not only more serious, but most beautiful also, with its fluted pinnacles built of rich red sand, so Mr. Malcolm made me climb one of its pillars and took another picture.

Our next point of call was the Alobane coal-mine under a hill on the summit of which the Zulus inflicted a nasty little defeat upon us and where Buller won the V.C. by dragging to safety men who were un-horsed and wounded.

But my object now was to examine a remote colliery, for Ballinger had told me that here the conditions were appalling, or so he heard for he had not been able to get there. It seems strange to see the gear of a coal-mine, so much connected in my past with the gloom of crowded black industry in and around Sheffield, held up aloft against the African sky on the slope of a lonely kopje. Whether there is some-thing in the nature of coal that invites sordid conditions I don't know, but here, almost unimaginably in its rural setting, I came upon one of the foulest slums.

We began by reviewing the school, run by the Dutch Reformed Church (what does this Church educate the Africans *for?*), and then went to the married quarters. These were tiny shacks, all but window-less and divided into two, a whole family in each single room. The huts were in a state of disrepair and their interiors, which were bare of all but dirty litter, showed signs of utmost poverty. Piles of ashes and rubbish lay outside the doors. But worst of all was the stench. A few, tiny, filthy runnels crept between the houses, and from the smell of these, half-blocked by rubbish, I assumed that they were the chief means of sanitation. The Indians, who are generally at least super-ficially clean, and often much more than that, were the shabbiest I have seen, the women's long dresses filthy and dragging about in the dust and scum. From the doorsteps, and from inside the crowded huts, came the sound of quarrelling and it was certainly the gloomiest African village I had ever seen. Yet when, after I had poked a nose into one of these dens and was just going, Mr. Malcolm remarked in Zulu that I was from England, there was a shout of wonder and joy and they rushed out to have a better look at me. This happened in more than one hutment and it was impossible not to ponder upon the tones of affection and admiration in which they repeated the word 'England'. Alas!

We went on to the single men's compound where they had about a thousand, a mixture of all tribes. There were heavy wire entangle-ments round the place. Why? Here, too, were foul, evil-smelling, broken-down huts, sixteen men to one smallish room, and a system, or lack of systems, of sanitation that made it unbearable to breathe in the compound. The men came in just as they were from the mine, brown bodies black with sweat and grime and lay down at once on the dark floor to rest. The African is so naturally cheerful that the dullness and silence of these men was startling. We questioned one who had been in the place for many years. He came from Nyasaland. He did not know whether he would ever get back home because he could not eat the food and had to spend his wages buying his own. There were other long-term men who said vaguely that they had wives at home.

It was quite clear that no attempt had been made to give these people any education. There was an entire lack of imagination. There was unlimited space round the mine and each cottage could, and should, have had a garden round it, for a garden is a source of pride and self-respect, and to have even a few maize stalks waving round the house must make an African feel more at home. And there could have been ground put aside for sports, to get them away at times from that dark, stinking compound.

The boy who took us round told us that there were quite a lot of desertions but that the men were generally caught and brought back. It must be remembered that to break a contract of work, as also to strike, is in South Africa, for Africans, a penal offence, so that the man can be fined or sent to jail. If fined, he must work longer than his contract in order to pay it. You may ask why he goes to such a bad mine since labour is legally voluntary. The answer is that in his ignorance and simplicity he may know no better: or he may be the prey of unscrupulous white labour-recruiters who get a large bonus for each man secured and who have under them native assistants who get 10s a head per recruit. The possibilities opened up by this can be imagined.

I was interested to find that my opinion was not that of the ignorant outsider and that Mr. Malcolm fully shared my indignation. Indeed the blackness of the mine cast a shadow over both of us which we could hardly throw off and we discussed what could be done as we drove off into the veld. He decided to approach the Inspector of Labour for Natal. I contemplated a letter to the *Natal Mercury* but in the end decided that, from an outsider, it would do more harm than good.

We had had our reminders of war with the Zulu: we now drove for a hundred miles through country made historic by the operations of the Boer War. We lunched at Vryheid and passed several battle-fields. We saw where the Boers closed in on Dundee and we followed up the British retreat upon Ladysmith. We dined between great pictures of the famous relief of that town by General White and Baden Powell. The town hall clock, which was long kept as it was, broken by a Boer shell, has now been repaired at the request of the Dutch, and the growing number of Dutch in the district may make the celebrations of the famous Relief next year rather embarrassing.

So came to an end this rather grim, disturbing tour through the country of a famous warrior tribe whose warlike traditions and resistance had only made their defeat more bitter and their subjection more complete. I parted from my guide and companion with deep gratitude, not only for all his untiring help and efficient guidance but even more for the sympathy and deep sense of agreement which he, as a South African and I as a passing observer, had shared.

Durban

January 1930

I arrived in Durban very tired, rather late and with no idea where to go and spend the night. Then I remembered a hotel-keeper I had met on the Perth–Durban boat who had once treated me to champagne. So I went to his hotel. He was out but they gave me a room. When he came he made a great fuss. He had me moved out of my room and gave me a suite looking over the sea. He proudly showed me round it. It led out of his own suite in a separate block from the hotel and I began to wonder if I was in for trouble. However, when, with much pride, he showed me his own suite I was relieved to see that it showed all the signs of his being married.

After dinner on the verandah, word having gone round that I was studying native affairs from England, I was attacked by the Natalians, and listened while I was told that (1) I had no business there; (2) I was quite incapable of judging until I had been ten years in the country; (3) the natives were spoiled; (4) education was at the root of all the trouble.

Having been on the go since five in the morning I put up a very poor defence and retreated to bed.

A long and exciting day today, 1 February. A stifling night made sleep difficult so I got up early and worked and dashed up the town to buy a dress and get money from the bank.

Back at 9.30 to find Durban's Superintendent of Native Locations and his car waiting for me. He took me first—very honestly—to see one of the bad parts, a long row of single-room hovels, with mixed Indian and native families bulging out of the dark doorways. Then we went to see the compounds, where he can hold 3,000 natives and is always needing space for double that number. (Where do the un-accommodated live and sleep?) Here are endless boards on iron bars for 3d a night: there are boards with fairly clean bedclothes for 6d: here is the disinfectant well in which the boards are dipped every week: here is the more permanent quarter, with a few possessions hanging over each bed, the sort of aimless variety you find in any boy's pocket, string, whistles, mouth organ, but also paper flowers, and here and there a rosary or a text. Each aperture is closed and all cracks covered by newspaper. African labourers never seem to want fresh air in their sleeping quarters.

We then went down to the headquarters of the native trade union, the Industrial and Commercial Union. It is in a very low part of the town reached through crowded slums of mixed races. We found it hard to discover as the last I.C.U. premises were wrecked by the whites in the recent serious anti-native riots, when there were deaths on both sides. The Natal I.C.U. is the most militant of all and, under its Zulu leader, Champion, has broken away from the main stem which Ballinger advises. But just because it is violent it attracts more support and has a large income. The I.C.U. premises, which are masked behind a warehouse door, are enormous, an old sweet factory, dark and inclined to rot, but with several huge rooms.

Champion is the arch agitator of the Union. He was once Mr. Taberer's 'boy' in Johannesburg. His master sent him to spy on seditious meetings but the speeches converted him so he deserted to the other side. He is responsible for the present boycott of the municipal beer-halls. The City Council made many thousands a year out of them: now they do not make as many pence. It was his activities that a few weeks ago led to the Minister for Justice, Pirow, flying to Durban and leading a raid of armed police to overawe the Durban Zulus. In June this year the white mob tried to storm these I.C.U. headquarters of Champion's and there was loss of life upon both sides. In September the Zulu women attacked the beer-halls. It appears that the authorities would like to see Champion's arrest and deportation. That seems sure to come. One question for the police must be how to get him out of this rabbit warren in the underworld without serious bloodshed.

We found Champion in an office blocked off from an upper room in the factory. We went through crowds of natives to get there. It was an act of great courage on the part of Mr. X, my guide, and an official, to bring me here. I am afraid, if it should get out, he will be in for trouble, for of course, to white Durban, there is only one opinion about Champion and that is that he should be put up against a wall and shot.

Champion is a big Zulu. He greeted us with some ceremony, more especially directed to me and made a little speech. When I held out my hand he put his behind him on the grounds that I was breaking the rule of the whites in offering mine to a black man. He is very clever. That impression is immediate. He has all the African's command of words, tones and facial expression, added to the alertness and cunning engendered by adversity. He is so embittered and reckless that he did not try to placate Mr. X, my official guide. He looked him straight in the eye and accused his department of various serious faults, mainly of refusing him any place to live in spite of repeated applications. I felt hot for my companion and hoped he would be able to stick it, for any sort of explosion under these circumstances would be most unfortunate. He kept his head, however, and disclaimed any idea of penalizing Champion for political reasons. He had no room for him in the married quarters.

'And so I, a married man, am divorced from my wife by the municipality. That's very moral!' said Champion, who has great command of English.

Perhaps my readers, not having spent the last three months in South Africa, will not realize the extraordinary nature of this visit and this scene in which a senior white official was put through it by a native agitator in the latter's own office.

I intervened, before worse could occur, and asked Champion a series of questions. He proclaimed it as his main object to raise the wages of the workers. One Commission has accused him of 'poisoning the minds of his people against the Europeans.' 'That I glory in,' he said. 'Up till now, though they were oppressed, they did not understand how or by whom. Now, thanks to me, every native in Durban knows. The only hope lies in discontent, because discontent produces organization.'

'But do you not want to co-operate with the whites?' I asked.

'Miss, I do. But *they* will not co-operate; they will not even speak to a native. From first to last in all our troubles here, has any official ever thought of asking the natives their opinion? Do we ever go near their Native Department except to stand about for hours until we can get a pass or get fined for not having one? The Native Affairs officials in this city are absolutely unapproachable and unsympathetic. *Of course* I would co-operate. I know we cannot do without the whites in this country. But the white will do nothing for us until we can organize and speak up for ourselves. It is sympathy and understanding we want. We get it from you. Do you know that your coming has achieved something that has never happened before: that the Superintendent has come down to the I.C.U. It was worth while your coming to Africa just for that achievement.' Here my companion hastily disclaimed any official significance in his visit. 'I know, I know,' Champion said, 'but all the most important things in the world are done unofficially.'

I then sat back while the two went at it and discussed the whole range of differences and the possible formation of a new joint advisory committee of town councillors and natives that is on the cards at present.

Watching, I could not *like* Champion. I suppose it would be hard for any white person to like a native agitator. His position must be too much for his character in this generation. He breaks into stump oratory, shouting and banging with his fist at the least provocation. His head is swimming with self-esteem and his outlook distorted by egotism. Moreover, as I turned over his pamphlets I found a vicious attack on my friend Ballinger. Ballinger draws his money from mysterious sources because he lives on the occasional gifts of trade unionists and friends in England and South Africa. After Champion broke Natal off from the I.C.U. he challenged Ballinger to confess where his funds came from. Ballinger declined. Champion drew the worst conclusions, the least damaging being Moscow.

Champion, at the end, turned to me and said there would be a huge gathering on Saturday night of natives of every sort and kind. Had I the courage to come? To the native population of Durban it would be a great event that a white woman, and one from England, should come down to their gathering. I did not know what to say. I was attracted and frightened. And I could feel the horror of the official at my side. I hedged and said I would let him know and I saw he feared this was a refusal. Outside we saw rows of clients waiting for Champion. He escorted us through the great, mouldering, dark, barrack-like place and into the sordid street.

I need hardly say that my official guide said that *of course* I was not to accept Champion's challenge. He said it would be quite impossible even for him to go to such a place at night.

We went on and visited the married quarters area and poked into houses. I won't describe them, though I have made careful comparisons and mean to write something on the housing of natives. He admitted that he had only a hundred houses and that he had thousands of applications. He charges them £1 a month, and they cost him £2 7s.

Now he cannot build any more, because without the help of the profits from the beer-halls the Council will not face the capital expenditure. Those profits must have been enormous for out of them night-schools were run, and welfare work and even a hospital were financed. In other words, the native pays out of his wretched wages. The whole economic-financial situation strikes one as being unsound. But if you say that it amounts to subsidizing the employer and allowing him to pay inadequate wages, the answer is that all whites are directly or indirectly employers and that the present arrangements are better for the white community than a general rise of wages which, it is *said*, would cripple South Africa. I have looked into wages a bit here. The Zulu 'boy' who does my hotel room gets £2 a month, the docker £2 to £2 10s. Indian waiters in this hotel get about £5 a month. The manager admits that they have not risen since he first went into business many years ago although the cost of living has risen so enormously and the needs of the natives, with education and urban life, have also increased.

I spent the afternoon writing to Mr. Coates, ex-Prime Minister of New Zealand, about Samoa. (What a contrast the word calls up!) In the evening I trammed around Durban, having another look at it and calling on people. I was thinking all the time, however, of the night, and being torn between fear and attraction. I have no doubt that Champion, from a white man's point of view, is an unprincipled and dangerous man. Having brooded on ways and means and not liking the idea of going down into those parts with an Indian taxi-driver I decided to get hold of a reliable white driver who would take me and fetch me away. So I rang up Champion, who said he was already making preparations, counting on my coming, and that he would see to my being fetched and taken back. That cut out my plan for possible retreat. So I fell back on another. I left for the hotel-keeper a note giving the name and whereabouts of the place to which I was going and saying that if I were not back in the hotel by 11 p.m. then arrangements would have gone wrong and I must be fetched. It was all rather like an Edgar Wallace novel but I had to be mysterious as I did not want to be stopped from going.

It was a stifling night, loaded with wet heat, and all the hotel people were sitting out along the *stoep*. A woman who heard I was interested in natives came up and sat beside me, and proceeded to blackguard them and, by inference, me, in the most outrageous manner. She was a handsome, white-haired woman, in a beautiful evening dress, and loaded with jewels. I really felt quite sick as I listened to the usual flow of words—spoiled—lazy—animals—keep them down. She knew nothing—nothing. She boasted a life-time in the country, and knew not the first fact of the situation. And the unprovoked vindictiveness with which she attacked me for daring to study the question! 'You wait until you have been ten years in the country before *you* advance an opinion.' I don't know whether I was a bit tired and therefore nervy, but I could not stand it. Argument was useless, and I did not want a scene on the *stoep*, especially as Champion would shortly arrive and run the gauntlet. So I got up and said it was useless to answer her, so wide apart were we in outlook. Then I went to another seat. Presently a smart new Buick swung up to the doorway with some natives in it and Champion came out. Fortunately no one recognized him and I hurried into the car before people had time to realize what was happening.

The Africans drove off at most furious speed. Not even in Paris have I been driven so fast through a town. The streets in the Asiatic and Indian quarters were crowded and when at last we drew up at the I.C.U. there was a dense crowd of natives round the door and along the pavements. Champion shouted and swung his arms to make a lane and they parted, staring in silence. The building, a large disused factory, was like a hive of bees, every part of it packed. There must have been several thousands of natives there and the heat and smell were overwhelming. Champion took me to an upper room where several hundred natives were already sitting on benches and many more standing and squatting all round. He sat me at a table in front of them and got up to make a speech. For my benefit he spoke in English and had it interpreted. He said that already they all knew about me as he had addressed them earlier about my visit. He paid various compliments to me and my country and the idea that I should 'tell England' of their wrongs roused, alas!, a cheer.

'Our visitor has come tonight to learn about us and we want to teach her all we can. But most of all, let us show her that, in spite of having black skins, we are human beings, with the desires, the faults and virtues of our species. General Smuts, in one of the extraordinary series of addresses he has lately been giving in England and America, said that we are as patient as donkeys. Has he read his Bible? Does he remember that the time came when a donkey opened his mouth and spoke, and, yes, even refused to go any further? Well, we are beginning to speak and we mean to be heard, or we shall refuse to go any further, and what will happen then ?

'We want our capacities recognized. There is nothing an African cannot do if he is given a chance. You, Miss, were driven down here by a black man: that man is also a skilled mechanic and he can take that whole car to little pieces and put it together again. We have started an all-black clothing factory here, and this suit I am wearing, and Mr. London's (the man beside him) were made there.' (Quite well cut navy suits.) 'I have yet to learn that any of our men who have been to London or Edinburgh or even Oxford have failed to pass their examinations in the usual time.'

But I lost half the speech as I was gazing at the audience. It comprised every type, young bucks in short-cut double-breasted waistcoats and Oxford trousers (these *very* popular with the Bantu) through all possible grades and shades of shirts and collars to the collarless and the coatless, to men with hair plaited in porcupine spikes and women in nothing much but brass wire and beads. They sat or stood, shining with sweat, staring at me with their big black-brown eyes and absolutely dumb. Then the choir, probably from some secessionist church, and looking highly respectable, appeared and at Champion's order, since they were to sing to *me* and not to the audience, stood right on top of me and sang an anthem about the captivity of Sion. Champion, evidently deeply moved, or acting, rose to say that for Sion he read Africa and asked when God would turn *her* captivity.

The whole audience now stood up and, singing in harmony, roared out the Bantu national anthem, 'Africa'. It was most inspiring, the word itself kept recurring in different tones, mournful or defiant. I must try to get the words.

It was now my turn to speak. I got up, fully aware how careful I must be in what I said. I was greeted with stimulating applause and Champion came forward to interpret. The pause, for interpreting, checks the flow, but enables you to keep them waiting for the point in a way that with practice, I imagine, could be made very effective. This was my speech as far as I can remember.

'Tell your people not to be afraid that I am going to make a long speech. I only want to tell them why I am here. I should not dare make a speech. Africans are so much better at speech-making than white people.' ('I don't agree with that,' said Champion.) 'I had the privilege of hearing Dr. Aggrey speak and he was the best orator, white or black, I ever heard. But I have also heard old chiefs up in the Transkei and in the Basutoland mountains make speeches I could never hope to equal.

'Why am I here tonight? It is not because I agree with Mr. Champion. I don't agree with him, with much of what he is doing, and much of what he has said. But I have come because I want to learn. I want to see all sides of this problem of South Africa and it is a great pleasure for me to be able to spend an evening here among you, in your own place, and see how you enjoy yourselves.' Then I told them something of my travels and of my hope, when I returned to England, of lecturing and perhaps writing on what I had learned. I finished up by telling them about Fort Hare and warning them about the difficulties of education, and the danger of thinking it was a cheap or easy thing to gain but that, in the long run, it was the only salvation.

The next thing on the programme was a European dance. I was made to sit in the middle while the couples circled round me. They dance very well though the women's bad figures show up in their scanty, thin dresses. They all moved slowly and decorously and exactly on European lines though they certainly grapple together with a completeness unusual in our ball-rooms and cheek to cheek is the rule rather than the exception. A row three or four deep sits round the hall and I was told that is always so and that the spectators are content to pay their entrance and sit all night long just gazing at the dancers. I suppose anything is better than lying in congested heaps in their minute houses and hovels. But no wonder so many are accused of being stupid and sleepy next day.

But the big event was preparing below. Soon a muffled noise I had been hearing began to grow and grow, and Champion came and asked me if I were prepared to see what they had got up for me. 'It is the real thing, you know,' he explained, half apologetic. I went down and found the huge hall that is the entire ground-floor of the factory filled literally to suffocation. They must have run into hundreds, though it was difficult to see them all in the big, half-lit space. They were all men, and all naked but for a thong round the loins and metal armlets and anklets and on their heads a few trimmings of metal and fur such as suited each man's fancy.

The great bulk of them were squatting at the back in ranks, each armed with a heavy stick, with which he struck the floor as he shouted his song. There was hardly room between my chair and these men for the first dance team to come in, especially as they must dash in at a gallop, and whirl their sticks round their heads. 'Don't be frightened,' said Champion. 'However near they come to you, they won't hit you.' But I remembered this from Somaliland and how men, frenzied with the dance and apparently quite unseeing, will, with quite reliable accuracy, miss you with their spears by a few inches.

Well, the dance was really splendid. One after another the teams, each about two or three hundred strong, replaced each other. They got more worked up as the night wore on. It was impressive, almost beyond bearing, to have a row of a hundred or more naked brown men, leaping and yelling within a few inches of you, their faces drawn into terrific grimaces, their eyes glassy with excitement, their mouths wide open to shout and scream and their whole bodies contorted with movements that demanded their whole strength to perform. I thought the rickety old floor would give way under the crash of their feet, especially as each crash was accompanied with the pounding of hundreds of sticks, and a simultaneous shout so that the rhythm was deafening. One team did a dance founded on the British Tommy, and evolved, I suppose, by a native labour corps in France. It was a priceless burlesque. They marched in ranks, formed fours, saluted, bringing their hands down with a resounding smack on their bare thighs, carrying their sticks like rifles, whistling famous half-remembered tunes of the war, and trying to imitate the stiff march of the white man, so unlike their own gazelle-walk.

But their own war-dance was the best of all. There were about three hundred dancers, all wearing white fur rings round knees, ankles and wrists, and carrying sticks festooned with white feathers. The joints of their arms were bound with gold and silver wire; some wore baldrics of leopard or catskin or embroidery of white and scarlet beads. The Zulu physique can be magnificent; many were slim and tall and some looked more Hamitic than Negro. Certainly this dance showed the Zulu off in all his glory.

The impressiveness became almost overwhelming. I was surrounded by these flashing brown bodies with muscles running up and down skins glossy with sweat. Yet it was beautiful, this living frieze of dark bronze bodies. Now they advanced, singing with sticks levelled at me like spears. Champion shouted the translation in my ear:

Who has taken our country from us?
Who has taken it?
Come out! Let us fight!
The land was ours. Now it is taken.
We have no more freedom left in it.
Come out and fight!
The land is ours, now it is taken.
Fight! Fight!
Shame on the man who is burned in his hut!
Come out and fight.

I was relieved when, with one great final roar, the dancers all fell flat on the floor, their bodies nearly dovetailed into each other and the sticks laid out in a long straight line. Champion said that the dancers were mostly men who had lately come in from the kraals, the majority of them working as house-boys. I could see another line of young men in the red-bordered calico of domestic service filing in, each carrying a little bundle containing the precious trappings of tribalism.

As I looked it suddenly struck me that these splendid young men could be the grandsons of the Zulu warriors who inflicted such a terrible defeat upon British regular troops at the battle of Isandhlawana in 1879, killing with assegai and rifle 800 regular British soldiers and as many native levies. Did they ever recall those days of their great military power as they stooped to menial tasks under their white masters or were nagged in the kitchen by white housewives? How those Durban matrons would have stared to see how their docile house-boys spent their Saturday night!

I had lost all sense of time. I looked at my watch. It was well after eleven! It was a terrible moment—I had far more to fear than Cinderella. I remembered my note on the manager's desk which told him where I had gone. Suppose they sent police to fetch me out of here—if police dared to come. 'Take me to a telephone,' I shouted in Champion's ear. He read my face: he asked no questions. We rushed up to his office. I found the number but in the continuing din from below I could neither hear nor be heard. Champion guessed the danger: in a few minutes I was in the car with him being raced through the docks and slums—now mercifully empty—until I jumped out of the car and ran into the hotel. I rushed to the manager's room. There on his desk lay my note—unopened! Clearly he was having a night out! I felt faint with the realization of what might have been. My only defence was that I had not realized the extent of recent disorders, of how police and unofficial white men had lately used their revolvers on Zulu strikers with loss of life on both sides, nor had I any idea of the kind of entertainment Champion had prepared for me.

Bechuanaland

February 1930

My time in South Africa is coming to an end. I have left Durban, feeling a little battered after my night out with the Zulus and deeply shocked by the disgraceful housing and starvation wages of the African workers. So on via Johannesburg and to the train that runs far north to Bulawayo. A long night in the train as we skirted along the eastern edge of Bechuanaland. I was up early to alight at Palapye, the junction for Serowe, headquarters of the largest tribe in the Protectorate, the Bamangwato.

I think I must pause here in order to explain why I was so anxious to break off my journey north and call in at Serowe in the Bechuanaland Protectorate, one of the three native territories retained under direct British rule. The Bamangwato, the leading tribe in the Protectorate, threw up in the last century a great chief and a great Christian, Khama. He and his fellow-chiefs managed to save their country from Cecil Rhodes and annexation to South Africa by going to London, putting on frock-coats and top-hats and sitting on Chamberlain's doorstep until at last he agreed to annex their country directly to Britain. When the great Khama died in 1923 and his immediate successor died a year or two later, his direct heir was Seretse, his grandson, a minor. His son Tshekedi, who was just about to take his matric at Fort Hare, was therefore called in to act as regent. He was then nineteen years old.

I was naturally eager to meet the best educated chief in Southern Africa and to learn how he was facing the threat from Hertzog's South Africa to take over his country along with the other two High Commission territories. I knew, too, that, linked with this, was another threat. The powerful British South Africa Company had long held concessions for mineral rights in Tshekedi's country and now it appeared that there might be gold not far from Serowe and the Company wanted to assert their rights. Tshekedi knows only too well what a young Johannesburg would mean to his people, no less than their demoralization and ultimately their annexation, and he is fighting tooth and nail to beat off the concessionaires. His strong will plus his education make him no mean antagonist. But the odds against him are huge.

It so happened that when I was in Capetown and as I was going up the stairs to call on the Imperial Secretary, the Honourable Bede Clifford, at his office, I was passed by a young African rushing down the stairs two steps at a time so that he very nearly knocked me over—a strange event in South Africa. He checked his headlong descent and apologized with much *savoir faire* and in perfect English. It was not difficult to guess that this was Tshekedi, so I told him of my wish to visit his country and explained about myself. He had already heard of me and warmly invited me to visit him. When I went on upstairs I found the entire staff wilting over their desks in a state of exhausted exasperation. They had never met with such suspicion and obstinacy from an African. It appeared that he had almost come to an open breach with Captain Clifford and was now demanding to see the Governor-General—and alone!

I felt very worried about all this, knowing Clifford and the strength of his will. So I went to find Ballinger with whom I knew Tshekedi was in touch and who was in Capetown. I have a great respect for Ballinger's knowledge of the Africans, his defence of their rights and also of his distrust of the Union Government. But I was not so sure that he was right to extend his distrust to the Imperial authorities, all the more as Tshekedi would need their support against Hertzog's annexation claim. But I found Ballinger obdurate. He believes that the chief has a strong case in law for breaking the mining concession and he is advising him to fight to the last ditch. He rejected my idea of relying on the Colonial Office. What pressure, he asked, would they oppose to the might of the British South Africa Company, backed by Hertzog? Nor had he faith in Clifford. It is a hard lesson to learn that in politics—especially in the international sphere—one must guard against allowing personal friendships to colour one's assessment of men and measures, especially men.

This, then, is the background to my visit to Serowe. It meant that I should have looked at two of the three African states threatened by the South African Government. Unfortunately, as an experience, flat, dry, Bechuanaland could offer nothing comparable with Basutoland's mountains. I decided to break my journey north to Bulawayo at Palapye, the nearest station—or rather halt—to the Bamangwato headquarters at Serowe.

When I got off the train I found that I had to go on some thirty miles or so on the track to Serowe in charge of the official District Commissioner of that area. I therefore had the chance to learn all that the official most intimately concerned with the crisis would tell me. I found that his sympathies were very much with Tshekedi but that he thinks his fight is hopeless. Especially now that he has antagonized the strong man on the government side, Captain Clifford.

I had a lot to learn at Serowe. I first visited the native school. This, in striking contrast with the Zulu school I had recently visited, has been built and is entirely run by the people themselves without any help or supervision from the white man. As far as buildings, equipment and cleanliness are concerned, I have seen very little to touch it in South Africa. Instead of all the classes being in one room there are separate form-rooms with excellent desks, wall-maps and spotless, painted walls. I had not time to watch the actual teaching but I found that the staff of six teachers were all at work at the early hour at which I called. I was told that the government inspector, who came the other day at their own request to inspect the school, was delighted with it. It is the most encouraging witness to what Africans can do unaided. But, of course, Tshekedi, like Khama, is a very exceptional man.

I went on to visit the royal Kgotla. This is an open space at the foot of the central kopje. The chief holds his court under the trees in front of a half-circular palisade. The people bring their little carved stools and sit about in the shade of some large trees. Here, the other day, some of Tshekedi's enemies, belonging to a rival line of the royal house, crept up and suddenly opened fire upon him. He was shot through the thigh and some of his followers were hit. The would-be assassins—rivals for the regency—were caught and it speaks well for the self-control of the natives and of Tshekedi himself that they were not lynched. The chief immediately and formally proceeded to burn down their houses according to native custom. Only it happened that these men lived in brick, semi-European houses. They therefore appealed for damages. The local British magistrate decided in favour of the chief. They took the case to the Special Court. Here the judge is Patrick Duncan. He decided for the would-be assassins on the ground that native law was here repugnant to the laws of civilization, and that, anyhow, it applied to huts, not houses. Tshekedi has now appealed to the Privy Council and the case comes on in March or June. (So, if any of you who read this diary note the report, please keep the cutting for me.)

The chief's relations and servants live in pleasant-looking huts. He himself has a European-type house with two or three cars in the garage. He was not in when I called so we decided to climb the kopje and see the memorial to Khama that the tribe has put up. Nothing but the best would satisfy them so they got Sir Herbert Baker to plan it and the best South African sculptor to do the statue, which is a bronze duiker, that lovely little antelope being the emblem of the tribe. All is spoiled, however, by the statue standing on a base of sepulchral white marble, instead of on the rough stone of the kopje itself, which would have been marvellous, for the hillock is a pile of glorious red-gold rocks standing over the wide, flat sea of veld. The marble looks prim and ridiculous. To crown all there was a glass bowl of artificial flowers at the foot of the monument. However, it represents their affection and respect for their great chief Khama.

Tshekedi now came looking for me. He took me to his office where we had a long talk and, with his permission, I took down all he said. It was all very interesting. I questioned him closely about his juris-diction and the methods he followed. He is a slender, handsome, keen, taut young man, highly strung, and quick in his replies. He answered me freely and frankly and seemed to feel no constraint because his British official, the District Commissioner, was present with us. Their relations, in fact, seemed excellent. But I felt that this man was almost too sympathetic, and that, as he does not seem to be a very strong character and as his powers are limited, this alliance could be rather unhelpful. He even seems to share the Chief's resentment against the High Commissioner's office in Capetown and yet feels hopeless of staving off the day of doom. Moreover, in long conversa-tions that I had with him, he seemed to waver in his opinions and sometimes to think that it was better that the country *should* be opened up. At other times he seemed to hint that the chief was right to fight the British South Africa Company. I could not help feeling that at this crisis of his fortunes the chief wanted, in this mediatory position, a very strong, self-confident man to advise him, one able to choose a good line and stick to it.

But perhaps Tshekedi can fight his own battles. I am immensely impressed by him and feel drawn to him. He has character as well as intelligence. It is impossible not to admire his strength of will. But he can be pleasant, too, when he likes, and he was open and friendly to me. But he would not admit that, following his father's example, he was about to journey to England to lay his case before the Secretary of State. But then the District Commissioner had told me that I had no business to know that as it was a secret.

The chief's attitude is this: 'Give my people a chance to develop a little further before you push this industrialism upon us. The gold will keep. In fifty or a hundred years we shall be ready at least to co-operate in its mining and the whole thing will injure us far less than it will today. But if I am to develop my people I must have more funds. Give me back some of the taxation to spend upon education and agriculture. Try me, and I won't fail in the trust.' But will Sir Ernest Oppenheimer wait ? Not he!

I persuaded the Chief to let me take his photograph. He agreed, but rather reluctantly. The District Commissioner told me that Captain Clifford was the last man who took his picture after a painful interview and the chief's face came out angry and sullen. He thought mine would be a good one!

The really wonderful thing about the chief is that he keeps off wine and women. He lives with his mother ('the only real Christian I ever knew' said the D.C.) and seems devoted to her. He refuses to marry and seems to lead a chaste life. His mother says he is too busy to bother with women yet. How far is this model behaviour the result of education ? It must be put down partly to the example of the father he so deeply reveres. The sad part is that as soon as he is fully experienced, in fifteen years, his nephew must come of age and succeed him. A British official here told me that he cannot believe that Tshekedi, or, at least, his friends, will allow the child to grow up: he lives conveniently next door to the Regent. But Tshekedi has recently sent the child all the way to Capetown to have his tonsils cut out by the best possible doctor, so it looks as though this grim expectation will not be fulfilled.

I think that the time I spent talking to Tshekedi in his house was, in political interest, the high-water mark of my visit to South Africa. It was not that he was the most fully 'westernized' African that I had met during these months, if I must use an unsatisfactory term. I had met a number of men with whom I could talk 'on the level' in Johannesburg. But the combination of this young man's intelligence, sensitivity, good looks (by our standards) and the fragile cause of independence for which he was fighting against such odds, all made a strong appeal to one's mind and heart. I looked round at his considerable library. He has a good collection of *Africana*, including the blue-books and official reports which he needs so much if he is to understand the complex dangers which threaten the status of his country. I could hardly realize that, outside, his house was encircled by a vast mass of little huts representing no great population in numbers and yet the largest purely 'native' town in all southern and eastern Africa. Beyond that stretches a vast dry region, the pasturelands of his tribe and the home of the remaining Bushmen and of wild animals. It did not seem much of a base from which to fight South Africa. Yet he can still laugh. 'Look,' he said, 'what happens to the gold that is dug up out of the earth on the Reef at so much cost in human toil and dislocation. Most of it goes off at once into deep vaults under the earth in America, Britain or elsewhere. Why not get expert geologists to estimate roughly how much gold lies under my people's land, make a nominal distribution between the Company and my State and leave it there until we are sufficiently advanced to carry out its excavation ourselves.'

I discovered an interesting fact here about forced labour. The men of the tribe are divided into 'regiments' according to age and by native custom and the chief can call on them to work for the tribe. He thus makes roads and even erects buildings at small expense. He is contemplating a system of sanitation for Serowe which will cost hundreds instead of thousands of pounds, which it would without 'forced' labour. The District Commissioner is a staunch upholder of the system. So, of course, is the chief. And both are furious with the International Labour Office at Geneva for interfering. The Imperial Secretary, Captain Clifford, to carry out our obligations, undertaken at Geneva, has had to publish the fact that no man need any longer work for his chief without pay. This has been a serious blow to Tshekedi but he carries on as best he can, relying on his prestige and the loyalty of his men. There is a great deal to be said for a labour tax. Under tribal conditions here, with cattle the main product, the men at times have little work to do: the conditions and length of forced service are never onerous and it is a way of showing loyalty and getting important work done. It should certainly be watched as at any time it might become a burden, but at present it is very necessary in these parts. So does a close-up of the facts lead one to qualify Geneva principles.

This afternoon we went to a church meeting. The church, a very big building, made of the yellow-rose stone of the district, was crowded. It was built, and is run and financed, entirely by the tribe, and all the congregation had, apparently, gone into committee for a week. The women separate themselves from the men. The open arch at the back showed a glimpse of the veld, level and blue-green like the sea, and the sun slanting through caught the head-dresses of the women, orange, blue, yellow and purple silk. Men and women listened keenly to every word, and the sub-chief, who was in the chair, invited and obtained opinions from them on many points. I could not, of course, follow this discussion. Tshekedi sat with his mother and myself at the back. He spoke only twice and was listened to with deep respect and attention. He urged them to provide more liberally for their church and to help the deacons when they visited outlying villages. His mother is a fine-looking woman. I had a talk with her afterwards. Two very aged ladies, hearing I was from England, asked permission to shake my hand. Once more I felt the weight of the moral responsibility Britain has undertaken.

On the way back we saw a splendid creature, naked but for a skin cloth and carrying a water-pot. She was evidently not of the trible. To my surprise Captain Nettleton answered that she was a slave, a Bushwoman from further into the interior, whom the tribe had subjected. With some difficulty I took her photo and learned that these slave people, the Masarwa, were quite numerous and that it was useless to free them as they had nowhere else to go and nothing else to do, and that they would refuse to be freed. I wonder! Well, the answer to that, of course, is that in spite of the obvious difficulty, a beginning could be made with the children. It was the second time I had come face to face with slavery but this seems to be of a milder sort than the Abyssinian.

I now had to return the forty miles to the railway halt at which I was to catch the north-bound train. Here there was a police post and the police officer had asked me to dinner. Between Serowe and the railway the land is worthless. Covered with grass and with small trees and pulsating with butterflies and grasshoppers, it is yet all waste from lack of water as is so much of this whole region. We discussed South African politics on the way back and I found that my host, though South African born himself, was an enthusiast for the Imperial Government and dreaded the possibility of the Union taking over the three Protectorates.

Arrived at the railway and the little tin house of the police officer, we found him in a befuddled state, though he claimed his distress was due to his acute sympathy for the wife of the Dutch veterinary officer next door whose eyes had been blacked by her husband. The result was that he babbled on with the whole sordid story instead of ordering dinner. Possibly he was also celebrating his appointment to accompany the British Museum Verney Expedition into the Kalahari in order to see they slaughtered the right game and not too much of it. But I should imagine from what I saw that the members of the expedition will not find him an invincible obstacle if they want to transgress. When at last, hungry and overwhelmed by his apologies about his bachelor establishment, we had just sat down to soup full of grit and had swallowed one mouthful, a yell from a watching boy announced the coming of the train. We dropped our spoons, tumbled into the car, and made off into the darkness. There was no road or else he missed it. We zig-zagged through sand and scrub and drove almost into the train. Any luggage was somehow thrown in aboard and I was hoisted up on to the high foot-board amid shouts of regret from my host, who was in tears, and the train pulled out en route for Bulawayo and the Belgian Congo.

Note added in 1973 by the Author
The visit to Serowe was the last incident of my South African travels. But it did not, of course, mean the end of my interest in the sub-continent. With regard to the three High Commission territories I found on my return to England, late in 1930, that the controversy about their transfer to the South African Government was still dragging on. Hertzog's Government continued to press its claims and British ministers, supported by such public opinion as there was on the issue, continued to use evasive tactics. Public opinion was suddenly concentrated upon Bechuanaland by the action of Tshekedi in 1933 in sentencing a white youth to flogging for assaulting a native woman. Tshekedi, as acting-chief, had shown a very strong and independent spirit. This was regarded by the British authorities as the last straw. At the time of the incident it happened that a naval officer was acting High Commissioner in South Africa for Britain. He sent a naval party up to Serowe, complete with guns which were dragged with difficulty across the soft sand. Tshekedi was temporally deposed. The incident roused very wide interest which in Britain was favourable to Tshekedi because of the dignity of his bearing through the incident.

Meanwhile the issue with South Africa over the future of the Protectorates dragged on. I did what I could, working in a junior capacity in a movement led by Lord Lugard and also by Lord Selborne, who had played a major part in the achievement of South African unity and in the definition of the status of the Protectorates. I wrote articles for *The Times* in 1933 and 1934[1] and found myself crossing swords in its pages with a distinguished opponent, Mr. Lionel Curtis, one of Lord Milner's famous 'Kindergarten' which had played such an important part in constructing the Union. Mr. Curtis wrote a series of articles in *The Times* in favour of transfer on the grounds that the Afrikaners would respond to a policy of trust. I continued the argument in person, Mr. Curtis being a Fellow of All Souls. In the end we decided to put our opposing views together in one book in which he generously allowed me to have the last words.[2]

I met Tshekedi and Seretse in England and had the pleasure of entertaining Tshekedi as a guest staying in my house. His story and that of his nephew, Seretse; of the latter's marriage to an English girl; of the reaction to this event in South Africa; of the exiling of both men by the British Government; of their reconciliation; of Tshekedi's premature death in London in 1959, are fully told in a book written by my god-daughter, Mary Benson.[3] With the Rev. Michael Scott, she was one of Tshekedi's closest friends and allies. It is the dramatic and moving story of a great man, worthy of a great father. His nephew, Seretse, aided by his English wife, is now the successful Prime Minister of the independent state of Botswana, formerly Bechuanaland which, with mingled poverty and promise, shows what Africans can do even under the shadow of a powerful neighbour which denies both the human rights and the potentialities of their race.

I could not resist referring in these few words to the story of Bechuanaland and the remarkable man I met there in 1930. It is a story which throws light upon so many aspects of the subject of race-relations which I had been sent round the world to study. For myself, my meeting with Tshekedi was perhaps the most important of many impressions made upon me during my time in South Africa. Here I had seen, if only in random glimpses, the problem of black peoples caught within the grip of a white ruling minority determined upon a

---

[1] 28 September 1933 and 6 July 1934. Reprinted in the book of my collected papers *The Colonial Sequence*, 1967.

[2] M. Perham and L. Curtis, *The Protectorates of South Africa*, 1935.

[3] Mary Benson, *Tshekedi Khama*, 1960.

lasting maintenance of its supremacy. North of me were states, some of them based upon the same principle of permanent racial stratification, some under the rule of a distant colonial power acting upon a principle of trusteeship the future of which they were hardly yet able to define but which seemed likely to produce a very different Africa north of the Zambesi, or perhaps of the Rovuma, than that which was developing south of the line of these rivers.

The Industrial Congo

February 1930

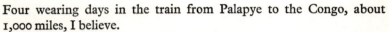

Four wearing days in the train from Palapye to the Congo, about 1,000 miles, I believe.

We arrived at Sakania on the frontier in the evening. It is an insignificant frontier, a mere clearance in the bush with a make-shift little station. The Belgian flag, hanging limply from a pole, first told me where we were. Then I had to adjust myself to the French notices, with their instructions to passengers and their promises of the *brasserie* and the *patisserie*. One connects the wilds and the natives so much with Anglo-Saxon domination that it is with an effort that one accepts 'the Continent' in Central Africa.

Two rather cheeky young railway officials in splendid uniforms lounged round the train and inspected tickets. Then came a Customs man. Then, for passports, a nice-looking youth but churlish in the extreme and with a pipe that seemed a fixture in his mouth. He accepted my passport until he asked me why I was coming. With an audacious whim I answered in my best French: 'Pour étudier l'administration indigène.' He then at once changed his attitude and said, 'Go to my office—I shall call the magistrate.'

I went to ask help of the only Englishman I could find at the moment, a representative of the Rhodesian railways. But though he had grovelled before the Rhodesian General Manager's letter, he said he could do nothing for me with the Belgians. He said this magistrate had a military manner and was a terror.

He certainly was. I was treated with the utmost abruptness, kept standing about in the office and then informed that I was to be turned back. Why, I could not discover, as I had a visa from the Capetown Belgian Consul. My protests were snapped off very short. And there was not even a train going back. I should have to stay the night at least at a foul little hotel attached to the back of the station. The Rhodesian railway man came and pleaded timidly in French worse than mine. I sat helplessly while the hideous martinet of a magistrate turned back other British subjects, rough-looking miners, hoping for a job on the copper mines. (Afterwards I learned the reason for this last rejection.)

I gathered up all my energy for a final effort and talked big about the Governor expecting me and bade him get him on the telephone. No telephone at this hour, it seemed. But I shook him a little and in the end he wrote me out a paper allowing me entry for four days only.

I went back to my train and up to the engine to find out if there were really black drivers in unsupervised charge of it. There were, and though it was interesting to me professionally, personally, and shamefully, I felt a faint tremor at the sight.

I picked up on the station with a South African manager from one of the Rhodesian mines who asked me to dine with him on the train. I accepted and roped in a Belgian woman who looked rather nice. Is it always I who raises the native question? I don't know, but it inevitably crops up. I suppose I question the first contemptuous reference to 'the nigger'. We went at it very hard and soon our colonial was saying:

'Of course *I* haven't got any education. I only happen to have known the native all my life. He is a hewer of wood and a drawer of water' (how sick I am of that expression!) 'and he always will be. On my mine I don't allow any of this magistrate business. I say to my boys "You can get a whipping or get out. Which will you have?" And they always choose a whipping. But I believe in justice. My boys never complain. Treat the natives hardly but treat them justly.'

I told them something of Fort Hare. But it was no good. The Belgian woman was also very extreme in her views and the dinner ended in controversy and coldness. The man was so moved that he kept coming back to my compartment when I was trying to go to bed to reiterate caustically the fact that of course *he* was not educated.

We got into Elizabethville before 6 a.m. the next morning. I had no idea where to go and, chastened by my first experience, and thinking I knew nobody and would have to creep to some place for a bath and breakfast, I resumed my crumpled dress and did not even powder my nose. I had no sooner got on to the platform than something like a deputation closed round me and there were speeches in French to be followed, and (Heaven help me!) to be answered. It seemed that the Governor was all but there in person. I said '*Mille remerciements*' over and over again to all the beards, though aware that the right rule about thanks, according to Oscar Wilde, is that 'one is enough, if it is sincere.' Everything, even my coat and purse, was seized by native servants. I was put into a car and taken twenty yards to a hotel, where the manager appeared, all servility, with confirmation of having kept me the best room. The deputation, with more speeches, warned me to be ready by half past eight.

There was a balcony, a bath with hot *'eau courant'*! (only the tap, which was made at Hanley, came off in my hand), and breakfast on the pavement. Then, at half past eight, M. Van Hoof, representing the Governor, came round with a car and took me to a series of interviews with heads of departments. It was all rather terrible. I was so tired and bewildered after those long days and nights in the train, that my French simply could not be found. I floundered about helplessly. I knew lots of technical nouns and adjectives about native administration but somehow all the little verbs and pronouns which are necessary to string them together refused to come. Moreover the whole system was so strange to me that I could not ask intelligent questions. I think M. Van Hoof's report to the Governor upon me for the morning's work must have been pretty poor.

I must say here that the whole Congo is divided into four parts, each enormous, with a Governor over each. The Katanga province, where I am, is the industrial one, with a rapid development of the copper industry begun on a large scale only since about 1920. This district is probably one of the richest in the world as far as the variety of minerals is concerned, gold, lead, zinc, tin, cobalt, coal, radium, but, above all, copper in abundance and in very rich ore. And it is not yet fully prospected. Most of the minerals are worked by one big company which has a monopoly, the Union Minière du Haut Katanga. This company naturally dominates the province and, as my main object in coming to Elizabethville was to study the industrialization of the native here, the U.M.H.K. managed my programme. My interviews, therefore, were with officials charged with watching over the operation of the special industrial laws which apply to Katanga.

At noon the Governor received me. He has a beautiful office and ceremony surrounds him. I passed to him through a series of grades until I met the Commissaire Général, Colonel Dufour. With him I discussed native affairs for about half an hour and then passed into the Presence. (I never cease to marvel at the wonderful reception I am getting in Southern Africa—except from the Afrikaners.)

Gaston Heenen was quite impressive. He is a thin, middle-sized, thorough-bred man, with piercing blue eyes, a nervous, highly strung, intelligent person. He looked rather worn out by his own energy but the shadows under his eyes and the lines on his face rather added to his distinction. If people can be divided into cat and dog types, he is very much the cat, watchful and subtle, though not in a deprecatory sense. However this was not an interview, it was merely a first formal presentation. He made a graceful and not unconvincing little speech and suggested that I might prefer to talk to him after I had seen something of their work. Meanwhile, as a basis for future discussion, he handed me one of his books on the problem of the industrial native.

I went back to the hotel and as soon as I had lunched, Dr. Mottone, who is the director of the whole of native recruitment and welfare for the Union Minière, arrived in his car. As he drove me out to the neighbouring mine of Lubumbashi—what a sinister sort of word!— he sketched in the native policy of the Union, which proved all the more significant against the background of South African industrial conditions.

What is so important to realize in judging Belgian policy is that when these vast riches were so recently discovered the whole area was almost desert. It is not agricultural country and the people around were scanty and unfitted to form a labour supply. The Union had therefore to transport large numbers of natives from great distances in this immense Congo state. There can be no doubt that, partly by profiting from South African mistakes; partly from the clear-sighted, logical outlook of these people; partly, I expect, to erase the scandal of 'red rubber'; this company, helped by its size and its despotic Government, can make and carry out a unified policy. Certainly they have evolved something which I cannot help thinking is better than anything South Africa can show.

First they organized recruiting on a scientific basis. A proportion was worked out by which the health of the tribe was regarded as resting upon a basis of 25 men (aged 16 to 45) to 75 children, women and old men. The local native commissioner must make his calculations and must refuse to allow more than the *surplus* men to be recruited. This is not to say that they *must* go. Recruiting is entirely voluntary (on paper at least).

Once recruited, the most elaborate laws govern the transport of the workers. They are collected at a camp, medically examined and then, accompanied by a native health officer, they set out on defined routes, with camps every thirty kilometres. That is, if they walk. For every effort is being made to transport them by lorry, train and river-boat. Arrived at the place of labour they pass, under another long law invented by M. Heenen, into a camp of 'acclimatization'. Here, generally, they spend about one month, carefully inspected by the doctor, given various injections that they have not had before setting out, and allowed to work a little more each day. Some are weeded out and sent home.

But the most important feature of all is that the Union has definitely decided to recruit married workers. This is where the system differs so strikingly from South Africa. So hard have they worked at this that now 40 per cent of their men are married and they are trying to raise the proportion even higher. They expect in two years to have 60 per cent, quite a natural proportion when it is remembered that many of the men are very young and not yet able to buy wives. The service is extended in every way to meet the needs of the women. There is special transport for women with child and for young children. The Union recruiters even offer to 'buy' wives for the men before they set out on their journey.

Dr. Mottone explained all this with the greatest enthusiasm. He is, indeed, largely responsible for the organization of the whole system in all the mines and has greatly influenced policy by his reports. It is he who draws up rules, appoints welfare officials, designs housing, etc.

He took me first to the compound, or rather the camp as it is called here. I could only stare with delighted surprise. For there are no compounds in the South African sense, no long barracks with dormitories like great concrete honeycombs. There are, instead, separate houses, one for each family or for two bachelors. These houses compare very well in size with those provided in South Africa and it must not be forgotten that relatively they are much bigger, since these people are much more primitive than South African tribes, and live themselves in tiny, shaggy grass huts. These mine houses have a deep overhanging roof which gives shade under which to sit. Behind the main rooms are two smaller rooms, a kitchen or store and a poultry house if they care to use it as such. It is impossible to exaggerate the neatness and cleanness of everything. Rows of banana trees make avenues and here and there are open spaces with gardens full of flowers. Behind each small group of houses is a large dust-bin, painted spotless white, and above it a shining glass fly-trap. Latrines, shower-baths, washing stands, water taps are all in perfect order and adequate number. One hesitates ever to apply the word perfect but here it had to be used for the housing and equipment. The women and children looked well dressed and healthy, a pretty good test.

We went on to see the school. The Union provides schooling for every child in their camps. But education is only just beginning in the Congo; all the camp-children are very young and it is difficult as yet to judge what the standard is. At least the buildings and equipment were excellent. Unlike South Africa, boys and girls, even the smallest, are divided. I gathered that the teachers had had no special training. The children rose like little soldiers at our entrance, piously folded their hands, bowed deeply, and chanted their greeting in bad French.

From there we went to the hospital. I must have been wrong to use the word perfection before, for now I have no better word with which to describe this marvellous place. Separate wards, connected by paved cloisters and surrounded by roses and canna lilies, with a central fountain playing. Inside, every sort of modern installation and all clean and orderly by the highest standards of hospital cleanliness: operating theatres, violet-ray department, and all the rest of it, with glittering metal, white porcelain and rubber flooring.

Then we visited one of the wards and saw row after row of black bodies lying numb and silent upon white beds, surrounded by vases of flowers and plants. One ward was entitled 'Petites Blessures', another 'Grandes Blessures'; then pneumonia, dysentery and the maternity wards. These are always interesting. Black babies have an air of being made all at once in one piece that we never seem to achieve. That is, all except the most new-born blacks. These always look rather horrible: they are much more red than black and for some reason are more like European babies, being, in fact, like caricatures.

The convalescents were having tea: fifty husky blacks all in very small tight uniform tunics of cheap cotton and all rasping out in sing-song the proper responses to a little white bird of a sister, following the time of her severely pointing finger, all with longing eyes upon the plate in front. More flowers, polished wooden tables and chairs. There is something almost ludicrous about it. Ten, five years ago (now, if they get the chance) these men were indulging in tribal warfare, perhaps in torture or cannibalism; now they look as docile and lifeless as bullocks at a fat-stock show.

After the hospital the acclimatization camp, with the medical inspection of new recruits. Then to the central office of the mine. Here organization has reached an American standard. Every man has a nail and a number on the wall of a big office. Here every day he brings his little book of work tickets and the half is torn off and stuck on the nail. At the end of six months the whole book goes on. Then there are a whole series of other labels, a red one when the man is on holiday and a blue one for bad work and so the reduction of pay: a yellow one for absence at hospital: a green one for prison, etc. It is possible by looking at a man's nail to see at a glance his whole industrial history, while he himself keeps a duplicate history. He has also a most elaborate 'fiche medicale' which contains in great detail his physical history, with date of various vaccinations and treatments, etc. Of this, too, he keeps a duplicate.

Dr. Mottone is a most galvanic person. He drives his car furiously from point to point, leaps out, darts at his objective, and after a rapid and brilliant exposé says '*Maintenant—allons !*' and darts back to the car. He now shot me into the big factory where the copper is smelted. I will spare you any attempted description of this vast and modern plant. I will only exclaim at the beauty of the flames springing up in the copper furnaces, green, and blue, and at the way in which I had to pass doors seemingly through a hail of red hot coals, stand under a rain of pulverized ore and climb up and down iron ladders at high speed. The dump here is most impressive, being made of the refuse of copper ore, which is a red-black carrying a high polish. At last it was over and, feeling quite burned up, with dress and stockings spoiled, I went back to dinner at the hotel.

As I was shaking hands and thanking my guide I was suddenly aware, out of the corner of my eye, of a very obvious Englishman striding into the hotel, a tall, lean, red-burnt person with golden hair and blue eyes and wearing his well-cut shirt and shorts with a difference. We picked each other up without hesitation and I found myself very much in luck. He and Captain Swettenham, who also appeared, proved most congenial, all the more so after the avalanches of continental politeness I had been accepting all day. They belonged to a commission for the delimitation of the boundary between the Congo and Northern Rhodesia and they have a moving camp out in the bush 180 miles away. Captain Swettenham is seconded from the Army for the job; the other, Dr. Evans, is a man about whom I have often wondered, for he is District Commissioner for a unique district, one formed out of twenty glorious little islands that lie east of Fiji. The District Commissioner there, quite isolated, must always be a doctor. I had read the book written by his predecessor about this glorious district and the beauty of the island and islanders, utterly untouched by civilization. So when he said he was a District Commissioner and named his region I said 'You mean you are the D.C. of Paradise ?', and of course he said 'How did you know ?' It turned out that he had been on his way home on leave when a cable met him at Capetown giving him the offer to do a stint as doctor with the boundary commission in Central Africa. So up he came.

They were a delightful couple. We had a drink and then dined together and we discussed the Samoan question and it was great to find someone with whom I could revel in eulogies of the South Sea islanders. I was very tired but I could not resist an invitation to go to the pictures with them, for they were in Elizabethville for dissipation and had bumped nearly 200 miles on a lorry to get it. Unfortunately it was the film *Verdun* and we gazed in gloomy boredom at exploding shells, falling aeroplanes and marching troops.

They proposed that I should come back and stay with them at their camp. They promised to show me the real, raw native and big game too. You can imagine how agonizing it was to have to refuse such a chance but the next day I was under the Governor's orders to proceed by car on a five hours' drive through the bush to Panda, the biggest centre of the mining industry.[1]

I had to get up at six in the morning to meet Dr. Mottone for breakfast at six-thirty. Then we got into his car and went rattling over an appalling road at high speed.

Elizabethville is very new and has been run up in the continental Cubist style with steel frames and cement. As there are plenty of trees and flowers and the houses are rather nice with their vivid paint and fancy tiles, the whole place looks quite cheerful. But the minute you leave the last house, the bush closes in upon you, the same African bush that seems to stretch in a hardly broken sheet for several hundreds, perhaps thousands of miles in all directions.

It is a new kind of bush to me. It is not the thin thorn scrub that you see in much of South Africa, nor the real tropical jungle as I imagine it to be, but a thin forest of medium sized trees, growing fairly sparsely out of very thick tall grasses and with a slight undergrowth of shrubs. The trees have a generally European look, though

[1] A year or so later Dr. Evans came to see me in Oxford and we luxuriated in talk about the Pacific islands and islanders.

every one is strange, and the red track twisting among them might be a lane in Devon rather than in Central Africa. Impossible to believe that this woodland is the haunt of lions and buck: impossible, indeed, to imagine oneself in the Belgian Congo. But as you look into the verdure you see that the grasses, very beautiful ones, are all strange and that a rule seems to obtain that the bigger the trees the smaller the leaves, the smaller the trees the bigger the leaves, until you get little sticks supporting a dozen huge lobes like the flaps of elephant's ears. Then you see, every fifty yards, regularly, the only architecture in the bush, that of the ants, ant-heaps, cone-shaped, and as tall as cottages, whose builders have incorporated perhaps half a dozen small trees, and on whose walls, instead of the ordinary grass, hangs a thick, feverishly bright growth. And as you pass mile after mile of this rich vegetation—rich in comparison with most of South Africa—you wonder why it is utterly neglected by man, even by the natives, who in tiny, rare villages, snatch a corner of a glade for maize. The answer is the fly and the mosquito, fever for man and death for beast, and you realize that this tame, monotonous country is a dangerous zone. The trees are all half-rotten with damp, their bark covered with mosses and lichen and often peeling away.

About thirty miles out from Elizabethville we stopped at a new mine, only just discovered. There was a slight rise in the ground here and on the slope where the trees were scant you could see the regular gashes made by the prospectors, as they groped for the seam. They struck it, too, for we climbed down the first shaft and saw the gleaming stratifications banding the rock. Jade-green malachite and beside it the cobalt, the valuable ore used for making steel stainless. Here and there is a space in the rocks; the malachite had been able to ooze about before it hardened and it could be taken out of these grottoes in convolutions like intestines, truly the bowels of the earth. Copper, it seems, can take on many colours, red, green, golden-bronze, and red-black. I was much impressed by this mine in the bush, this first hole in virgin earth, with one white man in a little shanty and a hundred natives. This is probably the nucleus of a big town, and in fifty or sixty years this copper will create round itself hotels and cinemas and trams, all that goes with such a town, drink, and prostitution and literary societies. And the Africans — ? My appreciation of the dramatic was cut short by some kind of machine dropping some ore on my head in this makeshift gallery. Two natives extricated me and after a bit we went on.

We now visited another big mine where 500 natives were employed. The danger here was dynamite. Explosions were going off in all directions. But Dr. Mottone seemed to think we bore charmed lives and, since mine was not to reason why, we plunged on. American shovels, huge, dragon-like machines, were eating into the earth, five tons to a mouthful, and all the processes of stamping, pulverizing and washing were going on with the highest speed and efficiency. Natives everywhere, dragging off their hats and bowing as we passed and staring with a dog-like look of incomprehension. But the conditions are good, mostly open-air work, and only eight hours a day, as against nine in the Union.

On again. We passed a gang of prisoners working with rings round their necks and each chained to the other. They are road-workers and live in moving camps. I compared the Basuto prisoners wandering about freely and hardly guarded; still more the Samoans. I asked to see the prison-camps so we dug out the police sergeant and made an inspection. Nothing here to complain about, the conditions excellent, food good and the prisoners very healthy looking.

Now we made a long stretch, and reached Panda about five o'clock. The land rises at Panda and it is with an extraordinary sense of relief that you find yourself above those smothering, blinding trees. Looking back they stretch for ever like a blue-green sea and even where the ground humps a little it does not throw off its heavy cloak. A spire of smoke alone told us where the last mine, Luisha, lay buried in trees.

But now Panda demanded all our attention, for this, too, rose just as suddenly out of the bush, with all its refining factories, mills for making sulphuric acid, and all the range of boilers, sheds, shafts, cranes and chimneys that express modern industry.

First we inspected the native villages, all the houses the 'type Mottone' of which my guide is justly proud. Before he came they sent for a Johannesburg expert to advise and he started them off on the compound-barrack buildings. Dr. Mottone came in time to stop them before they got very far. He hates them. Quite apart from the problem of celibacy, he says that it is bad to crowd people together. That, in itself, leads to quarrelling and crime. But most of all to the spread of disease and bad habits. So he uses these few barracks already made when he came as schools and offices.

Passing through these villages we saw something of the work done for the women. Every woman gets 10 francs a month for keeping her house clean and her family; another 10 francs for each child between five and fourteen; another ten when she is with child. This amount is taken away for an untidy house or for neglected children. We saw the women filing up to draw their money. There is also a special welfare service for women and children. The women have to bring their babies twice a week to be weighed, washed and medically inspected. As a bribe they get a cup of sugar and a bit of soap and a money prize for regular attendance over a long period. A trained woman in each camp supervizes and keeps records of the growth and health of each baby. It was rather jolly to see dozens of squalling black babies being dipped. The mothers looked on uncomprehending.

We examined the hospital and here found very serious cases of dysentery and tuberculosis, the result of the frightful famine in Ruanda-Urundi last year which has reduced these people very seriously in stamina. Round the hospital in all camps is a group of very much bigger houses. Into these 'expecting' mothers are temporarily moved in the last week or two, so as to have good conditions, to draw a special ration and to be close to the hospital in case of need. I came away feeling positively crushed by the elaboration of organization. What a contrast with South Africa where, of course, they say that the native up here is 'spoiled'.[1]

Tonight, Dr. Mottone and I are at the guest house of the Union Minière, a very fine house, in beautiful order, but, apparently, with no servants. All happens by magic. We had dinner in a private room of the Mess. I now write in a suite of rooms that was prepared for the King and Queen of the Belgians when they came here recently and very luxurious it is. It is very late. The sirens have gone for the midnight shift to come on and from my verandah I can see the entire valley lit up. The whole place reverberates with the stamping machines and the green flames can be seen leaping inside the factories. There are explosions every now and then and much whistling and panting and stamping. Dr. Mottone has gone to bed and given orders that I must be up at six. So I must turn in too.

A very long and busy day. I can only pick out a few points in it.

[1] I must add a footnote here to recall the scandals of the 'red rubber' in the Congo early in the century and the attack upon it by Morel and other Britishers. I could remember playing on the sands of Blankenberge with my brother and when the Belgian holiday-makers recognized our nationality they made a demonstration against us. Could reformation go further, I now asked myself?

One was a visit to the research department. They have a staff of about fifty geologists of all nationalities and their sample room is indeed a place of beauty. At the first blink you imagine you are in a butterfly room, or an exhibition of those marvellous fish that gem the South Seas. But it is simply rock and mostly copper. Some pieces are like red-gold sunsets; some like jade; there are 'amethysts' as big as your head. Such shapes and patterns, too, and the most lovely spars like shining hoar-frost. A very nice Dutchman from the University of Delft was showman and he loaded me with specimens, including a lump of ore from the radium mine containing a high percentage of that precious substance.

The next item in the programme was deeply interesting, especially to anyone from South Africa. We went to the workshops where the men are trained in skilled work. The difference made here by the absence of a colour-bar is, of course, fundamental. Here the native is urged and trained to improve himself progressively, to invade the preserves of skilled mechanics. Here my ignorance of technique prevents me talking with much assurance. But I saw natives working large and complicated machines for the manufacture of iron, milling and grinding machines, planes and lathes. They were under supervision but I saw only one white man to eight or ten machines. It was the same everywhere, in the moulding, casting and forging shops, while in the carpentry there was one white man to about eighty natives. Some of the natives were making furniture, simply working from a paper plan. I could not help comparing in my mind what I had seen of technical instruction in South Africa where the missions try to run workshops to instruct the boys. There is in all of them an atmosphere of unreality, a lack of vitality, because there is no certainty that the boys will be able to continue that work but every certainty that they will never be able to go very far with it. But here I saw genuine apprenticeship, with no limitations upon the native except those inherent in himself. It is the same in all sections, electrical, motor, etc. The reason is quite simple: it does not arise from the greater humanity of the Belgian. But it does arise from policy. There is no permanent white working class to feel themselves being ousted. The white workmen are imported from Belgium and go back to Belgium. They have no stake in the country, they are well paid and presumably content. In the early days when they employed South Africans they had a strike so they simply pushed them all back across the border. Now they tell me that, although they would prefer English-speaking workmen for some reasons, they will never have them again because of this 'colour-bar mania' and trade unionism. (Hence the rejection of South Africans I saw at the frontier.) And clearly they don't want to import a Belgian working class community.

We lunched with the head of this mine, Mr. Moore, an Australian. I had a talk with him but he was naturally very guarded in his replies, being in the employ of the Belgians. He said that as far as human foresight could reach the work in the Katanga would go on increasing though 'unlimited' was a word he would never use, and of course production must be regulated according to the world's need. He had not been short of labour so far. They had given him all he asked, but that was mainly owing to the ability of Dr. Mottone.

It took us nearly five hours banging through the monotonous bush, thirty-five miles an hour over an appalling road, to get back to Elizabethville.

On the way back I took a picture of my guide and host whom I now called Bluebeard—he likes it!—a man who enjoys enormously showing off his work.

I had dinner at night with some Belgians, the chief interest of which was that one, an *avocat*, inveighed furiously against the Government for its pro-native policy and the injustice towards the European. Many white men had been ruined because the laws were so absurd. He gave the instance of a man who was starting some enterprize and who provided each native with a blanket of extra quality and extra size according to the law. They promptly sold them and next day the inspector came round and fined him heavily for each of 500 natives found without blankets. Result, bankruptcy and disappearance. Other stories of the same kind gave the impression that the government, if Draconian towards white men, at least used its pro-native laws for more than window-dressing.

Next morning I was taken to the office of the Conseil Général de Travail, a recruiting organization for all firms in Katanga. Here I made inquiries in order to discover where the labour came from, how much of it was married, and how much was induced to stay to form the new permanent population for this future black country. I was given about 20 lb. weight of reports and charts which I hope some day to digest in the comparative leisure of Oxford.

One thing I saw they were not keen either in explaining or showing me. That was the Force Publique, the conscripted native troops. These are raised through the chiefs and used, also, on public works.

However I got my way and we went to the barracks. They admitted that the chief sent his enemies, or slaves, and that the pay, 40 centimes a day (the franc is 1½d) was lower than any other rate and that the term is seven years. I interviewed two officers whom I did not like at all. They told me most of the men wanted to sign on again when the seven years were up and that they had only had one desertion last year. One can have no better reason than instinct for disbelieving that. I was told later by a District Commissioner in Northern Rhodesia that eight deserters fled to him and that he put them in jail and wrote to their O.C. The Governor wrote to their Governor, everyone wrote on and off for eight months, and there never was and never will be any reply, for the obvious reason that they will not let it get on to their official files that their men did desert. All the better for the deserters, who lived happily ever after. I thought the military quarters were very bad and could quite understand why infant mortality should be high and natality low in comparison with the Union Minière.

Then we inspected the native location, which was airy and middling good. It is in process of being pulled down and re-built, so it is not quite fair to judge it. A marvellous hospital, of course, and very handsome schools, but with rather too much bowing and scraping and sing-song recitations for my taste.

After lunch I went to interview the Governor. The more interesting questions and answers went as follows:

Q. 'I see that you have a Conseil Régional upon which prominent citizens are represented. Has it any great influence?'

A. 'Influence? No. It is purely formal. It is a useful way of giving information, etc.'

Q. 'But in British colonies as soon as you have a handful of settlers, they begin to criticize the government and to demand at least some measure of control.'

A. 'No, we have nothing of that sort here.'

Q. 'I have been much interested in the wonderful organization you have for the recruitment and treatment of labour. But I am not sure if such conditions could be produced except where you have a practically despotic government working through a few large and wealthy corporations.'

A. 'I think you are right. I think it would be difficult for small men to keep our regulations.'

Q. 'You are deliberately building up an artificial collection of peoples. Do you think that the different tribes you are mixing

P   225

are close enough to make their conglomeration possible and desirable?'

A. 'Yes, they are all more or less akin, except those from Ruanda-Urundi. We encourage them to mix and break down tribal feeling by the way we distribute them in our native towns. We are thus never likely to have faction fights as they have on the Rand where they have tribal barracks.'

Q. 'These people, taken away from their own society and rapidly industrialized and educated will soon demand some sort of expression, some say in their own destiny.'

A. 'I am aware of that. When that time comes, according to my policy, they will be allowed to form some sort of council, but always under closest supervision and control.'

In reply to questions about a prophet who had raised an anti-white religious movement and was now imprisoned for life, he said:

'Yes, he was some kind of Protestant. That is why I do not like the Protestant religion for natives. I consider the Catholic very much better suited to them. It tells them what they must believe: it is dogmatic. The native is not yet ready to think for himself. It is true that there is no such thing as a native priest who has relapsed. But he is under close supervision. As the bishop said: "*Il est prêtre, mais il est noir: je le garde*".'

Q. 'I thought that on the mines your own people seemed to be under very good discipline, better than on the Rand.'

A. 'There I do not agree with you. This is something that you cannot say but I can. Our people have not the temperament to govern natives. The Englishman is calm, always the same. The native respects that. Our people are excitable: one minute they are too familiar, the next they are in a temper.'

The Governor's wife now arrived to take me out to see various things. I asked the Governor if I could visit the prisons. I don't think he liked this, but he rang up the Commandant and the Native Commissioner and asked them to go there to receive me.

I had a long round with Madame, seeing classes, schools, welfare centres, clinics. At the jail we found excellent conditions and all the prisoners very fat and placid in spite of their chains. I asked to see the prophet and found him in the kitchen. He was the most intelligent-looking native I had yet seen here. He told me he had been in the jail ten years and thought it was time he came out. No one had been killed because of him. He beckoned me into a corner and showed me his

Bible hidden inside a kettle, with all the marked texts. We asked the others what crimes they had committed, and when one said, with cheerful candour, that he had assaulted a white woman, Madame nearly had a fit, and backed out of the cell, crying '*Monstre !*' We met a woman who had tried to poison her white master; another intelligent creature insisted on retailing the crimes of all her colleagues. I suppose we must punish by our standards but it seems rather absurd to coop all these people up for doing what in their society might be the normal or necessary thing.

In the native city they are allowed, as at Bloemfontein, to build their own houses, renting a site for a small sum. It is noticeable they always build bigger houses than we provide for them. The Governor does not like this native 'town' and is by way of pulling it down, and building a model municipal location. But it compares well with the Rand towns.

We went back to the Governor's house where we met the Bishop and others, but they all talked too fast for me. The Governor has adopted two black orphan children who trotted into the room, little creatures of five and six, in immaculate clothes, and stared at us all with a solemnity I never saw equalled even in children. I was much interested in the fact of this adoption. I can't imagine any English governor doing it, at least to the extent of having them in the drawing room.

I questioned the Governor about the attitude of Belgium towards the Congo. He said it had changed enormously since the War but there was still a great deal of ignorance and prejudice about it and he had evidently small respect for parliamentary supervision. People in Belgium still said when they met a man from the Congo, 'What have you done ?' Also there was far too much desire to come out here and get rich quick and then go back. People would not leave Belgium to settle down to farming in Africa as the British did. Asked if the Congo was a white man's country, he said, 'Probably not.' (This, from the point of view of its future, is very important.) I certainly noticed that all the children looked pasty. Katanga, at least, seems to be a difficult country for farming and they draw their food from the Rhodesias.

At night I dined with the British Consul, who was formerly Secretary of Native Affairs in Northern Rhodesia and whose main duty here is to watch over the interests of the many 'British' natives whom the Belgians attract to their mines. In view of the growing importance of the Northern Rhodesian mines the Government there are going to stop recruiting by degrees in five years. But this will not stop the natives going voluntarily if they prefer Katanga conditions. He boasted that the natives preferred working under bad conditions with the British than under good ones under Belgians. I wonder! He also claimed the credit for the good conditions on the Katanga mines on the grounds that his Government demanded a high standard of conditions before they would allow their natives to go at all. He and his wife were very critical of the Belgian administration, partly, it seemed, on the grounds that they do too much for the native.

I left early next morning, 6.30 a.m.—the Governor's representative seeing me off into a special single compartment tacked on to a goods train. We dragged along very slowly, which at least had the merit of giving me time to think.

What do I think of Katanga? I hardly can come to any valuable conclusion after so short a visit but a few ideas suggest themselves that I may correct later.

The Belgians are on their mettle after the 'red rubber' scandals and are genuinely trying to do their best to clear their reputation. Their methods are a world away from ours. They believe in centralization and in the most elaborate and logical code of laws and regulations, covering every detail of administration. We, in contrast, tackle each problem as it arises and show a great trust in our officials. We, secure—too secure, perhaps—in our reputation, do not worry much about a few abuses; we feel that with Britons, these could never go far, and if on some mines, a manager does beat his natives against the law, the magistrate, if he knows this man, will probably look the other way. As for hospitals and housing, our standards, even in England, are far behind the Continental standard in many ways: we don't care much how things look if they work. And when we hear the Belgians praised, we just smile, so sure are we that these Continentals are 'no good with natives', and that we alone have the art.

But seriously, while granting all I have to the Belgians I must make some reservations. I had the impression that those thousands of natives that I saw, men and women mostly of a very primitive kind, were inhabiting those model huts and standing in queues at clinics etc. with about as much comprehension of what it all meant as sheep dipped and clipped and put in the pens of a model stock-market. That, you may say, is inevitable at present, and no reason why their bodies should not be cared for. But I very much doubt whether the Belgians want, or know how, to develop African initiative and individuality. In their own service I observed a discipline of an almost military kind, junior officials were ordered about in the tone we keep for natives across the border, while the native—well it is very hard to define his position or attitude. I could see, for one thing, that my attempts to get into conversation with some of the skilled natives to discuss their work, find out where they came from, etc. was a novelty. These men are developed more as tools than as human beings. It was with more scientific than human interest that the doctor asked me to observe the dawning intelligence on their faces. But this difference, which is more subtle than I have been able to show, becomes more clear when we turn to education. All the schools I saw were Roman Catholic with children doing meaningless recitations, learning perfect handwriting and hem-stitching and behaving with robot-like docility. There was a good deal of exclaiming over the little ones, (the sort of attitude expressed by the exclamation 'What a little poppet!'). I think the black has a certain fascination for the Latin. My guides would stroke the children's heads and even playfully smack the mothers and pull their plaited coils. English officials would never do that, though they will probably never take so many blood slides. But sometimes— not always—they accept that the native is a man, with all a man's mysterious potentialities. With our official his instinct to share his ideal of self-rule wars with his (apparent) interest in keeping the native down. So, while we have colour-bars and bad housing, we have schools where the prefect system obtains, and we have native commissioners who respect (almost love) the native, not as a fascinating curiosity, not for his music, art and strangeness (as many French do) but as a man who may have a right to be consulted, within reason, as to his own destiny. So under the Anglo-Saxons with their varieties of Protestantism, none very sure of themselves, the traditions and restraints of law and high valuation of freedom, the native develops somehow, anyhow, sprawling uncertainly all ways. Even in the Union, so long as British influence lasts, though half the Europeans distrust and condemn Ballinger and Champion, they are still neither deported nor jailed and the I.C.U. develops apace. They would get short shrift, I think, under Belgium. I am pretty sure that that prophet with a Bible in a kettle would not be in prison on a life-sentence in the Union. That is the difference between the rule of law and *droit administratif*. But, in uniform and far-sighted hygienic efficiency, the contrast is all in favour of the Belgians. Educationally, as I have said, we are embarked on an experiment that leads—no one knows where.

The differences between Continental and British Africa will be immense one hundred years hence but what they will be we cannot foretell. But in all this I am groping in the dark of half- or quarter-knowledge and I should put question-marks after every sentence in the hope that as I grope further into Africa I may remove them one by one.

Northern Rhodesia

February 1930

———————————⊷◆⊶———————————

I think the last instalment ended with my leaving Elizabethville early on the morning of Saturday, 15 Feburary. I was in a goods train and it was terribly hot and there was nothing to eat or drink. I had brought with me a food parcel from the hotel but it proved quite uneatable and gladdened the stomach of a grave piccaninny squatting at the railside. My torments were not made any less by the white guard, who had been quite insulting when I first boarded the train, but who had crawled when the Governor's representative, coming to see me off, had arrived and cursed him. He had then found a whole compartment for me (having earlier assured me there was no room) and now hung about the door telling me what a lonely life was his. I had not been able to resist the temptation of a Capetown peach which he had offered me and which had blessed my parched mouth and now in return he expected to be able to converse with me all day through. He rather fancied himself as a squire of dames. I expatiated on the value of the habit of reading and offered him a book on which to make a start. It was all in vain. I could not move him and snubs of the most direct kind had no effect.

By the evening he was in a condition in which he could only repeat again and again how much he wished that I would turn back at Sakania and so remain on his train. When at last we made Sakania, the frontier halt, I quickly walked off up a track into the *brousse*, anxious to get a little exercise before I boarded the Rhodesian train. It was very dark, though anything but silent, for the frogs were popping like a gargantuan champagne supper and the crickets were screaming until it seemed as if a needle was piercing your head from ear to ear. Imagine my annoyance when I found the guard insisted on accompanying me into the bush! I have never seen anything quite so funny off a musical-hall stage as the picture of him sighing and making absurd faces up to the last possible moment. I got something out of him beside the peach, though not much. I asked him about the railway regulations for white employees, including one which forbade them to strike a native. Were they kept? Not by him, it seemed. If he told a native to do something and he did not obey, he told him to come and stand in front of him just *there* (this was acted), and then he struck him five times over the face, like *this*, as hard as he could.

At the frontier station I saw my friend the Belgian magistrate and his assistant who had given me so much trouble on my arrival. Now they dropped their eyes and walked away. I had reported them to their chief at Elizabethville; he had—apparently—been furious and had told me that, quite apart from the importance with which they had endowed me, my papers were quite in order.

And now I am spending a night and a day and a night on the train, darning stockings and reading Congo laws and looking out at the eternal ant-heaps and trees and the long waving grasses which no cattle eat. There is no sign of life, only at night, above the roaring of the train, the ceaseless shouting of the frogs and the screaming of the crickets.

We got to Broken Hill, the big Northern Rhodesian lead and zinc mine at seven in the morning. Here I looked out anxiously for I hoped to be met by the Provincial Commissioner. On the platform we passed each other once or twice, for I had never expected a P.C. to be so young, and he expressed much the same notion himself. His car was there and he drove me off through the staked and taped outlines of a future town to have breakfast.

There is no type of British Colonial servant, only a bewildering variety. I cease to expect anything and just open my mind like a plate of wax and wait for the impression. This one was cynical and mocked both me for my interest in his work and himself for doing it. He professed neither to know what he was doing nor where it would all lead and he laughed to scorn what I told him of the elaborate methods of the Congo which, by the way, he had never visited in spite of long service on the border. Most of what we do for the native, he said, has no relation whatever to his mind or life, just as he knows nothing of us. After twenty-five years of experience in Northern Rhodesia he felt he knew nothing of the native, neither the working of his mind, nor his customs. He told me of life on the mines, of the breakdown of tribal discipline, of the crowd of women who hang about to be temporary 'wives' to the miners while these do their contract. He declared it an excellent plan. It suited everyone, including the mine managers.

But he was very pessimistic about the type of man Britain was sending out now, both to the mines and the Colonial Service. The only things they asked when they came up was what the games were and whether they could get dancing. They did the minimum amount of work and then rushed off on noisy motor cycles. Where is to be found the man who could safely be sent off to a lonely station for a year?

He took me to see the compound. Here were separate huts, not compounds, but the place was a striking contrast to the Congo. Water, baths and latrines were scarce and primitive, the whole place messy and unkempt. The P.C. laughed at me. 'They like it much better like this. They hate being fussed over and kept hygienic.' But there are so many things they hate that we impose for our own good that I do not see why we should not impose some for theirs.

Then it was on the train again for Northern Rhodesia's capital, Livingstone.

I had luck again on the train with two rather good encounters. One was with a water engineer who was up there advising the Northern Rhodesian Government how to get water for the new towns that are going to grow up round the mines. He had been for many years advisory expert to the Union government. The stories he told me of Dutch graft since the Nationalist Government came in left me gasping. Yet it was difficult to disbelieve. He was a gentleman with a quiet convincing manner. It must be remembered that water schemes mean:

(a) A lot of money to contractors.
(b) Benefit to individual farmers.
(c) Labour for poor whites.
(d) The chance to move voters into areas where they will prove most useful to the party in power—the Nationalists from now on?

He instanced the cost of wasteful irrigation dams, costing the country millions. He told me of direct offers of bribes to himself to give a favourable opinion upon a scheme that he knew would not pay; of money passing into the hands of members of the present cabinet; of municipal councils bribed to put schemes out on contract that they could have done more cheaply themselves. He was extremely gloomy about the future of South Africa and the absolute helplessness there of the English-speaking element at present. On the native question he made one rather interesting contribution. He has had to handle big

233

quantities of native labour and has never yet had a native beaten. This question of controlling labour is all a question of temperament, it seems. Some men can do without the stick, others can't.

We had some meals together on the train. Then a very lusty, fair-haired person, McGillivray by name, got hold of me and asked me to dine with him. He had been five years doing architecture at Liverpool under Patrick Abercrombie (the brother of one of my greatest friends) and was now hoping to have a hand in building Northern Rhodesia. But chiefly, having heard of my journey and its purpose, he wanted to bully me. His father was an M.P. in the young Parliament of Southern Rhodesia and father and son were infuriated that through the Secretary of States's veto an ignorant, sentimental British public could, and did, interfere with Southern Rhodesia. He told me of attending in England a Students Christian Movement meeting at his university and how, out of their utter ignorance, the speakers presumed to dictate what should be done in Africa: 'and now *you* —!' It was quite comical to see the contrast between his political resentment and his social friendliness towards me. Eating his dinner and drinking his wine, I humbly said I was only here to learn and perhaps he would teach me. And teach he did all through dinner and very long afterwards, though what he said I really cannot remember, whether because of the wine—and liqueur—or because I had heard it all so often before. Not that there is not a great deal of truth in what I am quite sure he must have said. Savagery has to be seen to be believed, and even seeing it as I do is not the same as living with it, making it work, having it in your kitchen. But that only means that there is a responsibility almost more than they can bear put upon people in these countries and that they certainly need the stimulus and the restraints of external and informed criticism. But there's the rub. How to make the criticism informed? Southern Rhodesia is at present embittered over the outcry raised over the Juvenile Offenders' Act and the name of J. H. Harris of the Aborigines Protection Society makes all her people see red. Well, my talk with this man was *all* very interesting as, with all our differences, he was a most likeable person, lusty and good-looking, and representative of a small young nationality, transplanted into the heart of south-central Africa.

We arrived at Livingstone about 6 a.m. this morning. I easily distinguished the Governor's A.D.C., from his uniform. We got into the

Governor's Wolseley and went off to Government House, a big rambling place converted from a hotel and half smothered in its abundant garden. Here, after the prolonged discomfort of the train, I slipped happily into Government House luxury—a suite of rooms, a glorious bath, two white-and-scarlet clad Africans and an English maid.

I went in to breakfast to find the Governor's wife, one of those big overwhelming, rather old-fashioned-looking women. I can only compare her with the photographs of Mrs. Baldwin, or with a large, splendid cabbage rose just tumbling over its prime. Sir James Maxwell, one of Lugard's pupils from the West Coast, was—had to be—all that she was not, in order to complete the married unit—small, silent, restrained, intelligent, cautious. As for the A.D.C., there seemed nothing left for *him* but to imitate non-existence to the utmost that a living man may do. Lady Maxwell was extremely kind. From the moment that I had made my curtsey to His Excellency beside the bacon-and-egg-loaded sideboard, she boomed at me plans of the most attractive kind and my protests about my own ideas of work were simply smothered. However, I caught the Governor's eye and one glance told me that all was well. So, immediately after breakfast, I was taken over to the government offices and introduced to the Secretary for Native Affairs, Mr. Moffat Thompson. He proved a stiff character. At first I thought he was the most jaundiced and bad-tempered official I had met. He had a bull-dog face and he barked out a series of questions about my business. There is nothing like this sort of treatment, as Jane Eyre remarked about Rochester, for putting you at your ease, so I stood my ground and made my face and eye as hard as his. Besides, I thought, he could not be quite so grim as he pretended. I was right.

'All right,' he growled, 'you'd better stay here. You can work in this office.' Then he went barking all over the place and white clerks and black porters got a table and chairs in the room leading out of his own and ran about for documents and codes and reports until I and the table were buried under them. 'Will *that* be enough for you?' he asked. I got down to work. I worked all morning from eight-thirty to one (and no morning tea) and from two to four. I worked with one half of my head and with the other listened to the business of the Secretary for Native Affairs coming through the door, every word of which interested me for it was a great chance to study native administration in action. (Was this his intention?) I noted that he spoke to everyone who came as harshly as he had spoken to me. He seemed pretty busy and as soon as he went out of the room there were streams of callers coming into mine and asking for him. When he came back and I reported them, he said:

'That's all right. The rumour has gone round about you and they are all coming in to find out who *you* are. Mr. X heard you were my new typist but said you couldn't be as you were too polite. I suppose what you really are is one of these people from Geneva coming to teach us our business. Or do you come from the Aborigines Protection Society? We spend half our time here answering questionnaires that show the utmost ignorance of all our conditions and the deepest suspicion of our characters.'

'But don't you think', I said, 'that it is a healthy restraint for brutal officials in the Native Department to know that they are being carefully watched from London and Geneva?'

That set him off. He leapt up from his desk and walked round and round my table, waving his arms until I thought he would strike me in his wrath. He shouted for the Assistant Secretary, Mr. Horne, to second his curses and I could see officials at all the windows opposite looking out to see what the row was about. He had an extraordinary way of clearing his throat in the middle of a sentence that was exactly like the growl of a wild animal.

Well, of course we became great friends and I got to like him enormously. The only trouble was that I was never allowed to do much reading for he would look over my shoulder at what lay on my desk and start talking and arguing. In fact, he gave up three whole days to my education and was indefatigable in looking up old laws and obtaining new reports.

At four o'clock yesterday afternoon Lady Maxwell kindly arranged for me to go up the Zambesi to the Victoria Falls. In order to waste no time I was to interview the Director of Education and the Head of the Public Works Department *en route*. So, with Captain Hopkins, we all four motored to the river and there boarded the Governor's very smart launch.

It was really a tragedy not being able to give all my attention to that noble river, nor even to be able to be silent and alone for five minutes to accept its impression. After the thousands of miles of scrub and desert which I had passed; after the miserable trickles which the Afrikaner calls sluits and which are—mostly—the South African 'rivers'; it was like a miracle to see the land held apart by this vast shining width of water—a mile and a half! Not that I could ever see its full expanse for long slender islands cut it up. The banks are crowded to the rim with growth of intense greenness and, among the mass of undistinguished vegetation, tall palm-trees, almost blue in colour, bring that touch of the romantic that seems inseparable from the palm. Small white egrets and black divers fly on sudden short busy journeys up the edge of the river or cross from island to island.

It is not, as I had expected, a music like thunder that warns you that soon the river is going to fling itself four hundred feet over a precipice. The first sign that answers your expectancy is a cloud. At first, approaching, you hardly notice it; then you wonder why one white cloud from the sky should have fallen so low. The cloud is the spray hanging in the air, a thousand feet in height.

I will not dare to compete at length with the many descriptions of this wonder of the world where a river 1,900 feet wide is suddenly compressed into a space of 200 feet and falls nearly 400 feet throwing up a cloud of vapour which the Africans called the smoke that sounds. But I must, for my own memory's sake, get down a word or two which readers might well skip for nothing is duller than descriptions of scenery that either you have seen or can never hope to see.

I think that one thing that makes these Falls so impressive is the contrast between the utter placidity of the wide river, moving smoothly, sleepily between low banks, and the sudden inevitable crash over the precipice into that terrible depth. Gazing at it, one reads human sensations into the river. What a terrible awakening! What frightful, helpless falling! What fury and agony in that gulf where, blinded by spray, the flood fights and roars as if in an effort to escape, and striking the drenched black walls of its prison breaks upwards in pillars of foam. For there is only one way of escape: the river that spreads itself over a mile and more of its bed must now find and force its way through a single exit barely 200 feet across. No wonder that the depth of the gorge here has never been plumbed: that even iron railway lines dipped into that water were twisted like corkscrews. You can see the old waterfalls which, through age after age of geological time, the river has made, as the strong water, groping for a fault in the dolomite has found one and gnawed a new chasm for itself.

Another feature of the Falls is that you walk right along the river-bank sheer in the face of the drop, so that even with my small camera I could take a picture of the very centre of the mile-long cataract.

But no photograph can show, except in the dry season, the full drop of the water, because the base of the pouring columns is generally veiled in spray. This has bred a forest on the opposing cliffs called the Rain Forest, soaked with the ceaseless spray and shot through with sunlight. It is worth while to walk ankle deep in the spongy earth with the water, tossed from side to side by the wind, pouring down upon you, now in sheets, now in mere rain, to get the impression of these glades. Here and there you can creep to the edge and see how on every bit of earth, every rock between the falling water, the spray has bred a luxuriance of trees and bushes. It is this that soothes the starkness of the Falls. It makes a deep frame of colour for the water which is yellow-white, like a polar-bear, where it springs from the brink, and pure white where, in falling, it separates into millions of separate drops. There is one place where, according to the experts, the river has found a flaw and is beginning to cut a new chasm which in a million years or more may run behind the present one.

All the way back, with a stormy sunset frowning over the broad river, I longed to be alone with it, but must carry on with my interview on education, an excellent thing at the right time. Then, at a sundowner on the verandah of Government House, I must try to tell Lady Maxwell what I thought of the Falls. That was quite impossible, as it has been impossible in this diary-letter, for their beauty and terror reach depths of you where interpretation becomes beyond your power or wish.

Last night, after dinner, Lady Maxwell having retired and Captain Hopkins, having learned with long practice to sleep with the inconspicuousness necessary to an A.D.C., the Governor and I talked. I count those long nightly talks with him as one of the most interesting events of my journey. In all the vagueness and variety of the views I have heard he was like a rock. Trained as a doctor, he brings something of the scientific spirit to a problem so much the sport of prejudice and sentimentality. Behind him lies the powerful tradition of Lord Lugard—from whom I get letters as I travel—and his own apprenticeship in native territories which are not rent by the disharmonies of European settlement. He has a slow, deliberate, resolute way of speaking, with his eyes holding yours and watching half sarcastically for your response. Not altogether an attractive man, too cold and dogmatic, but that does not matter, although in these late talks I found that I disagreed with him on every point but one that we discussed.

Firstly, he supports the Hertzog scheme of differentiation in politics and segregation in social life. Here, I think, he brings a mind moulded on the West Coast to deal with a problem that he does not know at first hand. He flatly refused to believe in my semi-Europeanized, urbanized, detribalized native as the van of a following host which will be content with nothing less than equal political status and who can never hope to get adequate consideration without it.

Secondly, he resents and discredits the control attempted in native policy by Westminster and Geneva but accepts that of Whitehall. He claims that native policy is one of the most expert subjects in the world and the opinions of a Wedgwood, a J. H. Harris, and the representatives of Liberia and Esthonia—and presumably of myself?—are negligible except to confuse and embarrass. I accused him here of distorting the record, and quoted historical parallels to show how influence, from Britain at least, had been vital in the past, and asked him whether the League of Nations did not make another Bondelswarts suppression unlikely.[1] We hammered away at it without coming any nearer agreement.

Thirdly, he is an intense believer in the 'indirect' system of government: as a 'Nigerian' that goes without saying. He would carry it all lengths, is so carrying it at this moment, some would say. For I come to Northern Rhodesia at the very interesting moment when he is crystallizing a system of native courts and native councils. He is calmly prepared for all and any but the very worst resulting abuses. My heart agrees with him but I am less sure about my head. For he is doing this at the very time when large-scale industry is being introduced into the country by the opening-up of mines whose wealth, we are promised, is all but illimitable. Is he not launching two policies that will ultimately be irreconcilable? Under prolonged imperial government it *may* be possible to give segregation without its dangers, industrialism without its corruption of native life. More for the sake of argument I opposed him. But, meeting on the politically virgin country of Northern Rhodesia, he with West Africa behind him and I with South, here, too, we failed to come to terms.

---

[1] The horrible incident when, in its mandated territory of South West Africa, the Afrikaner Government bombed dissident Africans from the air with heavy loss of life.

Today I interviewed the head of the Mining Department to learn something of the industrial possibilities of the country. Then back to Moffat Thompson's office once more, to be nagged and bullied and instructed. He came to tea at Government House with Mr. Horne, so we continued our arguments at the tea-table and in the car to the river and in the launch and all round the lovely verdant tangle of the island of Kandahar. And when Moffat Thompson dropped back exhausted Mr. Horne took up the barrage and again I longed for a moment in which to drink in and keep for ever the picture of the glorious river, sprinkled with palmy islands and, as evening came on, carrying on its surface legions of coloured clouds.

Back to a sundowner at Government House where His Excellency joined the already strong forces against me and drove me into impossible positions which I had never intended to take up. Well, we can but speak from what we are and what we think we know and both are limited while in this case we are up against an unknown factor that mocks all our gropings after wisdom—the potentiality of the African. It is easy for the eye of faith to magnify it. The vast majority are primitives, their minds imprisoned by notions of magic that block the need or effort to reason; their characters moulded by unknown centuries of tribal life, the virtues of which are not ours, nor the vices. That the tribe will not and should not survive I have now come to believe, and also that the man, torn from his tribe and thrown into our individualistic civilization, is, and for long will be, a man without a home, literally, politically, economically, spiritually. I do not believe that we can adapt those elaborate, rigid tribal sanctions to his new position. As well might a man who has trodden down a cobweb attempt to reconstruct it. The Church says that to this spiritually homeless man Christianity will supply all the needs. But Christianity grows more and more suspect to the educated native in very proportion to his education. He regards it as the gilding of his chains; his growing anti-white attitude identifies the parson with the employer and the policeman who is to him the closest manifestation of the State. Not that I depreciate the missions. I do that less and less as I see their work. But the 'new native' demands justice as a man, not only charity and conversion as a soul. What, then, can we do? Hold up the process of 'civilization' where the effects are obviously harmful? Try to raise whole communities where communities can be kept whole and, for the rest, study and watch and control the points of contact so that the least evil and the most good can come of them?

But I digress shockingly and I must come back to dinner at Government House, with Lady Maxwell extolling Northern Rhodesia as a white man's country to the embarrassment of the aide-de-camp who carefully keeps his wife and child out of it in England.

At night the Governor again, and long hours of sitting and talking, almost forgetting the way in which the mosquitoes were gorging themselves upon my ankles. Alas, there is never time nor strength at the end of such days to record them in this diary.

Next day a long morning's work and a quick dash by car to say good-bye to the Falls, this time from the bridge, surely the most dramatic bridge in the world, with its arch doubled by arches of rainbows spanning the foam.

In the afternoon I sat again in His Excellency's office and he honoured me by going through his correspondence with the Secretary of State on native policy. It was so enthralling that I almost missed my train. Laden with documents and bitterly upbraided by His Excellency and Moffat Thompson for the scanty time I had given to their domain, I was rushed to the train by the A.D.C., spruce, kind, soothing and self-effacing to the end.

Heavens, how I appreciate these moments when I find my reserved compartment and spread myself in the luxury of being alone, while Africa—bush and grass and sand—spins past by the window! Yet I felt warm with gratitude towards Livingstone for the kindness with which I had been treated and for all that I had been helped to learn.

Torrents of rain darkened the country and swilled round the little grass villages. In the dining-car was a woman I had seen in Livingstone. Her face had haunted me. She seemed to have been closely in touch with me at some time in my life and yet was now a complete stranger. I gave up my seat in the train to enable her to sit next to her friend. Suddenly I heard a loud, excited cry, 'Margery! *Margery!*' and a hand gripped my shoulder. She was shaking with excitement and calling out in this excited way 'Margery!' and then her own name. Then it flashed upon me. As a very little girl at the Harrogate Ladies (!) College she had been a Sixth Form prefect and I had adored her from afar. I had in the terminology of the time been 'gone on' her with an adoration so common then in schools, the only adoration of its kind which had ever distressed my mind. I remembered how I had worshipped her, collecting little bunches of flowers to put in her way, getting behind her at prayers, gazing at the hairpins in her 'bun' and hoping one would fall out so that I could treasure it for ever. And now my goddess, kind and comely but also stout and matronly, had lost all her divinity. Our minds were far apart, yet for the sake of that past, for which I blushed, I had to sacrifice my precious evening on the train, which I so much needed for making notes and resting, to reminiscences that to me were now, shorn of magic, sad and rather embarrassing. Yet magic it had been and for this she had a claim upon my gratitude.

Southern Rhodesia

February 1930

I arrived at Bulawayo early in the morning and went off to what is supposed to be the best hotel to get breakfast. It was a dirty, sordid sort of place. With unusual foresight, I had long before made an appointment for 9 a.m. with Colonel Carbutt, head of the Native Affairs Department, the headquarters for all Matabeleland, and I was able to keep it.

Colonel Carbutt was quite the least responsive official of any with whom I have had to deal. A shy, heavy man, who hid behind his reserve a lifetime of interest and adventure passed in Rhodesia. Was it, as it well could have been, that he resented being ordered by the Governor to give up three days to my education or whether he was just like that. I never knew. At any rate, merely being with him was extraordinarily hard work. And presumably it was the same for him.

In the morning he took me to the native location where I saw Africans building new houses without any supervision at all and, apparently, building them well. I mention this because in South Africa natives are not allowed to build even their own locations because of the colour-bar. White men build them at three or four times the expense and the unfortunate native, on his low rate of wages, has to pay the rent.

You may have noticed not long ago in the newspaper that very serious fighting took place in the native location here between the Matabele (the ex-overlords, a military tribe, off-shoot of the Zulus) and the former serf people, the Mashona. Colonel Carbutt appears to have handled the crisis well but Bulawayo had rather a panicky moment. All is quiet again now and a commission is to inquire into the the situation in the location. This looked a moderately decent place with fair-sized houses, dismal as they all are. One single man—a printer's hand, I think—had built himself a house and railed and beflowered it to show what a native can do. It showed the kind of self-respect and rapid assimilation of at least one side of our civilization that has struck me so often on this tour.

At the location we found a parson of the African Methodist Church, an all-native organization, affiliated with a similar body in America. The parson, Mr. Tehwelo, though this was a surprise visit, took us into a house that was in perfect order, swept and garnished in the highest degree. He had also an office with desk and neatly filed papers and printed charts showing the system of church administration. As far as I can make out this church functions quietly and successfully. It has its yearly synods in Capetown, or, less frequently, in America. The bishop in Africa is an American Negro; Colonel Carbutt tells me he is an able and well-educated person. In fact this native organization seems an exception to the general rule of awkward compromise between Christianity and paganism plus financial scandals all too common among young independent African churches.

The parson, a Cape man, showed us the very excellent church they had built with all native labour, helped by boys brought up from Lovedale.

When he heard about my being English and the purpose of my mission, he asked the familiar question, 'What are you going to do for us in England, Miss?' I explained that I was only a student and that South Africa was independent and Rhodesia almost so. 'But surely you could see the King?' I asked what their grievances were. But in front of Colonel Carbutt he was tongue-tied and the Colonel did not seem at all inclined to walk away. The parson told us that he had not enjoyed his visit to America. He felt that the American Negro had nothing in common with the African whom he despised and of whom he was largely ignorant. He was very glad to get away from there.

We went on to the beer-hall where the municipality sells beer, as in Durban, and makes the African support his own amenities from its profits. Then on to the law courts. Here a very interesting case was going on. They have just introduced a system in the High Court by which a native can elect to be tried by a judge and two assessors— always native commissioners—instead of by a jury. This man had so chosen. He had knifed another fellow and pleaded self-defence. In contrast with what I had seen in South Africa I felt that he was getting the maximum of consideration and even indulgence, both in the handling of the case and in the sentence, for the three judges called it culpable homicide and gave him six years. So the wind of British justice is tempered and most native murder cases get changed to homicide if native experts have any say in the case. Some, I have heard, object even to this and maintain that it is a scandal to put splendid fellows, whose only offence is to have killed another man in a beer-brawl, into the corrupting society of habitual thieves in a prison. This man, the judge later told me, had evidently stabbed to kill, for he had worked the knife up and down in the wound to make sure. But only very foul or cold-blooded murders or, of course, murders of a European, get the capital sentence. It is the same in most parts of British Africa. In Somaliland (a Protectorate) until lately we used their law of paying compensation in camels, a hundred camels for a man and fifty for a woman.

I went to lunch with the Chief Justice and very charming I found him and his family. They were as liberal as myself in native matters— and at greater cost! It is deeply encouraging to find a man like that in a high place. He teased me a good deal for having broken every precedent in Rhodesia by holding up a very important murder trial, that of an extensive poisoning plot that had created a great stir. Colonel Carbutt was assessor for the case but said he had the Governor's orders to take charge of me for three days. In vain they remonstrated with him, urging him to find a substitute. He defeated them and the trial was postponed for two days. The Chief Justice illustrated one useful feature among Rhodesians, a sense of superiority over the Union in matters of native policy. This makes the Rhodesians inclined to do the opposite from what is being done over the border.

The afternoon was given up to work in Colonel Carbutt's office and I had tea and talk with him at his house and have come away with a good sheaf of notes on Rhodesian native policy as seen from Bulawayo and much gratitude to my rather reserved, informant, who has grown hourly in my estimation.

Next day we both set off early on a long day's motoring expedition in cold wind and driving rain. As I had left all my warm clothes in a trunk at the station and had only a silk dress and a macintosh, I was perished with cold all day which rather blighted things for me. No one had told me that it could be so cold in this part of the world.

We first visited a very interesting London Missionary Society Mission called Hope Fountain. The main interest here was that they are launching out on what is called 'Jeanes training', a copy, or rather adaptation, of the training of 'Community Workers'. Selected women, with at least a basis of the three R's, are put through a year's course of nursing, dressmaking, cooking and infant welfare. They are expected to marry—some are married already—and then they are stationed in the villages and are paid by the Government. Their role is to raise the standard around them by example and precept. They plan to do the same in the Transkei and have already, I hear, started in Kenya. The whole thing is too young for us yet to judge the results but it is an entirely new departure in native education, a break with the old literary tradition and an attempt to educate the group instead of the individual. I had already studied the system in the United States from which the scheme has been borrowed. It is an attractive idea, but one must not expect too rapid results from it, or, indeed, from any comparable initiatives in Africa.

I saw the little model village where the women work and watched the cooking class. The scheme demands a very exceptional woman to teach the teachers, one who knows native life from A to Z and will not impose a standard they cannot yet apply under their own conditions. I fear the woman in charge of the experiment, fresh from England, is hardly the right type. They are to have a small hospital soon.

In the London Missionary Society Mission School I talked to the girls and found them very gauche and backward compared with the South African girls. The latter's century of education and white contact accounts for that. But I saw some amusing essays on 'White People'. The girls seemed chiefly impressed by our wealth and such achievements as flying, and admitted that whites are immensely superior. But some girls were frank. 'White people are strange. They treat us as if we were dogs or pigs and did not feel.' One girl remembered one white woman who, in her small infancy, had treated her kindly 'like a mother' and given her cake and sweets. She was different from all the others, it seemed. Of course, they all politely excepted the missionaries from any criticism.

We had lunch at the school and then drove some forty miles through heavy rain to the Matopo hills. We passed Rhodes' country house from which he used to make those expeditions into the hills which he loved so much. The estate is now used as a government agricultural college which, as the soil is like nothing else in Southern Rhodesia, does not seem to be a great success.

The Matopos themselves are reserved as a national park. Very weird they are though today the effect was blurred by rain. There are hundreds of kopjes of all shapes and sizes, not the pyramid and table kopjes of South Africa, but something unique for the hills are made of flat slabs of rock, smooth as silk, softly rounded and, being now black with rain, they looked like a vast herd of sleeping sea-lions. But that is not all. With a freakishness that surpasses all one has come to expect of geology, even in Africa, nature has balanced round balls and cones on the heads of her sea-lions, or else built up block on block as bricks are built up by a small child. Some are black, some grey, and nearly all are splashed with chrome and green lichen, while the tumbling broken rocks at the base are knitted together by shaggy undergrowth, mahogany trees and also euphorbia, rigid as candelabra.

You must walk a mile among these displays to reach the rock into which they put Rhodes' body. We scrambled in silence up its gleaming flanks, as he must often have scrambled, and at the top, in the place where he used to sit and gaze at what he called the 'View of the World' we stood and peered through the rain at the endless series of kopjes—a whole school of sea-lions with balls and bosses—whose heads just emerged out of the steamy mist into which the rain was pouring. It is not, as I had once imagined, a very high place, but it gives an impression of height, of being lifted a little above the world and that a very strange world.

At this point, just beside a monstrous ball of rock that looks as if it would roll down if you stamped your foot, they have dug a grave in the rock and have put in the stone the name of Rhodes on a plain piece of bronze. A few yards away lies the body of Dr. Jameson of the famous—or infamous?—Raid. It was not a good day for a picture but I attempted one and stood a while trying to summons the appropriate thoughts. But they would not come; men's skeletons and dust seem to have so little significance. So I turned to look at the elaborate Shangani memorial which Rhodes insisted on having there though it screams aloud in incongruity. It is dedicated to the troops cut off and killed in the Matabele rising and has simply the inscription that was cut on a tree over their first burial-place on the field of battle, '*To Brave Men*'. Many Matabele were killed. They were brave too. I wonder when their descendants will set up a memorial.

Back through rain, wind and twilight to Bulawayo, chilled to the bone. I had dinner at my hotel, was grossly overcharged on my bill and shivered for two hours in the lounge waiting for it to be time to go to the station. I begged the staff to light a fire but they just laughed at me, so I sat miserably and watched hearty Rhodesians treating each other to whisky-and-soda, served by 'boys' who are under a prohibition law, and then, at last, the cold vigil ended. I do not think a crisis about luggage at the station need go down to history. I was seldom more glad to get to bed, even on a Rhodesian train.

I reached Salisbury, the capital of Southern Rhodesia, at 11.30 on Saturday morning, 22 February, and found a hotel. There were instructions to report on arrival to the Governor so I went round at once to see his secretary, made appointments for Monday and carried away a lot of documents. The secretary sent me straight on to see the Chief Native Commissioner, Mr. Jackson, who, strangely enough, has his brother as Assistant Chief, Major Jackson. By this time, to my horror, the post office was shut. I had had no mail since Capetown and was simply living for it. Now I must wait until Monday.

After getting in one set of tennis at Major Jackson's, only about the third time I have played since leaving England, I went to dinner at Government House. I had heard strange things of this establishment and the stories were not exaggerated.

Sir Cecil Rodwell had been Imperial Secretary in South Africa, Captain Clifford's present position; then Governor, first of Fiji and then of British Guiana. He is a small, compact, dapper man, with a very official manner, who appears to believe it important to retain every ounce of ceremony that his position allows. Perhaps it is, in the circumstances of Southern Rhodesia. Lady Rodwell, an ex-actress, said to have been married by a woman-hater immediately the curtain went down, seems to be a bundle of nerves and I find her intimidating. There was an old friend of mine staying at the house who was upset because I had not been asked to stay at Government House in spite of letters from the Colonial Office and Philip Kerr.

I sat next to His Excellency at dinner and drew him a bit. He had read my Samoan article and also seemed to know that I had been in touch with what must, to him, be the nefarious I.C.U. He seemed, not unnaturally, a bit suspicious and I wondered whether it had been by his orders that I had been forbidden to meet the branch of the I.C.U. in Bulawayo, 'political reasons' being the only answer to my protest. He seemed to know little or nothing of what his opposite number, Sir James Maxwell, was doing across the border in Northern Rhodesia. Afterwards he and his wife played bridge with the High Commissioner for Southern Rhodesia and the wife of the head of a large firm, the sort of woman who I did not think existed out of the pages of *Punch*. ('If you want anything while you are in Salisbury', she said, 'you apply to me. I have several cars and chauffeurs.')

Next day, Sunday, I worked hard and in the evening went to tea

with Major Jackson, who motored me out to his brother, the Chief
Native Commissioner, six miles out of Salisbury.

The Chief Native Commissioner is a great shambling mastiff of a
man, enormously tall, thin and stooping. He has intense blue eyes that
flash upon you from under shaggy white brows. His face is nobly
lined. He has strength, dignity and fire: these you see at a glance:
much more is revealed later. He at once took the offensive with me.
He was clearly ill and over-worked, yet he took the duty of talking to
me very seriously. He asked leading questions. What did I know?
Had I a preconceived attitude? If so, was I honest enough to throw
it away and start clear? At first his attitude puzzled me. Then he said
that J. H. Harris, Secretary of the Aborigines Protection Society, had
written to him about me, and had said that I 'should bring the wrongs
of the African prominently before the British public'.

This is hardly the best kind of introduction to a Chief Native
Commissioner, least of all in a country whose constitution still gives
Britain control of native affairs. And it could not have come at a worse
moment for J. H. Harris had been largely responsible for raising an
outcry in Britain against the Chief Native Commissioner's pet project, the Juvenile Offenders Act. What is a small event in Britain is a
big one in Southern Rhodesia which has been obsessed by the controversy and the alleged injustice and ignorance of British public
opinion. Therefore, as with Moffat Thomson, I had pretty stiff
going at first. But the Chief Native Commissioner is a darling. I took
to him from the first moment. In fact, I all but fell in love with him.
It was impossible not to feel the attraction of that magnificent head,
with a long and responsible career carved upon it, especially as it was
easy to guess that behind his stern demeanour he was romantic as a
boy, brimming over with human sympathy and endowed with the
temperament of an artist.

We engaged in deep and fascinating conversation. It was a delight
to be instructed by him, his policy, his natives, land, councils, justice
and comparisons with the Union. He justified the Juvenile Offenders
Act (by which juveniles, instead of going to prison, are to be liable to
summary whippings for petty offences) entirely to my satisfaction.
But there is a lapse somewhere—the objects and arguments for such an
Act should be written in a preamble, so that controversy need not be
stirred in Britain. A world of bitterness would have been avoided. I
must pause on this, for B. E. Gwyer, Principal of St. Hugh's, Oxford,
and I were interested in it and both misled. The Act is the attempt by

earnest and philanthropic native affairs officials to reduce to order the rabble of young juveniles who run away from their villages and pick up any work they can in the towns and become increasingly criminal in their way of life. It was hoped that by early light chastisement and a return to their villages they might be saved from the contamination of the prisons. I can't go into details here but certainly when you see the situation, and when you read the whole Act, with all its safeguards, instead of seeing isolated clauses picked out, it is impossible not to sympathize with the native affairs officials.

One lesson I am learning on this trip is that if there is one man whom you can generally trust it is the native affairs official. Unfortunately, in Southern Africa, they are not wholly free agents. But the good district commissioner knows the native as no one else can; his work brings him into contact with every side of the native's life from cradle to the grave. His interest and his career are largely bound up with the development of the Africans, and there are few men in the position who do not grow in some degree devoted to their charges, proud of their knowledge of their customs and language and eager to interpret and defend them. Of course there are exceptions and there are some errors in the policies they have to administer. But we *must* trust and support them for who else can we trust? The settler, the missionary, the educationalist, the humanitarian at home—there are obvious limitations and special interests in all these cases, though they all do and must count. But I believe that the improvement, if not salvation, of the natives in Africa—British Africa, at least—will be forwarded by this policy towards these officials:

(a) The greatest care in selection and training.
(b) Ensuring the utmost independence of political control.
(c) Proper conditions for service (i.e. not overwhelming them with office work).
(d) Arranging conferences both within a territory, and as between territories to stimulate and co-ordinate their work.

I have strayed away from the Chief Native Commissioner, talking in his deep voice, fixing me with his earnest, humorous blue eyes, and illustrating native policy by quotations from Shakespeare and Browning. His brother could hardly drag me away and back to Salisbury.

Up early to the post office to find a glorious batch of letters from Oxford, Hampstead, New Zealand, Zululand, Basutoland, Sydney and the Transkei, with thrilling news from the Governor of Tanganyika about his plans for me there.

Then at 9.30 a.m. I had an interview with the Director of Native Development, quite a young man, Jowitt by name, imported from Natal where he had been under my kind friend, Mr. Malcolm of Natal. He was very modern and clever, had read all the latest books on Africa and had produced a brilliant report with half a dozen graphs in pretty colours on native education. A new idea in Rhodesia is the consolidation of all native welfare services, education, agriculture, etc., in one department and under one head. The native affairs people are a bit suspicious about it and rather resentful as they say all the interesting work has been taken away from them. I generally find the educational people easy to get on with. They talk the same language as I do: they know what I want and they can generalize. But I never feel they have quite the grip upon native life that the administrative officers have.

Then I had an interview with the Governor. He was much better in his office than in his house and we had a very interesting talk, mainly about Samoa, and he told me he agreed absolutely with the opinions in my *Times* articles. He said that he had been prepared to help New Zealand in those early days of the Mandate and had actually found the right man for them but they would accept neither help nor advice. He has a great love for the Fijians and thinks they are the finest people in the Pacific.

On Rhodesia itself, unfortunately, he said little that was memorable. He said that he thought the tone on native affairs was high, immeasurably higher than in the Union. He thought that it had improved since the days when he was High Commissioner and he sent me away with a load of the local *Hansard* with references to debates on native affairs. He also fetched in the Prime Minister, Mr. Moffatt, to arrange an interview with me. He is grandson of the famous pioneer missionary.

I played tennis in the afternoon at Government House. It is a glorious house, built round a quadrangle, with cloisters of white columns over which fall curtains of bougainvillaea and golden shower, a creeper loaded with orange trumpets. In the garden were massed all those flowering trees which glorify the sub-tropics, the flame tree, the jacaranda, and a host of others, with the great ivory chalices of the moon-flowers hanging shyly downwards beneath the sun. It is a good setting for a governor, with black servants moving noiselessly about the house, spotless white *kansus* (long nightdress-like gowns) clasped by scarlet, gold-embroidered waistcoats. Something of the atmosphere of an oriental sultanate is brought into the place. The bedrooms open upon the gardens: there are summer-houses half-choked in blossom: tennis courts with little piccanins in uniform to fetch the balls: the arms of Britain emblazoned on the leather of the chairs, on the china and the panels of the car: huge portraits of the King and Queen: sentries to salute you at the gate. No wonder that a man, one moment a Provincial Commissioner or Chief Secretary, can assume on the next the almost god-like demeanour of the Governor. How pleasant, too, to fill the house with your friends and relations and let them share in the state and magnificence!

We played tennis. I was feeling rather queer by now and was hardly able to play. But I had to brace up because next day there was planned for me a most interesting expedition to Domboshawa, the school and native agricultural college. Mr. Jowitt was to take me.

Mr Jowitt called in the morning with his wife, a Dutchwoman, twice his size and full of energy and beneficence. We ran through plains of red earth and farms with the eternal crop of maize, until, as abruptly as if a line were drawn, rich red changed to dusty white and here the native reserve began. This is not quite so sinister as it looks at first sight—or at least so I was told—because the native with his inadequate implements generally concentrated on the white earth, granite sand, which, though poor, is easy to work. He could not manage the red loam. Now, when we have given him the plough, we have taken the best land.

Domboshawa has two sides: the training of teachers, Jeanes teachers, men who concentrate upon community work. There is also a school.

I expect the readers of this journal have had enough of my amateur school inspections but I must record that I was deeply impressed by this place. It is run by an Anglican parson, Brodrick, on public school lines. That means that they have prefects and they run the school on a self-governing system. The prefects make the rules and decide the punishments. The Headmaster stands in the background. The other day he handed a boy to them for punishment and they expelled him. He thought it a bit drastic but he upheld them. There is practically no trouble and no corporal punishment.

We went round the school and I had a long talk with the agricultural pupils who are just going out to be demonstrators in the reserves. They are mostly Mashona since the Matabele, like most military tribes who have lost their power, tend to be a bit stagnant and sullen, while the Mashona, broken and enslaved over and over again, are much more adaptable and keen on education. I thought they answered up well, far better than at the Zulu school. These people have made a late start but they seem to be very quick in the uptake. I asked them what they meant to do when they left school and they got up and gave an excellent account of their ambitions. They would teach their people to plough better, to rotate crops, to grow trees, etc. (Or were they merely being good?)

At night I had dinner with a man who had spoken to me in the hotel. Having heard my business he asked me if I wanted to hear something more than the official point of view about the native, because if I did he would tell me and would ask another man to dinner who would also tell me and who knew more of the native than any pooh-bah official.

The second man proved to be a brother of the Mr. Taberer who works for the Chamber of Mines in Johannesburg. (The man who called me 'girl'.) Well, these two went for me for three hours on end. It was the usual thing: natives have no capacity for advance: education is a danger: people like me are the worst danger of all. What was more interesting was the account he gave of the financial and general situation of the colony, the disastrous disease which has ruined the tobacco farmers, the serious plight of all farmers, no rich men in Rhodesia at all. Only the mines pay and the British South Africa Company take the royalties from them. Indeed, they were very bitter about the Company, which they said had a stranglehold on the country, whose real ruler was Mr. Malcolm, its Chairman.

That night and next day I had either fever or 'flu. Unfortunately Salisbury insisted on being most hospitable, and though I tried to get a day in bed and cancelled an expedition arranged by the Governor to Sir Francis Newton's farm, I could not get much rest as I had a stream of callers and invitations.

The next day, though I was still feeling rather ill, I went out on a long expedition into the reserves. We had two cars and in one of them was an American, an ex-missionary, and now the Director of Agriculture for Natives. We motored, in all about 150 miles, and considering a good deal of it was not on roads at all, but through swamps and high grass nearly over your head, it took from nine in the morning until eight at night.

It was all very interesting. The reserves are fairly crowded and they were drought-stricken. Mile after mile of poverty and inefficiency. I never saw such miserable crops, worse than anything I have seen in all South Africa, about one wilting and stunted mealie to four square yards; native millet and Kaffir corn mixed with ground nuts; the land exhausted by successions of the same crops; patches of agriculture haphazard in the middle of pasture. When you see this and realize that many of these men have worked on European farms and that their crops are life and death to them, you can plumb the depth of their lethargy and conservatism. Here and there, where they have sown in the manured earth of an old kraal-site, there is a tall island of prolific maize, thick and high above the surrounding poverty. Even that does not teach them. It needs the stimulus of direct intervention.

The work of the demonstrators who only started two years ago in this reserve is almost miraculous. One demonstrator may have thirty or fifty square miles. He goes out and starts one acre demonstration plots; he also advises any man who volunteers to follow exactly his directions. All that is done is to plough and cross-plough and to manure. I took a picture to show the contrast at one of these plots. What you see in front is the ordinary native crop, behind the demonstration plot. The difference in crop is between nine and ten bags an acre to one or two.

We saw the little kraal schools, tumble-down wattle and thatch buildings, with the single teacher wrestling with five or six classes littered about the dark interior, crouched on their little carved stools. The huts are rather miserable compared with those of other Bantu.

We had a picnic lunch under a big tree. As we motored along afterwards we saw a small buck. I was with the American and he seized his gun and shot. You could hear the loud 'spat' of the bullet striking soft flesh, a pause, and then a cry, half-groan, half-scream—a prolonged and agonized noise. It nearly made me sick and I vowed to keep clear of shooting while in Africa. They went and cut its throat and brought it back, a long-necked, long-legged little doe—well-named a stem-buck. Why must so many men out here want to kill almost every wild creature that crosses their path?

We did not get back until eight o'clock, whereby I missed playing tennis—of which I was quite incapable—with Bishop Paget whom I had met in Oxford and Capetown. I was by way of collapsing so I was given stiff brandy, and made to lie down at the Jowitts' house until I felt better, when they motored me home to the hotel.

I had a long busy day all day. I started off with an interview with the Prime Minister. He was most amusing—earnest, simple, rather woolly-minded. I imagine he is like a cushion, you can't fail to make an obvious impression but will it lead to anything permanent? Anyhow, he was very kind to me. He is evidently proud of Rhodesia's policy towards natives and brimming over with good intentions. He expressed a determination to develop native councils on the Kenya system and explained the whole policy of native reserves under the Lands' Apportionment Bill, a grossly unfair allocation. He has, alas! fallen under the spell of Professor Edgar Brookes' earlier views and would not believe me that Brookes had completely changed his mind about segregation. When I was in the Union I begged Brookes to publish, if only in pamphlet form, his lectures to our conference at Capetown. Now I feel I must write to him again as his existing book has an important influence and no one could credit that a man would go the whole possible range away from his first position unless they saw it in black and white.

What the Prime Minister told me in answer to my questions about Imperial control was deeply interesting. I knew that in the Cape, then in Natal, then in New Zealand, now in Southern Rhodesia, the Imperial Government, in handing over responsible government to the colonists, retained control over native policy by means of the Secretary of State's veto. Unfortunately this has never proved more than a temporary expedient and at the first real clash with the local whites the Imperial Government has given in. Sir James Maxwell was very contemptuous about the control, said it was a sham, a hypocrisy to soothe Britain's conscience. It merely served as an irritant to the colonials and led to an inevitable surrender that made Britain look ridiculous. I am not so certain about this. I think it has the effect of directing special attention to native affairs and as long as it lasts it can make the community concerned conscious of an external and impartial scrutiny on their policy.

I raised the question of imperial control over native affairs with the Prime Minister and begged him to talk frankly. The conversation ran as follows:

M.P.: 'Is there much resentment against this control by the Secretary of State ?'

P.M.: 'Practically none. It was part of the agreement when we were given responsible government in 1922 and it would be rather early days to evade it after eight years. (He then sent for the local *Hansard*.) You will see here that the Leader of the Opposition brought in a motion condemning it but it was not very serious and it was partly just for the sake of opposition.'

M.P.: 'But in your experience have you found it at all inconvenient or embarrassing ?'

P.M.: 'Not at all. In fact I value it. We have no second chamber and the Secretary of State thus fulfils the function of a revising authority. All bills are sent to him and he returns them with criticisms and amendments.'

M.P.: 'And do you find these are generally well informed and helpful ?'

P.M.: 'Yes, I do. As you have raised this point I think I might show you my correspondence with the Secretary of State about this very important Lands' Apportionment Bill. You will promise to return them ?'

There was more talk, all revealing his humane and liberal, if rather muddled ideas, and I went away with a sheaf of his highly confidential correspondence about native affairs with the British Secretary of State, intimate and confidential evidence which I read in my hotel bedroom. The papers certainly did throw light: they showed the Prime Minister arguing with the Secretary of State, defending and explaining his bill point by point and even accepting amendments. The P.M. had actually taken a debate in the House of Lords and answered the points raised in every speech, even that of his strong critic, Lord Olivier. He had not, however, pointed out that much of the area to be reserved for the African was very poor land, nor that the area for future determination was largely in the fly or dry belts. But, apart from that—a large exception!—he seemed to have put the matter fairly. As I left his office I had a talk with his secretary, Spicer, who turned out to be the brother of a girl who was at St. Anne's and St. Hugh's with me and is now a nun. He, and also the Governor's secretary, were clearly shocked at my having under my arm the Prime Minister's correspondence with the Secretary of State and I fear that poor old Moffat will get into trouble with them.

The next interview was with the local District Commissioner, rather a fiery person, who damned the native development department and gave a picture of the demoralization of the native in the town.

I went to lunch with a Mrs. Robbins, god-daughter of old Archdeacon Archer-Houblon, ex-chairman of St. Hugh's Council. She is wife of Colonel Robbins, the manager of the British South Africa Company, and has a beautiful house on a hill just outside Salisbury, built in the old Dutch style, with a grey thatched roof. It was the first cultured, rich English home that I have been in since that of the Cartwrights in Capetown and she and her house startled me by their quality of 'Englishness'. It is so difficult to realize what one's own society stands for until you have been long away from it. She complained of being rather stranded among the Rhodesians and I realized that, English as white Rhodesians are in comparison with older and more mixed colonial societies, yet they have already grown away from us, and the language talked by the upper-class Englishwoman is peculiar to her kind and has little in common even with her cousins over here.

In the afternoon I set out on a round of local exploration. First I went to look at native housing. The first thing we saw was about rock-bottom, even for Southern Africa. I cannot think what southern Africa can have been like before the advent of the petrol tin, for now its uses are universal and it has penetrated to the inmost bush.

The location itself presented various types, cramped little nondevals (round mud huts) with steep tin roofs and very horrid blocks of four, back to back, with only one room each. Where the new standard of civilization demands a double bed and a sideboard there is not room for much else. But the latest type was pretty good: three large rooms and a verandah, but unfortunately no garden. Rent at 17s 6d is not too heavy compared with South Africa's 25s a month. But then wages are lower here by a good deal.

We next visited the camp where the Rhodesian Labour Recruitment Agency collects all its men as they come down from Northern Rhodesia and Nyasaland. It had a fair hospital, very full. One boy, who looked about thirteen or fourteen and ought never to have been recruited, was dying. Inquiries brought out that the organization along the routes was far less elaborate than that of the Belgians and the quarters of the men much more primitive. The Belgians may believe too much in statistics but the British not enough and they seemed quite surprised at being asked if they kept records of health according to disease and tribe, etc.

We went on to the native hospital and saw the usual dreadful sores,

R

dysentery, pneumonia, and broken limbs. The hospital was crowded and the white sisters seemed very much overworked but it was a nice-looking place with a charming garden. I had tea with the Jowitts and went back to bed, feeling rather done in.

Next morning I had a long talk with the Chief Native Commissioner, who was now better and inclined to be very frank. I interviewed other officials during the morning, tried, and failed, to find a doctor for myself, and went to lunch with the Principal Medical Officer. He is about to retire, having been in his post from pioneer days, twenty-five years ago. He is, partly on these grounds, the subject of much criticism and when I praised the Belgian medical work in Katanga province he at once thought I was criticizing his administration and fiercely defended it. He said these people in Southern Rhodesia were not ready for any kind of medical training and that many instances of educated natives reverting to witch-doctors were recorded. His wife told me how their chief boy, one of the most advanced natives in the country, was very ill. She nursed him as if he had been a son, having special invalid food cooked. Then one day she found his swallowing a concoction made of putrid fur and other filth, with the witch-doctor at his side. By some miracle he recovered and told the witch-doctor to send the bill in to her!

An elegant young farmer there complained that there was no medical attention of any kind on the farms nor any kind of Government inspection of quarters. 'Of course', he said, 'I like the jolly old nig, but other fellows round me don't care if they lose a few now and then.'

I asked the Governor to put me in touch with an ordinary citizen who would represent public opinion. One, Y. Collings, was chosen, and with him I went to tea and found his wife was sister to Dr. Loram. I don't think they were at all ordinary: conversation revealed their passion to do the best for the native and a population made up of such citizens would bring a millennium. Afterwards they drove me out to the Chief Native Commissioner's house and left me to have a last conversation with this new key friend of mine. He told me of his measures to suppress the I.C.U. and we quarrelled hard about it. But he was unrepentant. Only discipline would do with children: they must be protected against irresponsible agitation that they can neither understand nor oppose. The stories he told me of the kind of speeches that some African visitors from the Union had made inclined me to understand his point of view, if not to agree with it.

With deep regret I bade good-bye to the Chief Native Commissioner and drove back in the dark to Salisbury. After dinner I went round to see the P.M.O. as I was feeling very queer and wanted him to pass me for my journey to Portuguese territory next day. It wasn't his business to doctor me but he was very kind. In spite of controversy with him, and as he saw it was useless for him to say I could not go, he concocted some sort of stimulant and his wife ordered a room to be made ready to which I could come if I did not feel better next morning and which they would still keep ready for me if I had to turn back from Beira. This was the finishing touch to all the kindness I had met with in Salisbury. I went home and struggled to pack. Unfortunately there was a big dance in my hotel and a whole series of visitors came up to my room to call.

Obviously there could not be much sleep for me. But Southern Rhodesia has provided me with plenty to think about as I lay awake. The Chief Native Commissioner had introduced me to the poems of Cripps, the missionary who had written that almost passionate plea for the land rights of the Africans, *Africa for the Africans*. Cripps' poems about Africans are piercing in their compassion, good reading for a sleepless night.

On the train to Beira. I am now writing on the train as we begin to crawl along the first lap of what is, I suppose, the approximately three hundred miles between Salisbury and Beira. I was feeling pretty ill last night as I boarded this train but I resisted the tempting offer of the Principal Medical Officer to take refuge in the bedroom which they had prepared for me. I expected I was in for a poor night on this very African railway. But soon after we started the guard brought me a note from Sir Dougal Malcolm who was on the train in his private coach and would like me to join him for dinner and bridge.

In spite of my feeling so low this was for me a royal command. For the Hon. Dougal Malcolm is a—I think *the*—leading member of the British South Africa Company which really created the Colonies of Northern and Southern Rhodesia. Though the introduction of self-government five years ago in Southern Rhodesia has changed the whole relationship, the Company still has its all important mineral rights and also an immense financial and political influence in the two states. Malcolm was one of that band of Oxford intellectuals who played such a large part in South African affairs as the so-called Milner's Kindergarten to which I must have referred in one of my diary-letters from South Africa. To his work with Milner, his first classes in Honour Mods and Greats and his Fellowship at All Souls, he has now added big business. In spite of feeling so low, his invitation was one I could not refuse.

For me to reach his special coach the train had to be stopped and I was helped by the guard to climb down on to the track and walk along in the twilight back to the last coach. In its luxurious setting, I dined and played bridge with this highly civilized and powerful successor to Cecil Rhodes. But though it was rash to challenge such a man who was also my host, I could hardly hide my own views and before I left I had committed the outrage of quoting the poem of Arthur Shirley Cripps, that saintly missionary and defender of African rights in Southern Rhodesia, in the magnificent verse in which he visualizes Rhodes in purgatory:

'God be with you in your need,
When God's mills have ground you through,
All the coarse, cruel chaff of you,
Be there left one seed to sow!
Which in season may unfold
Your visionary might of old,
Like some fecund vine to sprawl
On the width of Sion's wall,
In penitence imperial.'

'Magnificent', I thought as I spoke the lines. Yet I am Rhodes, beneficiary, travelling in his country, living on his money. What are we small people to think about the big—even bad—men who change and create the conditions within which we—prosperously—live? Malcolm thrust back at me quickly by quoting Kipling's estimate of Rhodes which is inscribed upon his grave in the Matopo hills:

'The immense and brooding spirit still
Shall quicken and control.
Living he was the land, and dead
His soul shall be her soul.'

Soon after this the train was stopped and I clambered out of the state coach and began to make my way alongside the track towards my carriage. It was now dark as I made my way towards the rest of the lighted train. Imagine my horror when long before I had reached what I judged to be my carriage the train began to move on. My cries were unheard. I looked wildly round in the star-lit blackness. There was no sign of human life. We appeared to be in an uninhabited level plain. Thousands of frogs were making their shrill assertion that here the line ran through a vast swamp. My host who had telephonic contact with the rest of the train must have assumed that the guard had received a message to fetch me back to my carriage. I could hardly think this was his revenge! The train was just slowly beginning to gather speed and would soon disappear into the darkness. My non-arrival would, I could hope, be noted at Beira but a night in a mosquito-infested swamp was not an attractive prospect. At least, I hoped, lions would be as averse to swamps as I was myself. It did not take long for these thoughts to rush through my mind. Yet it seemed long enough before I heard the rasp of brakes from the now almost invisible train. I went stumbling along the line after it and the guard hauled me up with a frightened but obscure explanation.

This was not quite the end of the story. As I awoke in the morning the guard handed me a note. Inside it was a Latin ode about Cecil Rhodes which Malcolm had composed, presumably after my departure. My Latin is of the minimum standard needed for Oxford entrance and Responsions but, with some trouble, I made out most of the erudite apologia Malcolm had composed about his hero who, I suppose, he thought for more than one reason ought also to have been mine.

I am writing this on board the S.S. *Madura*, steaming northwards up the west coast. I am still not quite recovered from what I suppose was malaria in Salisbury and still feel rather battered by a brief exposure to Portugal in Africa. Letters about my visit had gone before me to Beira. The Portuguese reaction was to put me into the solid, strict charge of the Chief of Police. In this one long day I do not think I was ever out of his sight except for one or two obvious moments when he remained close to the door. He was able further to protect the secrets of his empire by his inability to speak much English and my inability to speak any Portuguese. In his office he presented me with copies of laws and notices about the strictly humane treatment of the natives and—no corporal punishment! It was unfortunate for him that on approaching an office where a queue of Africans were lined up we heard from inside the sound of angry cursing, a resounding blow and the crash of a body to the floor.

Another unfortunate episode arose over a hospital. My guide pointed out an attractive-looking white building on a hill—all the buildings had a South European charm which shamed most of our erections in Africa—and proudly proclaimed this was the new hospital for natives. I said I would like to go up and inspect it. He said everything he could to dissuade me but this only made me more determined to go. When at last the door was opened it gave upon one very large room or hall in which crowds of Africans were lying or squatting all over the floor in utter squalor and disarray. There was no white person and hardly a bed to be seen. From this almost intolerable sight and stench I quickly backed out.

I do not pretend to judge a large European colony in Africa by such a brief and unhappy visit. On the credit side I certainly did see a number of very assimilated looking Africans walking the pavements from which they were not barred as in South Africa where no comparable assimilated class is allowed to emerge.

I am now bound for Mombasa with a brief stop at Dar es Salaam where I hope to make a preliminary contact with the Governor, Sir Donald Cameron, and arrange future plans. Upon his reported humanity and vision I have built great hopes. It will for me be the end of Southern Africa and the beginning of a study of Britain's three eastern dependencies.

Conclusion
Written in 1973

It was while I was in Southern Rhodesia that an idea which had been slowly gathering shape in my mind developed into a definite purpose. This was to devote myself entirely to the study of the government of 'native' races, especially in the African regions administered by Britain. The Principal of my college, Miss Gwyer, kept the many letters I wrote to her while on my tour and this year she handed them back to me. I find in one written from Salisbury on 24 February 1930, this first avowal of my new ambition:

'I had a long letter from H. A. L. Fisher today, four big sheets, defending Smuts against me. He says that Rhodes House is to go ahead as a centre of African studies but, of course, does not suggest that there is any place in it for me. I do not enlarge here upon my plans and hopes because you will know without my saying it that I want to go on with what I am only now beginning. A book on native administration, for me at any rate, would be a colossal enterprise and I should need to give all my time and strength to it if it is to be of any use. It is for you to tell me my duty to the College as at present I am, perhaps, a little overwhelmed by my duty to this work, this cause, if you like. The situation in Africa is among the most complex the world has ever had to face and some political machinery has got to be invented that will enable the twentieth-century European to live with "primitive" man without the latter swamping the former or the former exploiting the latter. So far our present machinery offers little help. There should be as many people as possible thinking, studying and writing on these problems. If I can go on with this work and have some status in the University and some connection with the College, so much the better. If not, I think I ought, as soon as the College can spare me, to leave and try to manage on my own resources. I know that it would be better for me to have some status, with a recognized obligation to get the work done in a certain time. Not that I fear I should ever slack but I might go on and on and be submerged by the size of the subject.

'I know that if you get the chance you will discuss the matter with H. A. L. Fisher or Reginald Coupland,[1] or both. I, for my part, must try to make an intelligible report for Philip Kerr as some proof that I have not been merely globe-trotting. That quoted remark by— as I suppose—some Rhodes Trustee, still stings—I never worked harder in my life. I know that.

'I don't think I write of myself in any egotistical spirit. I have seen something of the world now and I know how small in it are even the great ones. I can, however, see myself as one upon whom money has been spent and opportunities given that make it possible for me to offer some small contribution. But life is short and the flesh is weak and it seems a waste that I should not be free to make that contribution. But *you* see all round the subject—the College, Africa, me personally and officially, and your judgement I trust. I don't want you to rate too highly what I could do. It will be, and a must be, very little. But I have said enough. I am not holding you to ransom. I shall, if necessary, be ready to take up my work in October, in the right spirit.'

The sequel to this letter was in the form of two cables which reached me soon after I had begun to work in East Africa. One was from Philip Kerr to say that the Rhodes Trust were offering to extend the Travelling Fellowship for a further year. The other was from my College to say that if I accepted I must resign my Fellowship. I at once sent off two cables in the sense of 'Accept' and 'Resign' and then proceeded to rearrange my plans for East Africa upon a more thorough basis. The Rhodes Trust grant was so generous that I was able, after returning to England, to observe, and write upon, the Joint Committee of both Houses which considered the issue of Closer Union for East Africa. In 1931–2, as a result of economizing in the use of my second Rhodes Trust grant, I was able to spend the best part of a year in Nigeria and to write a book upon its administration.

---

[1] Beit Professor of Colonial History.

Index

Index